CARMELITE STUDIES

X

CARMELITE STUDIES

A BETTER WINE

Essays Celebrating Kieran Kavanaugh, O.C.D.

You have kept the good wine until now.
John 2:10

Kevin Culligan, O.C.D.

Editor

ICS Publications
Institute of Carmelite Studies
Washington, DC
2007

Cover painting: Juan de Flandes, *The Marriage Feast at Cana,* Detail
© 1998 The Metropolitan Museum of Art

Cover design by Rosemary Moak, O.C.D.S.

Portrait of Fr. Kieran Kavanaugh by R.B. Hill Photography (2006)

ICS Publications
2131 Lincoln Road, NE
Washington, DC 20002-1199

www.icspublications.org

Typeset and produced in the United States of America

Library of Congress Cataloging-in-Publication Data

A better wine : essays celebrating Kieran Kavanaugh, O.C.D. / Kevin Culligan, editor.
p. cm. (Carmelite studies ; 10)
Includes bibliographical references.
ISBN-13 978-0-935216-41-3 (alk. paper)
1. Discalced Carmelites--Spiritual life. I. Kavanaugh, Kieran, 1928- II. Culligan, Kevin G. III. Series.
BX3203.B48 2006
271'.73--dc22

2006009133

Contents

Preface

The chapters in this volume of Carmelite Studies were written or translated by members of the Institute of Carmelite Studies to pay tribute to their brother and colleague, Fr. Kieran Kavanaugh, O.C.D., for his significant contribution to the cause of Carmelite spirituality in the English-speaking world. Since 1957, Fr. Kieran has devoted his priestly life to the translation of the works of St. John of the Cross and St. Teresa of Avila from their original Spanish into standard American English. This year—2006—he will finish this project with the completion of Volume Two of *The Collected Letters of St. Teresa of Avila.*

The idea for this tribute came early in the new millennium. Originally we had planned to have these essays ready for Kieran's seventy-fifth birthday on 19 February 2003. When various delays kept us from meeting that goal, we decided to aim for the fiftieth anniversary of his ordination to the priesthood on 26 March 2005. Although that day too has passed, we nonetheless present this volume to him to thank him for his fifty years of dedicated service to the Carmelite family and the entire people of God. The completion of this book happily coincides with the fortieth anniversary of the founding of the Institute of Carmelite Studies and the completion of the final volume of his translations of the two Spanish Carmelite spiritual masters. Both the ICS and these translations have been an important part of his fifty years of priestly ministry.

I thank the many people who have helped prepare this volume through their enthusiastic interest, encouragement, and willingness to provide information about events and activities that Kieran has been associated with over the years. I am particularly indebted to: John Sullivan, O.C.D., Chairman of the Institute of Carmelite Studies, and my fellow members in the ICS for their support from the very first day the idea of this volume was presented; the contributors of the essays and translations for their patience with the many delays along the way; Barbara Oncay, O.C.D.S., for her valuable proofreading of the manuscripts and helpful editorial recommendations; Michael Berry, O.C.D., for his expert and ever ready technical assistance in resolving many computer glitches; Sal Sciurba, O.C.D., and Matthias Montgomery, O.C.D., for taking two of my retreat commitments that freed me to work on these pages; to Anthony Haglof, O.C.D, and Gilbert Tovares, O.C.D., my brothers in the Hinton community, who covered my house duties so that I could finally complete this volume. All of you share in the tribute we pay to Fr. Kieran through these pages. Finally, I thank Kieran himself, the most modest of men, for permitting us to honor him publicly and for his gracious help in preparing this book.

Kevin Culligan, O.C.D.
Hinton, West Virginia
Ash Wednesday, 2006

Acknowledgements

The editor gratefully acknowledges ICS Publications for the permission to quote extensively from its published books, which are all copyrighted by the Washington Province of Discalced Carmelites. He also expresses his gratitude to Ildefonso Moriones, O.C.D., for providing the text of Jerome Gratian's *Constituciones del Cerro,* published by the Teresianum in Rome, from which the translation in this volume is taken.

The painting of the Wedding Feast of Cana on the cover of this book is by Juan de Flandes. Originally from the Netherlands, he was employed by Queen Isabella and was appointed court painter in 1498. He died in Spain in 1519. The Wedding Feast of Cana was painted around the year 1500. It is now in the Metropolitan Museum of Art in New York City, and is used here with the museum's permission.

Abbreviations and Citations

Unless otherwise noted, all English quotations from St. Teresa of Avila in this volume are taken from Kieran Kavanugh and Otilio Rodriguez, trans., *The Collected Works of St. Teresa of Avila,* 3 vols. (Washington, DC: ICS Publications, 1976-85). The following abbreviations indicate St. Teresa's writings:

L=*The Book of Her Life* W= *The Way of Perfection*
F= *The Book of Her Foundations* C= *The Interior Castle*
T=*Testimonies* P=*Poetry*

In *The Book of Her Life* and *The Way of Perfection*, the first number in a citation refers to chapter, the second to paragraph. Thus, W.6.5 signifies *The Way of Perfection,* chap. 6, par. 3. In *The Interior Castle*, the first number refers to one of the seven dwelling places, followed by numbers for chapter and paragraph. Thus, C.7.1.2. is the Seventh Dwelling Place, chap. 1, par. 2. Citations to *Spiritual Testimonies* give the number of the testimony, followed by the paragraph; for the *Poetry* only the single number of the poem is given.

Similarly, unless noted otherwise, quotations in English from St. John of the Cross are taken from Kieran Kavanaugh and Otilio Rodriguez, trans., *The Collected Works of St. John of the Cross,* rev.ed. (Washington, DC: ICS Publications, 1991). The abbreviations for St. John's works cited in this volume are:

A=*The Ascent of Mount Carmel* N=*The Dark Night*
C=*The Spiritual Canticle* F=*The Living Flame of Love*
S=*Sayings of Light and Love* L=*Letters*

For *The Ascent of Mount Carmel* and *The Dark Night,* the first number refers to the book, the second to the chapter, the third to the paragraph. Thus, A.1.2.3 indicates *The Ascent of Mount Carmel,* book 1, chap. 2, par. 3. In *The Spiritual Canticle* and *The Living Flame of Love,* the first numbers refers to the stanza, the second to the paragraph. Thus, C.27.2 is the 27th stanza (or chapter) of *The Spiritual Canticle,* par. 2. Quotation marks are used for both "The Spiritual Canticle" and "The Living Flame of Love" when only the poem is cited. CB indicates specific reference to the second redaction of "The Spiritual Canticle," and, similarly, FB to the second redaction of the "The Living Flame of Love." References to John's *Letters* and *The Sayings of Light and Love* give the single number of the letter or the individual saying.

Finally, unless otherwise noted, English quotations from St. Thérèse of Lisieux are taken from the Institute of Carmelite Studies' translations. These are: *Story of a Soul: The Autobiography of St. Thérèse of Lisieux,* trans. John Clarke, 3rd ed. (Washington, DC: ICS Publications, 1996); *St. Thérèse of Lisieux: Her Last Conversations,* trans. John Clarke (Washington, DC: ICS Publications, 1977); *The Letters of St. Thérèse of Lisieux,* 2 vols., trans. John Clarke (Washington, DC: ICS Publications, 1982 and 1988); *The Poetry of St. Thérèse of Lisieux*, trans. Donald Kinney (Washington, DC: ICS Publications, 1995). The abbreviations for these works are:

S=*Story of a Soul* LC=*Last Conversations*
L=*Letters* P=*Poetry*

In citations of the works of St. Thérèse, the numbers following the letters refer to the page numbers in the ICS translations. Thus, L, 1181-3 refers to *Letters,* vol. 2, pages 1181 to 1183.

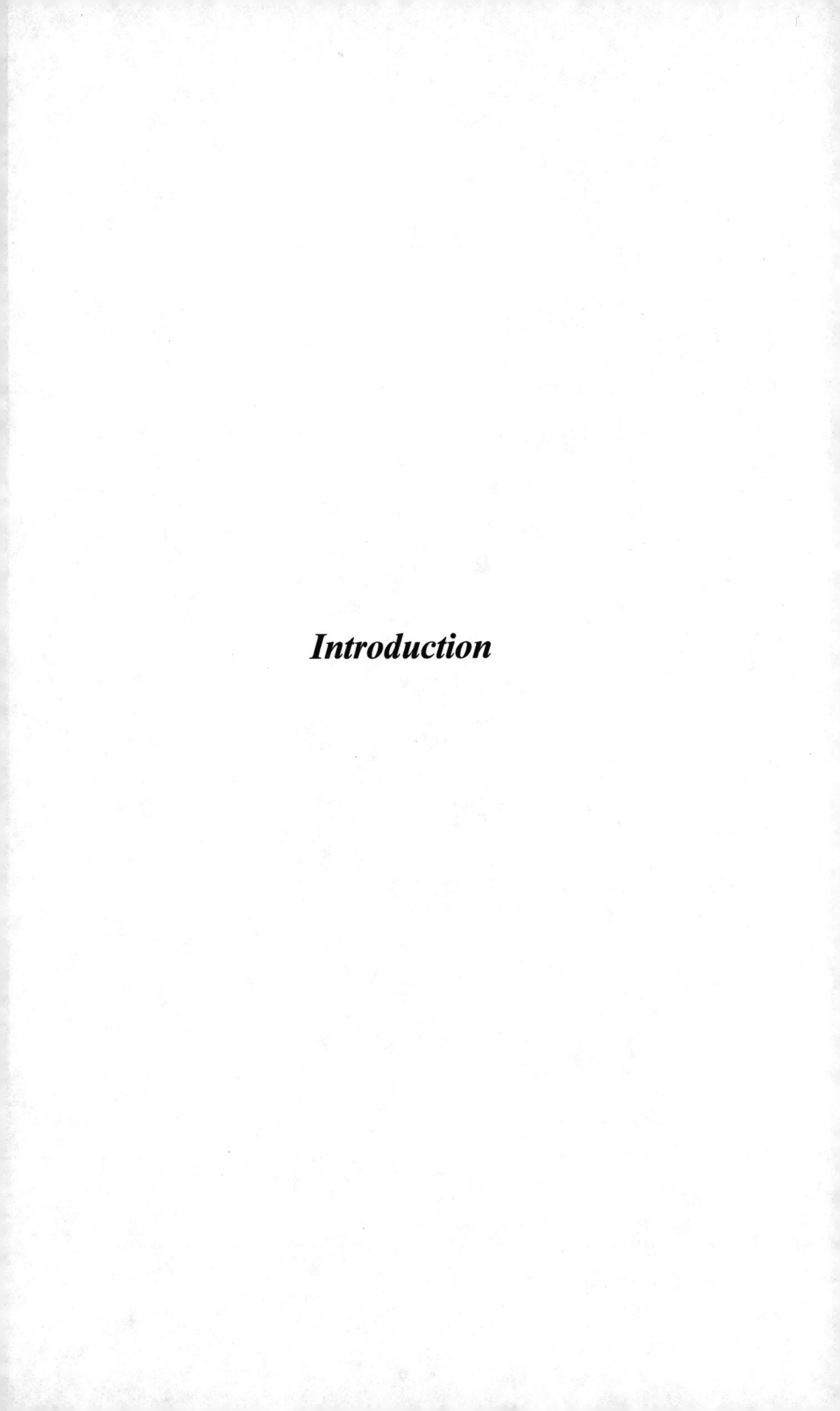

Introduction

CASA GENERALIZIA CARMELITANI SCALZI
CORSO D'ITALIA, 38
00198 ROMA

Reverend Father Kieran Kavanaugh, OCD
Washington Province
United States

1 January 2006

Dear Father Kieran

The Friars of your Province and of ICS have brought to my attention their desire to celebrate the work which you have done over the course of many years in translating the words and works of our Holy Parents. I wish to join my voice to theirs in acknowledging your significant and essential contribution to ICS and to the knowledge of the spirituality of Saints Teresa and John of the Cross in the English speaking world.

I have had the opportunity to meet you over the years in various circumstances. I know that in the course of more than 50 years of your priesthood you have served the Province and the Order in many positions and in different apostolates. It is, above all, your diligent attention to translating the works of Saint Teresa and Saint John of the Cross that will be your legacy. It is your testimony to the importance of Teresian Carmelite spirituality.

You began this work together with Father Ottilio Rodriguez in 1958. Your first publication in 1964 was the first edition of the *Collected Works of Saint John of the Cross* with Doubleday Press. It seems to me fair to say that your work and the promise of continuing translations of Saint Teresa over the next decades (in the 1970's and 1980's) was a large part of the stability of the Institute of Carmelite Studies that enabled ICS to publish your translations of Saint Teresa.

In 2002 ICS published the first volume of Saint Teresa's letters and in this current year of 2006 ICS will publish the second volume. This brings to fulfillment what has been the driving desire of your life, namely, to make the wisdom and insight of our saints available to a world in need. This apostolate that you have exercised over these years must have been at times exasperating and tedious, but I am sure, always challenging. The fruit of this work is not counted by the number of volumes printed or sold. It remains hidden. The real fruit is in the number of persons who discover the "power to converse with none other than God."

Congratulations Father Kieran, and in the name of the Order of Discalced Carmelites, I thank you for your significant contribution to the culture of our Order.

Luis Aróstegui, OCD
Superior General

Discalced Carmelite Friars
Province of the Immaculate Heart of Mary

Office of the Provincial
Tel: 414-672-7212
Fax: 414-672-3138

Reverend Kieran Kavanaugh, O.C.D.
Discalced Carmelite Friars
2131 Lincoln Road, Northeast
Washington, DC 20002-1199

Dear Father Kieran,

It is certainly an honor for me to write you this letter on the occasion of your fiftieth anniversary of priesthood. I know that all your brothers in the Province join me in asking God's special blessing on you. Because you have done so much to further the understanding of our Teresian and Sanjuanist spirituality through your English translations of St. Teresa of Jesus and St. John of the Cross, your brothers in the Institute of Carmelite Studies honor you with this *Festschrift*. It is but one expression of the esteem and respect your brothers in the Province have for you, Kieran.

Back in 1958 you and Fr. Otilio Rodriguez began working on the translation of the works of St. John of the Cross. From there you moved on to the works of St. Teresa of Jesus and even after Fr. Otilio died in 1994 you continued to complete the translation of her writings. This year, 2006, the last of these translations will be complete with the publication of the second volume of the Letters of St. Teresa. This is truly an amazing accomplishment! Even more, your dedication, perseverance and faithfulness have given the Province and the entire Church a great treasure in making these spiritual classics available in standard American English.

God has used your giftedness to touch the lives of people throughout the world, Father Kieran. For those of us who have lived with you in community over these years, you have also touched our lives with your witness to faithfulness, generosity and service as our brother. ***Ad multos annos!***

Fraternally and gratefully yours,

Fr. Phillip

Fr. Phillip Thomas, O.C.D.
Provincial

1233 South 45th Street Milwaukee, Wisconsin 53214-3693

Celebrating Kieran Kavanaugh

Kevin Culligan, O.C.D.
Carmelite Monastery
Hinton, West Virginia

This volume of Carmelite Sties celebrates the life and work of our brother, Fr. Kieran Kavanaugh, O.C.D. Beginning in 1957, he has devoted himself to the translation into standard American English of the writings of the sixteenth-century Spanish Carmelite spiritual writers, St. Teresa of Avila and St. John of the Cross. This year, 2006, nearly fifty years later, Kieran concludes that effort with the completion of the second and final volume of *The Collected Letters St. Teresa of Avila* by ICS Publications. These translations have made their way throughout the English-speaking world, leading to a deeper appreciation of these two doctors of the church and contributing to the current revival of Christian spirituality. Such achievement demands celebration. As his colleagues in the Institute of Carmelite Studies, we agreed there was no better way to show our admiration and gratitude for our brother's work than to offer these essays on Carmelite topics in his honor.

Life

Thomas Morgan Kavanaugh was born in Milwaukee, Wisconsin, on 19 February 1928. After attending Archbishop Messmer High School in Milwaukee, he entered the novitiate of the Discalced Carmelite friars in Brookline, Massachusetts, in 1946. During his novitiate year, the Brookline community received a pastoral visitation from the order's Spanish general, Fr. Silverio of St.

Teresa, the great Carmelite historian and editor of the writings of Sts. Teresa and John upon whose scholarship Kieran would draw heavily in later years. On 27 August 1947, he professed his first vows of poverty, chastity, obedience, and humility, taking the religious name Kieran of the Cross after the saintly Irish founder and abbot of Clonmacnois, a famous center of holiness and learning in sixth-century Ireland. Following the novitiate, he returned to his native state to begin his studies for the priesthood in the Carmelite house of philosophy at Holy Hill, Wisconsin, forty miles northwest of Milwaukee. Kieran's student master at Holy Hill was Fr. John Clarke, who would later join him in the translation ministry with his translations of the writings of St. Thérèse of Lisieux.

In August 1950, Kieran made his solemn profession of vows at Holy Hill's Shrine of Mary, Help of Christians. His superiors then sent him to Rome for theology studies in the Discalced Carmelite International College of St. Teresa. On the college's faculty at this time were Gabriel of St. Mary Magdalene, the renowned professor of spiritual theology, and the young Tomás Alvarez who would become one of the world's leading experts on St. Teresa. Among the students were Spaniards Federico Ruiz, Eulogio Pacho, and José Vicente Rodríguez, all later to distinguish themselves as St. John of the Cross scholars. In Rome, Kieran wrote "The Christology of St. John of the Cross" for his licentiate in sacred theology and was ordained to the priesthood on 26 March 1955. He was twenty-seven years old.

Before leaving Europe, Fr. Kieran spent one year in the desert monastery of the Discalced Carmelites in Roquebrune-sur-Argens in southern France. A "desert" in the Carmelite tradition is a community of friars devoted exclusively to the contemplative life without involvement in external pastoral ministry. Its purpose is to preserve within the order both the early eremitical life of first hermits on Mt. Carmel in the

Holy Land during the thirteenth century and the contemplative spirit of the sixteenth-century Spanish Carmelite reformers, St. Teresa of Avila and St. John of the Cross. At Roquebrune, situated in the rough foothills above the French Riviera near Fréjus and Saint-Raphaël, where the French-speaking provinces of the Discalced Carmelites maintain a desert in the chapel and hermitages of a former Camaldolese monastery, Kieran drank deeply of Carmel's contemplative waters.

Translations and Writings

Fr. Kieran returned to the United States in 1957. Shortly thereafter he was assigned to the College of Our Lady of Mt. Carmel, the Discalced Carmelite house of theology in Washington D.C., to teach both dogmatic and spiritual theology and to be the director of students. In the Washington community at that time was Fr. Otilio Rodriguez, O.C.D. Newly arrived from Spain, a protégé of Fr. Silverio, Fr. Otilio was a historian of the Carmelite order and dedicated student of the writings of St. Teresa of Avila. Eager to see the Teresian Carmelite heritage spread in the United States, Fr. Otilio recommended to Fr. Kieran that he translate the writings of St. John of the Cross for Americans. Initially, Kieran resisted, claiming insufficient knowledge of Spanish. After Otilio reassured Kieran that St. John's Spanish is not difficult and that, in addition, he would help him, the two friars began the translation in the fall of 1957.

The translation proved more difficult than Fr. Otilio imagined. What he thought could be completed in a few months took five years. Nonetheless, in 1964 Doubleday, the large secular publishers in New York, together with Thomas Nelson in England, published *The Collected Works of St. John of the Cross,* translated by Kieran Kavanaugh, O.C.D., and Otilio Rodriguez, O.C.D, with introductions by Kieran Kavanaugh. For the first time, readers in the United States had a modern American translation of the complete writings of the Spanish mystical doctor of the church in one 740-page volume. In addition, Kavanaugh and Rodriguez's work reflected the most recent research in the life and writings of St. John, a benefit not present in the earlier translations by the Englishmen David Lewis in the second half of the nineteenth century or E. Allison Peers in the 1930s. Also, being Carmelites themselves, the ones for whom John originally wrote, the translators had insights into the saint's words that came from living daily the way of life he was promoting in his writings.

In 1979, the Institute of Carmelite Studies published a second edition of the translation that included two hitherto unknown autograph letters of St. John discovered after 1964. In addition to stylistic and editorial improvements to the original translation, the translators also added a twenty-two page topical index and an index of Sacred Scripture. A decade later, in preparation for the fourth centenary of the death of St. John of the Cross in 1991, Fr. Kieran prepared a revised edition of the translation incorporating the results of the latest sanjuanist scholarship, adding footnotes that included helpful cross-references and a glossary of St. John's terminology. He also revised the text, replacing the generic masculine with gender-neutral language, while preserving John's references to God and Christ in masculine nouns and pronouns. Over the last forty years, this translation in its three editions has sold an average of 360 copies a month.

With their translation of St. John widely accepted by both scholar and general reader, Frs. Kieran and Otilio turned next to translating the writings of St. Teresa into American English. In the years since they began their collaboration, the Discalced Carmelites had closed their theological college in Washington and Kieran was now teaching spiritual theology at Catholic University of America. With the decision in 1972 to translate St. Teresa, he left the university to concentrate on his collaboration with Fr. Otilio in the challenging task of translating St. Teresa, a writer more prolific and complicated than John of the Cross. The Institute of Carmelite Studies published their translation of *The Book of Her Life,* together with her *Spiritual Testimonies and Soliloquies*, in 1976. This was followed in 1980 with their translation of *The Way of Perfection, Meditations on the Song of Songs*, and *The Interior Castle.* Finally, *The Book of Her Foundations* and minor writings, including her poetry, appeared in 1985. In each of these three volumes, Kieran wrote the introductions that provided readers with valuable historical and doctrinal background for understanding St. Teresa.

In the late 1960s, Fr. Otilio was called to Rome to head the Teresian Historical Institute at the Discalced Carmelites' International College, now named the Teresianum, where he was also later to serve as rector. He and Kieran continued their collaboration by mail and during the summer months when Otilio returned home to the United States. From this point on, however, Kieran assumed more of the responsibility for the translations, especially as Otilio's health began gradually to fail. When Otilio died in 1994 at the age of 83, his dream of promoting the Teresian heritage in the United States was largely fulfilled. At the time of his death, people not only in America but also throughout the entire English-speaking world were reading the Kavanaugh and Rodriguez translations of the writings of St. Teresa of Avila and St. John of the Cross.

Still, one significant part of St. Teresa's literary legacy—her letters—remained to be translated into American English. Teresa wrote thousands of personal letters, of which some 468 still exist. Considered by John Tracy Ellis, the late American church historian, to rank among the masterpieces of Catholic world literature, these letters reveal the woman Teresa in all her humanness in ways that her writings on prayer and Carmelite life do not. Now without Fr. Otilio, but with his skills as a translator finely honed and his reputation as a Teresian scholar firmly established, Kieran began in the early nineties to translate St. Teresa's letters. He has been assisted by Mrs. Tina Mendoza, who has compared his translation of each letter with the original Spanish, frequently suggesting more accurate renderings, and Dr. Carol Lisi, who provided editorial assistance in preparing the manuscript for publication. The first volume, consisting of 224 letters written by Teresa between 1546 and 1577, together with an introduction and brief biographical sketches of her correspondents and other persons mentioned in her letters, appeared in 2001. In 2007, ICS Publications will publish the second volume containing the translation of St. Teresa's remaining letters, thus concluding the major work of Kieran's priestly life, fifty years devoted to translating over 2500 pages of the complete works of John of the Cross and Teresa of Avila into standard American English.

Translating Carmelite classics was not Kieran's only literary activity during these years. To celebrate the fourth centenary of John of the Cross's death in 1991, for example, he translated *God Speaks in the Night: The Life, Times, and Teaching of St. John of the Cross.* Produced in Italy as a collaborative effort of many Spanish Carmelite friars under the direction of Fr. Federico Ruiz, one of Kieran's classmates in Rome, this is not a literary biography, but rather 387 pages of text and color photographs that provide the reader with the most reliable information available today about Spain's great mystic and poet.

In addition to his translations, Kieran has also contributed significantly to the current literature on Christian spirituality through his own writings. In 1959, he wrote his first article, "St. John of the Cross: On Faith." It appeared in *Spiritual Life,* the journal of contemporary spirituality that his own Washington province of Discalced Carmelite friars had inaugurated a few years earlier in 1955. Since then he has produced fifty titles, listed in his bibliography in this volume. Many of these writings comprise book reviews in *Spiritual Life* and *The Catholic Historical Review;* summaries of various aspects of Christian spirituality in the *New Catholic Encyclopedia;* essays on Spanish history and Carmelite spirituality in collections such as *The Spirituality of Western Christendom* by Cistercian Studies, and Crossroad's multi-volume *World Spirituality: An Encyclopedic History of the Religious Quest;* and introductions, prefaces, and forewords to works by other authors. In 1999, he authored *John of the Cross: Doctor of Light and Love* for Crossroad's Spiritual Legacy Series, and, in 2003, *Teresa of Avila: The Way of Prayer* for New City Press, both reviewed enthusiastically by Lawrence Cunningham in his "Religion Booknotes" in *Commonweal* (23 March 2001; 26 September 2003).

Ministries in Spirituality

In the early sixties, a handful of friars in the Washington province, including Fr. Kieran, prodded by Fr. Otilio, began discussing the possibility of establishing an institute to promote Carmelite studies through acquiring and maintaining Carmelite resources, research and publications on Carmelite topics, and conducting conferences, seminars, and programs on Carmelite themes. Fr. Peter-Thomas Rohrbach, O.C.D., then prior of the house of studies in Washington, organized this interest and won approval for the Institute of Carmelite Studies from the 1966 Provincial Chapter.

As a charter member, Kieran has been active in the ICS from the beginning. For example, he lectured on Blessed Anne of St. Bartholomew, St. Teresa's trusted secretary and traveling companion who carried the Teresian reform into France and the Netherlands after the foundress's death, in a 2004 symposium, "The Heirs of St Teresa." Held at Georgetown University, ICS cosponsored it with the

Carmelitana Collection of Whitefriars Hall, Washington, DC, and Georgetown's Department of Spanish and Portuguese. Currently, ICS members are offering a lecture series on "A Living Charism: Carmelite Spirituality for a Second Century" honoring the first centenary of both the Bavarian Discalced Carmelites friars' arrival at Holy Hill, Wisconsin, and the death of Bl. Elizabeth of the Trinity in Dijon, France. In this series, Kieran is lecturing on "Bl. Elizabeth of the Trinity and Silence." Over the years, Kieran has also dutifully shared the administrative burden of ICS, including taking his turn as chairman in the early years and, in fact, playing an instrumental role in establishing ICS Publications.

The impetus for the ICS starting its own publishing operation came in 1972 after Doubleday decided not to reprint the one-volume Kavanaugh and Rodriguez translation of St. John of the Cross. The publishers did, however, offer the Carmelites, free of charge, permission to reprint the book on their own. With this permission, but no money, Fr. Kieran and Br. Bryan Paquette, O.C.D., business manager of *Spiritual Life,* arranged for loans from a number of communities of Carmelite nuns to enable them to do a second printing. This appeared in 1973, the exact same book Doubleday had first published, but now a green-covered paperback under the ICS Publications imprint.

The proceeds from the sale of this volume enabled ICS to repay the loans to the nuns and to begin publishing other American translations of classic Carmelite texts. In 1975, ICS published Fr. John Clarke's new translation of St. Thérèse of Lisieux's autobiography, *The Story of a Soul,* from the original French manuscripts prepared by the Carmelite friars in France. This book is now ICS's bestseller. In 1976, ICS brought out the first of the three volumes of Kavanaugh and Rodriguez's translation of the writings of St. Teresa of Avila. Strongly committed to bringing Carmelite classics from Europe to readers in the United States, ICS subsequently published American translations of Br. Lawrence of the Resurrection, Bl. Elizabeth of the Trinity, and the German philosopher and educator, Edith Stein, now St. Teresa Benedicta of the Cross.

The income from the sale of these Carmelite classics now allows ICS to publish a limited number of current Carmelite books, such as the translation of *Awakening to Prayer,* by the Japanese Carmelite Fr.Augustine Ichiro Okumura, and Fr. Francis J. Murphy's work on Père Jacques Bunel, O.C.D., the Carmelite priest-hero of the Mauthausen death camp. ICS's most recent publishing venture is providing study guides for the already published classic Carmelite texts. Fr. Kieran led the way in 2000 with his study guide for St. Teresa's *Way of Perfection.* This was followed by Fr. Marc Foley's study guide for St. Thérèse's *Story of a Soul,* which appeared in 2005. From its almost accidental beginnings in 1972 to its current list of over fifty titles, ICS Publications has sold well over a million books, as well as some 35,000 audiocassettes and CDs of lectures, conferences, seminars, and other resources on Carmelite themes.

Kieran has also been a charter member of the Carmelite Forum, another collaborative enterprise in Carmelite spiritual ministry. In 1982, during the Washington, DC, celebration of the fourth centenary of the death of St. Teresa of Avila, Sr. Constance FitzGerald, O.C.D., prioress of the community of Carmelite nuns in Baltimore, and Fr. Ernest Larkin, O.Carm., the well-known Carmelite teacher, lecturer, writer, and retreat master, discussed informally the desirability of a group of Carmelite scholars working together to interpret the rich Carmelite tradition for contemporary Americans. When they presented this idea to Fr. John Malley, O.Carm., then Prior Provincial of the Chicago province of the Carmelite friars of the Ancient Observance and later the order's prior general, he responded favorably, offering to fund such an effort.

With this support, Sr. Constance convened a meeting of interested persons, including Fr. Kieran, in early 1983 at Whitefriars Hall in Washington, DC. From this meeting, the Carmelite Forum, a small group of men and women, lay and religious, from both orders—the Carmelites of the Ancient observance and the Teresian Carmelites—came into being. Their goal is to foster understanding and interpretation of the Carmelite tradition, particularly the spirituality of St. John of the Cross and St. Teresa of Avila, in light of the needs of the contemporary American church. Since 1985, the Forum's principal activity has been its annual summer seminar in Carmelite spirituality, sponsored by the Center for Spirituality at St. Mary's College, Notre Dame, Indiana.

At St. Mary's, through lectures, workshops, reading sessions, liturgy, prayer, and community, Kieran and his colleagues—principally Constance FitzGerald, Ernest Larkin, Vilma Seelaus, Keith Egan, John Welch, and myself—have presented and interpreted Carmelite spirituality to well over 1500 clergy, religious, and lay persons, whether Catholic or of other faith traditions. From these seminars have come numerous audiocassettes on Carmelite topics produced by Alba House and ICS Publications, as well as two collections of essays, *Carmel and Contemplation: Transforming Human Consciousness,* edited by Kevin Culligan and Regis Jordan and published by ICS Publications (2000), and *Carmelite Prayer: A Tradition for the 21st Century,* edited by Keith Egan and published by Paulist Press (2003). To these volumes, Fr. Kieran contributed "How to pray: From the Life and Writings of St. Teresa" and "Contemplation and the Stream of Consciousness" respectively.

Along with his involvement in the Institute of Carmelite Studies and the Carmelite Forum, Kieran has many other ministries. For years he has provided individual spiritual guidance for numerous persons. He frequently gives retreats, lectures, seminars, and workshops, both in this country and internationally. He has presented in Europe, Asia, and Africa. This year, for example, he will be off to Singapore in August to lead retreats for the Carmelites there. At home, he has served his brother and sister Carmelites in numerous ways. Over the years, his fellow friars have elected him to such offices as local superior, provincial councilor, vicar-provincial, and delegate to both provincial and general chapters. He has also held appointments as spiritual assistant to different Carmelite secular communities and the provincial's delegate to the communities of Carmelite nuns who have the provincial as their religious ordinary.

Currently, he is the Washington province's postulator or promoter of causes for canonization. In this capacity he participated in the medical verification of the illness and unexplainable recovery of the American child Benedicta McCarthy, the miracle presented in the canonization process of Edith Stein. Kieran described this exhaustive process in "The Canonization Miracle and Its Investigation" that appeared in *Never Forget: Christian and Jewish Perspectives on Edith Stein,* volume 7 of the Carmelite Studies series, published in 1998. He then had the privilege of concelebrating, with Pope John Paul II, the canonization Eucharist in St. Peter's Square in Rome on 11 October 1998. When not translating, writing, lecturing, sharing the burden of administration, and promoting the sanctity of others, Kieran may be found in his monastery in Washington, participating in the daily liturgies, praying, washing dishes, and answering the telephone.

To the members of his province, community, and especially, the Institute of Carmelite Studies, Kieran has become an older brother who daily shares his life with us, advising, encouraging, supporting, and inspiring us with his quiet presence, wise words, and good example. His legacy to our order will undoubtedly be his fidelity to the prescription in the ancient Carmelite Rule of St. Albert that calls each of us "to remain in or near one's cell, meditating day and night on the Law of the Lord and watching in prayer unless otherwise justly occupied." Kieran's fidelity to this directive has been a main source of his productive life. Although he obtained a licentiate in theology during his early years in Rome and taught spiritual theology for several years at Catholic University of America, Kieran's work has not been centered primarily in academia. Rather, his scholarship, translations, writings, and prepared conferences, preaching, and retreats have come from his devotion to his cell. He has thus left an example for us of the immense good for the order and the Church that results from following the ancient monastic custom of prayer and study in the quiet of one's own cell.

A Better Wine

To express our appreciation for all that Kieran has been for us and the Church in the fifty years since he was ordained a priest, the members of the Institute of Carmelite Studies have prepared this volume of essays and translations. Aside from the bibliography, which in itself is an eloquent testimony to his own accomplishments, the individual chapters are not about him. His modesty would not permit this. They are, however, about that which is so dear to him, the Teresian Carmelite heritage. The two opening essays by Daniel Chowning and Marc Foley offer interpretations of important teachings of St. Teresa of Avila and St. John of the Cross. Appearing for the first time in English, Michael Dodd's translation of Jerome Gratian's *Constituciones del Cerro* presents a humorous interlude in the lives of Gratian and St. Teresa when they were collaborating in the serious work of the Teresian reform in sixteenth-century Spain.

Moving into more recent times, the chapters of Emmanuel Sullivan, Salvatore Sciurba, and Steven Payne focus upon St. Thérèse of Lisieux, the most recently proclaimed and only truly modern doctor of the church. Steven Payne's chapter, in particular, tells the fascinating story of how Thérèse, who did not even graduate from high school, came to be proclaimed a church doctor, placing her not only in the elite company of her Carmelite spiritual parents, Teresa of Jesus and John of the Cross, but that also of such great lights as Thomas Aquinas, Bonaventure, Robert Bellarmine, and Alphonsus Liguori. The final three essays by John Sullivan, Denis Read, and myself speak of the heroic examples of faith and love in the courageous wartime lives of St. Edith Stein and Père Jacques Bunel during the Holocaust, the influence of the Carmelite mystical school on the late Pope John Paul II, and learning to meditate in Carmel. Finally, in the afterword, Fr. William Johnston, S.J., an author long admired by Fr. Kieran, contributes an invited essay on St. John of the Cross's potential contribution to the future of interfaith dialogue in Asia.

These essays and translations have been brought together under the title *A Better Wine*, an obvious allusion to Jesus' miracle at the wedding feast in Cana of Galilee. From the earliest days of Christianity, this event has symbolized the Eucharistic banquet wherein the priest's words transform bread and wine into the Body and Blood of Christ, our spiritual food and drink. Jesus' changing water into wine at Cana is also an apt symbol for the contemplative tradition of Carmel, in which God's grace transforms our human lives into the divine life. The wedding feast at Cana seemed the right image for the golden jubilee celebration of a Carmelite priest whose ministry for fifty years has been the transformation of our lives in God through love. We trust these chapters will please Kieran; we hope that in them our readers will taste "a better wine."

Essays

Jesus Christ, Friend and Liberator: The Christology of St. Teresa of Jesus

Daniel Chowning, O.C.D.
Discalced Carmelite Novitiate
Milwaukee, Wisconsin

Throughout the centuries the followers of Jesus have had to answer the question Jesus posed to his disciples in the Gospel of St. Mark: "And you, who do you say that I am?" (Mk 8:29). The response to this query led to hot debates, conflict, and even bloodshed and death during the great ecumenical councils from Nicea to Chalcedon. The answer to Jesus' inquiry that emerged from Chalcedon in 451 A.D. has shaped our orthodox understanding of the person of Jesus of Nazareth, the Eternal Logos of the Father, who became human; but the questioning did not end then. This question has reverberated in the hearts of Christians throughout the history of Christianity. Poets, mystics, artists, historians, and theologians have responded to this haunting inquiry according to their own age and culture with its particular vision of reality, language, problems, and lived experience. An examination of those in the past who have had the courage to reply to this great Christological question will deepen our understanding of Jesus and challenge us to respond both personally and collectively to that mystifying query: "And you, who do you say that I am?"

This essay examines the Christology of St. Teresa of Jesus to seek her answer to Jesus' question. Teresa's experience parallels that in the New Testament: her human need and search for redemption and liberation made Jesus above all her liberator and friend. At the heart of her knowledge of him is her human search for love and wholeness, her quest for God. The conflict, crises, and sufferings enmeshed in this search eventually forced her in 1554 to surrender all trust in herself and fall back on the power of the Risen Lord Jesus. This experience, which took place before a statue of "a much wounded Christ," marks a decisive turning point in her life. (L.9.1) She divides her life into two stages, seeing this event of conversion as the birth of a new and freer existence. The years of conflict and struggle in her search for love, intimacy, and God, as well as the trials and sufferings that followed this momentous occasion, form the very impetus of her search for Jesus and the source of her understanding and liberating experience of him. They are the starting point for her Christology. They led Teresa to an authentic, profound discovery of the humanity of Jesus Christ and the difference Jesus makes in our lives when we place our absolute trust and confidence in him and take him as friend and companion. Teresa's relationship to Jesus grew and developed from 1554 onward. In him she found the freedom to stand more confidently on reality, to live more fully, and to love and serve others more generously. She experienced the heart of what resurrection truly means for all Christians: that Jesus lives now for us in a new and dynamic way.[1]

The first theme that usually comes to mind when we think of Teresa of Jesus is prayer. Teresa has made a profound contribution in helping us understand the dynamics of an interior life devoted to prayer and contemplation. But if her doctrine is explicitly on prayer, implicitly her message is about the person of Jesus Christ and the difference he makes in our lives when we surrender completely to him. Jesus is the door through which we must pass to truly understand Teresa's charism.[2]

In the first section of this essay, we will study the history of Teresa's experience of Jesus and concentrate on the principal events and crises of her life that eventually led her to an encounter with the Risen Lord, first in 1554, and then subsequently in 1556.[3] Following a brief overview of Teresa's experience of Jesus after 1556, we will examine in part two the substance of her doctrine on the humanity of Christ and its implications for her spirituality. Finally, in part three we will discuss her experience of the Risen Christ to discern what her experience teaches us about the meaning of resurrection for us, and what the relationship of the Risen Christ is to her spirituality as a whole and its implications for our personal and collective lives as Christians.

1. The Mystery of a Life in Search of Love and Wholeness

When we read the New Testament, especially the four Gospels, we find that the primary source of people's encounters with Jesus was the human experience of conflict and suffering, the hunger for love and wholeness, the thirst for God, the profound human need for redemption and liberation from the brokenness and limitations of human existence in all its forms, whether physical or mental illness, material or spiritual poverty, alienation, and above all, death. The Gospels present us with concrete conflictual and debilitating human experiences that lead people to seek Jesus, accept his gifts of liberation and new life, and come away full of new meaning and hope. Life was changed dramatically by the experience of liberation found in him. St. Mark's depiction of the possessed man of the Gerasene territory who lived among the tombs, and day and night screamed and gashed himself with stones, portrays in a vivid manner the difference Jesus can make in a person's life. Therefore, we see the origin of New Testament Christology as the human experience of conflict and suffering that gave rise to an encounter with Jesus of Nazareth, which afterward was reflected upon and proclaimed as "good news." As Edward Schillebeeckx reminds us, "soteriology is the way to Christology."[4]

Paralleling the New Testament, St. Teresa's Christology is born from her experience of human limitation. When we examine her life, especially the first half from her birth on 28 March 1515, to Lent of 1554 when she was thirty-nine years old, we find a series of painful crises and conflicts, in which her search for love, friendship, and God, led her to a revolutionary discovery of the humanity of Jesus Christ. The first eight chapters of her autobiography narrate the life events that brought her to this discovery, culminating in chap. 9 with the story of her famous conversion of 1554 before the image of the wounded Christ. Let us briefly inquire into her interior state on the eve of her conversion. This will provide a focal point through which we can probe deeper into the nature of her long struggle. Following a discussion of the underlying issues, we can then proceed to a closer examination of how she lived out this dramatic interior battle through the three phases of her life up to 1554.

Inner Conflict

The symbols Teresa uses to describe her psychological and spiritual life on the eve of her conversion in 1554 poignantly reveal a state of inner conflict and fragmentation. The overall picture she paints of herself is one of being interiorly divided. She speaks of a "war so troublesome," a "tempestuous sea." (L.8.2) All the things of God made her happy, but those of the world held her bound. (L.7.17) She writes: "So, save for the year I mentioned, for more than eighteen of the twenty-eight years since I began prayer, I suffered this battle and conflict between friendship with God and friendship with the world." (L.8.3)

What was the nature of this battle between God and the world? The roots of Teresa's conflict lie deep in her personal life history and are woven into the very fabric of her warm and extroverted personality. Teresa possessed a profound capacity for love and friendship.

Love is the most important key for interpreting her life and message and for explaining her intimate conflicts and her "martyrdom" for years.[5] Friendship was the joy as well as the torment of her life. It led her to a crisis, first in adolescence, then between youth and middle age.[6] We need only look at the abundant references she makes to her relationships to perceive her natural disposition to establish warm and meaningful friendships. She frequently uses adverbs "much," "too much," and "extremely" to describe her relationships. Speaking of her family she writes: "He was the one I liked most, although I had great love for them all and they for me." (L.1.4) "I was the most loved of my father." (L.1.3) Following Teresa's illness at the convent of Our Lady of Grace, she went to recuperate at the home of her half-sister and brother-in-law. Their love for her reveals how cherished she felt in the family circle. "She loved me so deeply that if they had followed her wish I would have lived there permanently. And her husband also liked me very much. . . . But even this I owe to the Lord, for everywhere I was always loved." (L.3.3)

Even outside her family Teresa found herself surrounded by warmth and care. When Teresa's father, Don Alonso Sánchez de Cepeda, concerned about the company his sixteen-year-old daughter was keeping, entrusted her to the care of the nuns of Our Lady of Grace convent, Teresa found herself showered with love. "All were pleased with me, for the Lord gave me the grace to be pleasing wherever I went, so I was much loved." (L.2.8) Her relationship with the priest of Becedas demonstrates well her capacity to move outside herself in order to enter into the joys and sorrows of others. "He became extremely fond of me. . . . His affection for me was not bad; but since it was too great, it came to no good. . . . By reason of the strong love he had for me, he began to explain to me about his bad moral state. . . . To me it was a great pity for I loved him deeply. I was so frivolous and blind that it seemed to me a virtue to be grateful and loyal to anyone who loved me. . . . Once I knew about these charms, I began to show him more love." (L. 5.4&6)

Although Teresa's profound and natural capacity to give and receive human love was a God-given blessing and good, for her it had a dark underside that collided with her spiritual aspirations. Her search to assuage her restless longing to love and be loved, accentuated by her warm and extroverted personality, easily bound her in a state of dependency on others and ran the risk of her living perpetually outside herself in other people.[7] A few examples will illustrate her problem. She recalls the extremes to which she would go in pleasing others during a visit with her uncle Don Pedro at the time of her recuperation from her illness at Our Lady of Grace. "For in this matter of pleasing others I went to extremes, even when it was a burden to me; so much so that what in others would be considered virtuous, in me was a great fault, for I very often acted without discretion." (L.3.4) Teresa admits quite honestly that "she enjoyed being esteemed" (L.5.1) and was prone to follow the "way of the many." (L.7.1) Even her decision to enter the Incarnation manifests some dependency: "I had a good friend in another convent, and that was the reason why if I were to become a nun I would not have done it unless it were in the convent where she was." (L.3.2)

But Teresa confesses quite openly the heart of her difficulty in chap. 37 of her *Life.* "I had a serious fault that did me much harm; it was that when I began to know that certain persons liked me, and I found them attractive, I became so attached that my memory was bound so strongly by the thought of them. There was no intention to offend God, but I was happy to see these persons and think about them and about the good things I saw in them. This was something so harmful that it was leading my soul seriously astray." (L.37.4)

Considering the drive behind Teresa's search for God, we can understand the conflict she endured for many years. Her tendency to live outside herself in others clashed with her quest for the transcendent through interior prayer. Friendships, therefore, became a source of conflict because Teresa was unable to reconcile her need for human love and companionship with her thirst for God. She became divided and fragmented within herself, and a duality was set up between her longing for God and her need to give of herself in human relationship. Desiring to avoid her humanity, her spirit longed to fly to God, but her human heart of flesh and blood cried out for recognition and acceptance.[8] At one point Teresa describes her life as a "voyage on a tempestuous sea" (L.8.2), and tempestuous it was, for the waves of her desires for the Infinite would raise her high toward heaven, only to come crashing down to the earth in which she was firmly planted.

As we examine more closely the three periods of her life up to 1554, it will become evident that she suffered from the tension between her spirit, which longed to take mystical flight into God, and her finite, "earthy" nature, which clung tenaciously to the earth with its human loves and friendships, joys and sensuous pleasures. It is here that the meaning of the "world" emerges for Teresa. The world she speaks of, which she considers to stand in opposition to God, is not so much earthly reality, but rather her own inner "world of affective reactions and contacts" that held her dependent and made her live outside herself.[9] Teresa struggled for many years in this "war so troublesome" (L.8.2) between friendship with God and friendship with the world, between her "body and spirit," between her spiritual thirst for God and her natural thrust for human love and friendship.[10] In the three stages of her life from childhood to middle age, we will see this duality lived out in a pattern of alternating periods of intense religious fervor or conversion with periods of falling into what Teresa refers to as "vanities and pastimes" (L.7.1), "havoc" (L.7.11), and the pastimes of "conversations" and "friendships." (L.7.6) Not until her discovery of the humanity of Jesus Christ does this split within her find healing and reconciliation.

Now that we have discussed the nature of Teresa's long and arduous struggle that eventually brought her to her conversion experience of 1554, let us next examine her life from this perspective. I will divide her life from childhood to 1554 into three periods: 1) childhood; 2) adolescence, including her stay in Our Lady of Grace convent; and 3) her religious life from 1535 to 1554/56.

Childhood and Adolescence

The first period is Teresa's childhood. One Teresian scholar has compared the opening chapter of Teresa's autobiography to the beginning account of the Book of Genesis.[11] In it she describes her experience of "paradise," a harmonious life filled with intense religious fervor. Indeed, Teresa's longing for the infinite awakened within her at an early age. An experience she shared with her brother Rodrigo illustrates well this ardent desire for the absolute that possessed her from early childhood. She and her brother read the lives of the saints, and although the torture the martyrs endured terrified them, the thought of the glory awaiting them held Teresa and Rodrigo spellbound. They often spoke about this and would delight in repeating "forever and ever and ever." (L.1.4) Teresa tells us she wished to die in the same way in order "to enjoy very quickly" the wonderful things she read there were in heaven. (L.1.4) One day, she and her brother decided to run off to the land of the Moors to seek martyrdom themselves so they could delight in the wonders of heaven. Unsuccessful in their attempt, Teresa resolved to seek God closer to home. In a sense, this small childhood incident reflects an underlying pattern Teresa relived more than once: a premature, unsuccessful effort to seek an immediate vision of God, after which she would resign herself to searching for God closer to home—in nature, in history, in human life.

Teresa continued her quest for God and gave alms, sought out solitude to pray her devotions, and pretended to be a nun along with her other childhood companions. (L.1.6) She tells us she awakened early to the practice of virtue through the example of her parents and the good books her father provided. (L.1.1) In one short swoop of the pen, Teresa sums up her childhood in these words: "As I said over and over, the Lord was pleased to impress upon me in childhood the way of truth." (L.1.4)

Teresa's youthful, earnest search for God began to wane around the age of twelve. Puberty brought a new consciousness to her. Much like Adam and Eve, she was expelled from her "garden of Eden" and began her long toil to reconcile the forces of a divided nature. The last sentence of chap. 1 of her *Life* sets the stage for the second phase of her journey toward 1554. "As I grew older, when I began to know of the natural qualities the Lord had bestowed on me (which others said were many), instead of thanking him for them, I began to make use of them all to offend him." (L.1.8)

Not only did puberty bring all its physical and emotional changes, but it also introduced the world of love and friendships, "the pastime of pleasant conversation" (L.2.6), and her own propensity to immerse herself in a superficial and mediocre life. She describes three areas that brought her to crisis in adolescence. The first is books on chivalry.[12] Following her mother's example, as a young teenager she became "completely taken up" with the habit of reading these stories. (L.2.1) Second, she tells us she became overly fastidious and concerned about her looks, clothes, and how she pleased others. "I began to dress in finery and to desire to please and look pretty, taking great care of my hands, and hair, and about perfumes and all empty things in which one can indulge, and which were many, for I was very vain." (L. 2.2)[13]

But the primary source of Teresa's crisis in adolescence was her friendship with some cousins. Her ability to give and receive human love blossomed and she embarked upon that long period of conflict with her affectivity that would hold her for many years in a state of dependency and at odds with her religious longings. At some point around the time of her mother's death, Teresa became involved with some cousins, and one in particular, whose influence on her changed her desire for virtue and encouraged her in frivolous pastimes. "I imitated all that was harmful in a relative who spent a lot of time at our house. . . . My talks and conversations were with her, for she encouraged me in all the pastimes I desired and even immersed me in them by sharing with me her conversations and vanities." (L.2.3)

Teresa devoted much time to these relationships, listening to the accounts of "their affections" and "to things not the least bit edifying." (L.2.2) Despite the efforts of Don Alonso and her sister to divert her from the friendship, she continued on and strove to keep her actions secret. (L.2.7) In a short time, the effects of the relationship became evident. "And indeed this conversation so changed me that hardly any virtue remained to my naturally virtuous soul. And I think she and another girl friend of the same type impressed their own traits upon me." (L.2.4)

Teresa's friendship with her cousins so concerned her father that he entrusted his sixteen-year-old daughter to the care of the Augustinian nuns at Our Lady of Grace convent to free her from the company she had been keeping. When we read Teresa's account of her year-and-a-half experience in this convent boarding school, we find a resurgence of intense religious fervor, a conversion, followed by a vocational crisis that manifests her primary conflict. The good company, holy conversation, and fervent atmosphere of Our Lady of Grace touched the sensitive fibers of Teresa's own religious sentiment and deepest spiritual desires. "There was no time it seems to me when I was not happy to hear about God." (L.3.1) She met the saintly nun, Doña Maria de Briceño y Contreras, whose devout conversation on the word of God awakened within her the desire for "eternal things." (L.3.1) "Beginning, then, to like the good and holy conversation of this nun, I was glad to hear how well she spoke about God, for she was very discreet and saintly. . . . She began to tell me how she arrived at the decision to become a nun solely by reading what the Gospel says: *many are the called and few the chosen.* She told me about the reward the Lord grants those who give up all for him. This good company began to help me get rid of the habits that the bad company had caused and to turn my mind to the desire for eternal things." (L.3.1)

As a result of all this, Teresa "began to return to the good habits of early childhood." (L.2.8) Her spirit soared high in her search for God. She began to recite many vocal prayers and to ask others to commend her to God so he might show her the state in which she was able to serve him. (L.3.2) She envied those she saw with the gift of tears or other virtues because she herself could read the entire passion without shedding a tear, and this pained her. (L.3.1) It was probably during this period that she began to meditate on Jesus when he was alone and agonizing in the garden the night before his crucifixion.[14] "Most nights, for many years before going to bed when I commended myself to God in preparation for sleep, I always pondered a little while this episode of the prayer in the garden. I did this even before I was a nun since I was told that one gains many indulgences by doing so." (L. 9.4)

Teresa's renewed spiritual ardor, however, failed to deliver her from further inner conflicts; rather, it became the impetus for a new crisis, illustrating the interior division with which she struggled. Her conversations with Doña Maria de Briceño, her reading of the word of God, and her devotions freed Teresa somewhat from the "antagonism" that she felt toward becoming a nun. (L.3.1) Good thoughts of becoming a nun would come to her, but her will refused consent. Fearful of herself and her own "frailty" (L.3.7) (her tendency to throw herself into her relationships), she experienced a split between her intellect, which persuaded her that religious life was the best and surest path, and her heart, which longed for the love and companionship of her father, family, friends, and a less austere life.[15] "Although my will did not completely incline to being a nun, I saw that the religious life was the best and safest state, and so little by little I decided to force myself to accept it. I was engaged in this battle within myself for three months forcing myself with this reasoning: that the trials and hardships of being a nun could not be greater than those of purgatory and that I had really merited hell; that it would not be so great a thing while alive to live as though in purgatory; and afterward I would go directly to heaven, for that was my desire." (L.3.5-6)

There is definitely an element of force in Teresa's choice of religious life. She tells us that she "was moved more by servile fear than by love." (L.3.6) The war between God and the world waged on within her. She admits that since there was no love of God to take away her love for her father and relatives, everything so constrained her that if the Lord had not helped her, her reflections would not have been enough for her to continue. This interior battle led to a breakdown in her health and to her departure from Our Lady of Grace. "The Lord was more determined to prepare me for the state that was better for me. He sent me a serious illness so that I had to return to my father's house." (L.3.3) The period of recuperation apparently gave Teresa distance and time for reflection, enabling her to proceed with her decision to embrace religious life despite her father's disapproval. With a divided heart, afraid of herself and her own frailty, and of backing down, Teresa stole away from her family home and entered the Carmelite convent of the Incarnation in Avila on the morning of 2 November 1535, at the age of twenty-one. She writes of this experience: "I remember, clearly and truly, that when I left my father's house I felt that separation so keenly that the feeling will not be greater, I think, when I die. For it seemed to me that every bone in my body was being sundered." (L.4.1) Thus begins the third and longest period of Teresa's journey toward 1554.

Religious Life

Teresa's early years in religious life portray a woman of intense religious enthusiasm and, as a result of illness, profound spiritual insight. Her interior drama subsided shortly after her entrance into the monastery. Much like her early days among the Augustinian nuns, Teresa experienced in Carmel renewed peace, fervor, and consolation in the things of God. "As soon as I took the habit, the Lord gave me an understanding of how he favors those who use force with themselves to serve him. . . .Within an hour, he gave me such great happiness at being in the religious state of life that it has never left me up to this day, and God changed the dryness my soul experienced into the greatest tenderness. All the things of religious life delighted me." (L.4.2)

Sometimes while sweeping, during the hours Teresa used to spend "in self-adornment and self-indulgence," she realized that she was free of all that and felt a new joy that amazed her. (L.4.2) Even though she "suffered great uneasiness over things that in themselves were of little importance" and over "anything that seemed to be scorn," she felt great happiness in being a nun. (L.5.1) She envied the virtues of others, and even though a novice in the spiritual life, she had the "light that made everything coming to an end seem of little value" in comparison to the great value of eternity. (L.5.2) If Teresa's initial months and years in the convent reveal a phase of intense spiritual effort and delight in her quest for God, they were not, however, devoid of suffering. The change of food and lifestyle injured her health. "My fainting spells began to increase, and I experienced such heart pains that this frightened any who witnessed them; and there were many other illnesses all together." (L.4.5) Teresa's illness has been the object of much speculation, and it would take us far beyond the scope of this essay to discuss it at length. However, regardless of the nature of her mysterious sickness which took her to the brink of the grave, it became the providential means for a deeper experience of the Lord and to the discovery of what would become her special vocation in the Church.[16]

Unable to find a doctor who could provide a cure for his daughter, Don Alonso accompanied Teresa, along with another nun companion, from the Incarnation convent to a small town named Becedas famous for treatments of various illnesses. On the way, they passed by her uncle's house, Don Pedro Sanchez de Cepeda. Don Pedro gave his niece a copy of Francisco Osuna's work, *The Third Spiritual Alphabet,* which taught her the prayer of recollection. Before this she didn't know how to proceed in prayer or become recollected. We cannot underestimate the importance of the discovery of this book for Teresa's experience of Jesus, for it impressed upon her that the God she sought was not abstract or diffused but truly personal—the Incarnate Word of God, Jesus Christ, living within her. "I tried as hard as I could to keep Jesus Christ, our God and our Lord, present within me, and that was my way of prayer. If I reflected upon some phase of his passion, I represented him to myself interiorly." (L.4.7) As a result of this method of prayer, Teresa underwent a conversion. She took time out for solitude, confessed frequently, avoided serious sin, and experienced greater freedom. "I was left with some effects so great, and even though at this time I was no more than twenty, it seems I trampled the world underfoot." (L.4.7)

The solitude, silence, and confinement to bed during her long recuperation following the dreadful cures at Becedas, which left her paralyzed for nearly three years, led to a deepening of her spirit so zealous for God. She desired to be cured only to remain more alone in prayer. (L.6.2) She longed for deeper solitude (L.6.4), received communion and confessed often (L.6.2), received favors in prayer which made her understand the meaning of love for God (L.6.3), and enjoyed conversing and speaking about the Lord with others. (L.6.4) She read books and felt repentance after having offended God. The awareness of her infidelity to God tormented her. (L.6.4) Her love of neighbor also increased and she ordinarily avoided all faultfinding and speaking evil of anyone. (L.6.3)

Finally, Teresa regained her health through the intercession of St. Joseph. She had peered into the domain of death and had slowly returned to the land of the living. Her prolonged illness physically symbolizes the dramatic and mysterious dying and rising in the realm of her spirit. "I had seen myself almost dead and in such a serious danger of being condemned, after having been raised up body and soul, so that all who saw me were amazed to see me alive." (L.6.9)

Once again, however, Teresa's high spiritual aspirations and fervor came tumbling back to earth. There was no escape from her own humanity nor from a sinful and broken world, even in the convent of the Incarnation. The environment in which Teresa found herself was not simply an enclosure where all the nuns were caught up in an ecstasy of divine love.[17] Like any monastery of the sixteenth century, it was a place where worldly honors and recreations could be so exalted and people's obligations so poorly understood that they took for virtue what is sin (L.7.4); where a nun may have to be "more cautious and dissimulating in speaking about the friendship she desired to have with God than in speaking of other friendships and attachments that the devil arranges" (L.7.5); "where there are two paths (one of virtue and religious life, and the other a lack of religious life) and the greater number take the more imperfect path." (L.7.5) In this atmosphere, Teresa became enmeshed in the same conflict with which she had struggled in adolescence and prior to her entrance into Carmel. "Now then, I engaged in these conversations thinking that since this was the custom, my soul would not receive the harm and distraction I afterward understood comes from such companionship. It seemed to me that something as general in many monasteries as this visiting would not do me any more harm than it did others who I saw were good. I did not consider that they were much better and that what was a danger for me was not so much for others." (L.7.6)

Helpless to place any boundaries on her affective needs that held her dependent and kept her back from what she felt God was asking of her, Teresa lived for many years going back and forth from her convent cell to the parlor of the Incarnation. She had one friend in particular to whom she was especially attached. "No other friendship was as much a distraction to me as this one of which I am speaking, for I was extremely fond of it." (L.7.7) Once while engaged in a conversation with this person, Christ appeared before her with "great severity" making her understand what he regretted about the friendship. (L.7.6)[18] Although the vision of Christ frightened her, Teresa returned to "the same conversation and also at other times to other conversations." (L.7.7) On another occasion, she and those with whom she was visiting saw running toward them some creature that looked like a large toad. The presence of such a reptile in that place and time of day seemed quite unusual. The incident left Teresa with an ominous feeling. Nevertheless, she remained bound, even when warned by a relative in the convent of the danger of these relationships. (L.7.9)

Seeing herself so enslaved, Teresa feared the practice of prayer out of guilt and a false sense of humility and eventually abandoned it for more than a year. (L.7.1) The effects of her conflict extended further than this. She began to "lose joy in virtuous things" and in her taste for them. (L.7.1) In order "to be held in esteem," she decided to "go the way of the many" at the expense of her own inner truth and to plunge herself into the flow of a dependent, mediocre and "lax" existence. (L.7.1&14) "Since I thus began to go from pastime to pastime, from vanity to vanity, from one occasion to another, to place myself often in very serious occasions, and to allow my soul to become so spoiled by many vanities, I was then ashamed to return to the search for God by means of a friendship as special as is that found in the intimate exchange of prayer." (L.7.1)

Life became "extremely burdensome" and Teresa felt torn between heaven and earth. (L.7.17) On the one hand she felt God's call, and on the other, her heart made of flesh and blood desired to follow the world of her friends with all their sensory joys, pleasures, and pastimes. "All the things of God made me happy; those of the world held me bound." (L.7.17) Her confessors proved no help for her divided heart. They approved of her conduct and assured her that these "occasions and associations" would in no way harm her. (L.8.11) Even her prayer, to which she had returned after the death of her father, became a source of torture. "I was more anxious that the hour I had determined to spend in prayer be over than I was to remain there, and more anxious to listen for the striking of the clock than to attend to other good things." (L.8.7) Furthermore, sermons and conversations about God, although they delighted her, became a source of torment for she knew she was "a far cry" from what she should have been. (L.8.12) Struggling to reconcile her restless and fragmented spirit, Teresa found herself in a state of captivity out of which she saw no escape. "Would that I knew how to depict the captivity my soul was in during this time." (L.8.11). She paints a vivid and poignant picture of her inner conflict. "I voyaged on this tempestuous sea for almost twenty years with these fallings and risings and this evil—since I fell again—and in a life so beneath perfection that I paid almost no attention to venial sins. I should say that it is one of the most painful lives, I think, that one can imagine; for neither did I enjoy God nor did I find happiness in the world. When I was experiencing the enjoyments of the world, I felt sorrow when I recalled what I owed God. When I was with God, my attachments to the world disturbed me. This is a war so troublesome that I don't know how I was able to suffer it even a month, much less for so many years." (L.8.2)

Teresa sought to remedy her plight; she made attempts to help herself, but to no avail, for she still placed too much trust in her own power to lift herself above her human weakness. "I searched for a remedy, I made attempts, but I didn't understand that all is of little benefit if we do not take away completely the trust we have in ourselves and place it in God." (L.8.12) Life seemed to ebb away, and Teresa found herself groping in a "shadow of death," searching for someone who could lead her to reconciliation and give peace to her restless, torn heart. "I wanted to live (for I well understood that I was not living but was struggling with a shadow of death), but I had no one to give me life, and I was unable to catch hold of it." (L.8.12)

Surrender and Freedom

Liberation, however, came to Teresa in this state of complete helplessness and weakness, when she admitted her powerlessness. One day during Lent of 1554, she entered an oratory and saw a familiar statue of a "much wounded Christ." (L.9.1) The sight of Jesus' wounds, his neediness, loneliness, and brokenness, undertaken for love of her, struck a deep chord within her. Beseeching Jesus to strengthen her once and for all that she might not offend him, she threw herself down on her knees and, "with the greatest outpouring of tears," surrendered herself before the power of the Risen Jesus. (L.9.1) She told Jesus she would not rise until he had granted her request.

Teresa's surrender to Jesus before the image of his broken and suffering humanity brought about a profound change in her life. The days of her captivity ended when she ceased to rely on her human efforts alone, and instead, opened herself to the saving and healing power of Jesus. When she takes up the account of her life in chap. 23 of her autobiography, after having digressed for several chapters to discuss prayer, she begins by relating the effect this experience had on her. "I now want to return to where I left off about my life, for I think I delayed more than I should have so that what follows would be better understood. This is another, new book from here on—I mean another, new life. The life I dealt with up to this point was mine; the one I lived from the point where I began to explain these things about prayer is the one God lived in me—according to the way it appears to me—because I think it would have been impossible in so short a time to get rid of so many bad habits and deeds. May the Lord be praised who freed me from myself." (L.23.1)

"May the Lord be praised who freed me from myself." How often the word *libertad,* "freedom," appears in Teresa's works in reference to the transformation which transpired in her life through the power of Jesus.[19] "He gave me a freedom that I with all the efforts of many years could not attain." (L.24.8) A newer and deeper stage of the Christian life began for Teresa in 1554, and her quest for God became more and more concretized and personal in and through the humanity of Jesus Christ. Although new interior vistas opened up before her in 1554, Teresa still had not reached a complete freedom from her dependency on others. A much greater liberation would come in 1556 through the wise guidance of two Jesuit spiritual directors who advised her to meditate on the humanity of Jesus Christ.

During the summer of 1555, Teresa confessed to a young Jesuit priest named Fr. Diego de Cetina. Teresa sought out Fr. Diego with a certain amount of unrest and anxiety over her imperfections and attachments, but the confessor stressed the love of God, allowed freedom, and used no pressure if Teresa's love was not as free as she desired. Most of all, Diego de Cetina directed her to the humanity of Jesus Christ. "He told me that I should devote prayer each day to a phase of the passion, that I should benefit from this prayer and dwell only on the humanity." (L.23.17) As a consequence of this reflection on the mysteries of Jesus' life, Teresa began to improve and her love for the humanity of Christ deepened. "I started again to love the most sacred humanity." (L.24.2)

However, it was under the direction of Fr. Juan de Prádanos that Teresa experienced a definitive liberation from her unchanneled affectivity. Powerless to let go of some friendships which bound her, Fr. Prádanos directed her to pray for some days the "Veni Creator" in order to obtain light from God on the matter. One day, while devoutly reciting this prayer, Teresa experienced her first rapture. Deep within her she heard these words: "No longer do I want you to converse with men but with angels." (L.24.5) Terrified and frightened on the one hand, but full of consolation on the other, Teresa underwent a profound transformation. From that day onward, she became courageous in abandoning all for God. For years her overwhelming need to receive and give love, although a God-given gift in itself and a sign of her capacity for the infinite, had run the risk of her living perpetually outside herself in others in a state of dependency and restlessness. It had clashed with her spiritual longings for God. Now, all changed in a moment. The Lord Jesus gave her the strength and freedom that she could not obtain by herself. "May God be blessed forever because in an instant He gave me the freedom that I with all the efforts of many years could not attain by myself, often trying to force myself that my health had to pay dearly." (L.24.8) The words the Lord spoke to her heart effected what they expressed. "These words have been fulfilled, for I have never again been able to tie myself to any friendship or to find consolation in or bear particular love for any other persons than those I understand love him and strive to serve him; nor is it in my power to do so, nor does it matter whether they are friends or relatives." (L.24.6)

Sometime following this rapture, Teresa had a vision of the Risen Jesus that verified and confirmed her liberation. "After I beheld the extraordinary beauty of the Lord, I didn't see anyone who in comparison with him seemed to attract or occupy my thoughts. By turning my gaze just a little inward to behold the image I have in my soul, I obtained such freedom in this respect that everything I see here below seems loathsome when compared to the excelling and beautiful qualities I beheld in this Lord." (L.37.4)

Jesus satisfied Teresa's hunger for love. Her search for a love which could fully satisfy her heart found repose and an answer in Jesus of Nazareth. Furthermore, he freed her from the crippling power and attraction others had exercised over her. No longer would she live depending solely on the love that others would give her, but "on the one who never fails and surpasses all demands and needs to be loved."[20] In Jesus, Teresa found true satisfaction of heart. However, this liberation in no way destroyed her profound capacity for love and friendship; rather, it freed and channeled it. Now Teresa could love freely, with a more refined, mature love, rooted in God and free from egotistic demands. Furthermore, in and through him who is the perfect harmony of God and humanity, she could love others without a sense of being split within herself or with scruples and interior struggles.[21] Relationships would no longer necessarily appear in opposition to her search for God, but would become an important element of the spiritual life. "But a good means to having God is to speak with his friends, for one always gains very much from this. I know through experience." (W.7.4) To the very end of her life, love and friendship would be the hallmark of Teresa's life and charism, but they would have their source in Jesus Christ who is Incarnate Love. We need only read her letters and study her relationship with Jerome Gratian and Maria de San José to realize that her ability to establish warm and caring friendships never left her, but only deepened and became more human.[22]

Jesus, Teresa's True Friend

Also out of Teresa's long and arduous struggle with friendships emerged an experiential knowledge of Jesus as the true friend who accompanies us in all our undertakings and remains loyal to us when all others fail. The title of Jesus as friend is central to her experience of him and permeates all her writings and understanding of the Christian life. She conceives of the Christian life as a journey in the company of our good Friend Jesus who leads us to union with the Father and with one another. "Whoever lives in the presence of so good a friend and excellent a leader, who went ahead of us to be the first to suffer, can endure all things. The Lord helps us, strengthens us, and never fails; he is a true friend. And I see clearly, and I saw afterward, that God desires that if we are going to please him and receive his great favors, we must do so through the most sacred humanity of Christ, in whom he takes his delight." (L.22.6)

Jesus not only fulfilled Teresa's longing for a love that only God could satisfy, but in him she experienced the God for whom she had yearned since early childhood. Our study of Teresa's life up to 1554 revealed her struggle to reconcile her spirit that longed to take mystical flight into God with her finite, "earthy" nature, which clung tenaciously to the earth with its human loves, joys, and sensuous pleasures. Powerless to resolve the tension between these aspects of her personality, Teresa's quest for God became separated from and at odds with her humanity and all its affective needs and drives. God, therefore, appeared obscure and remote from concrete human existence with all its struggles. As one author has expressed it, how could Teresa give her human love to this mysterious, obscure God who so fascinated her and to whom she felt drawn?[23] The answer lies in Jesus of Nazareth. In the God-Man, Teresa experienced the gift of God's self-offer to her in a human way, and in and through him, she found a channel through which she could respond to God's invitation.[24] Teresa's discovery of the humanity of Jesus Christ thus gave her search for God concrete form and this in turn healed the division she experienced between her spirit that longed for God and her humanity that craved for the earth. We can say that Jesus grounded Teresa. No longer would her search for God seem in opposition to daily life or her humanity. Rather, it would be integrated into concrete bodily existence, for in Jesus, God has entered fully into human life and has become one of us. "We are not angels but have a body. To desire to be angels while we are on earth—and as much on earth as I was—is foolishness. Ordinarily, thought needs to have some support. If at times the soul goes out of itself or goes about so full of God that it has no need of any created thing to become recollected, this isn't so usual. When one is in the midst of business matters, and in times of persecutions and trials, when one can't maintain so much quietude, and in times of dryness, Christ is a very good friend because we behold him as man and see him with weaknesses and trials—and he is company for us." (L.22.10)

Shortly after Teresa's religious experience in 1556, she encountered a blockage in her spiritual life that served as a catalyst and foundation for her doctrine on the humanity of Jesus Christ. The Christology of her time was mostly from above, especially in the area of spirituality. Although Spanish religious piety and theological thought of the sixteenth century focused toward the humanity of Christ, there were different approaches to it. Almost all spiritual writers viewed the humanity only as the "door" that opened to the Father. A few others saw it as the "way," a stage that one must leave somewhere along the spiritual path in order to meet the Father. Few, however, understood the humanity of Jesus as the abiding place where one dwells all along life's journey to God.[25]

Furthermore, a strong antimatter Platonism impregnated almost all spiritual literature. Most spiritual works stressed a rigid asceticism in order to go to God and dichotomized life into the natural and supernatural, the corporeal and the spiritual with a great disdain for all corporeal matter.[26] Teresa, a woman of her times and avid reader, fell under the influence of this Neoplatonic doctrine through books belonging to the new Spanish Franciscan school, perhaps from Francisco de Osuna or Bernardino de Laredo, and most likely, from Barnabas de Palma.[27] Teresa read that anything corporeal would become an impediment to a deeper experience of the divinity; even the humanity of Jesus Christ was an obstacle at one point to perfect contemplation. Therefore, the spiritual person must leave aside all corporeal ideas and notions, even concerning the historical Christ, and remain absorbed in the divinity. Following this advice, Teresa turned away from the humanity of Jesus for a period of time. The result, however, proved other than she expected. She experienced dryness in prayer and difficulty in living out her daily Christian life with all its demands, obligations, and trials. She describes this experience with painful bitterness in chap. 22 of her *Life* where she takes up a polemic with these authors and actually goes contrary to many of her contemporaries on the importance of the humanity of Jesus Christ. Teresa profited doctrinally from this error and learned through her experience that the humanity of Jesus Christ is never an obstacle in Christian life to deeper levels of spiritual growth. If we are to arrive at the fullness of Christian maturity, we do so only in and through Jesus. If we are to knowingly and lovingly surrender to the mystery of God, this takes place in and through an abiding personal relationship with the Man-Jesus "in whom and in whom alone the immediacy of God is reached."[28]

From Teresa's conversion in 1554, she began to experience the powerful and transforming presence of the Risen Lord within herself and in the Church in ever more profound ways. The first experience came to her by surprise. In prayer one day, she had an intellectual vision of Christ by her side. The vision, which left her calm and free from fear, did not simply pass; rather, she felt that Jesus walked always at her side and witnessed everything she did. Therefore, she strove to perform all her actions to please the One who accompanied her in every facet of her daily life. Sometime later, Jesus revealed to her different aspects of his humanity. First she saw his hands, then his face, and then his entire person. (L.28.1-3) Finally, on the feast of the Conversion of St. Paul, 25 January 1561, Teresa had a vision of the sacred humanity of Jesus Christ in his risen form.

Her experience of the Risen Christ was one of an empowering presence that healed her affectivity, renewed her hope, liberated her from fear and anxiety, and increased within her the love of God and desire to proclaim the mercy and praises of God to the whole world. Furthermore, this presence gave her courage and enabled her to accept and face reality calmly and confidently. Teresa experienced the Risen Christ, not in an esoteric way, but amidst the realities of daily life.

A key to understanding her christology took place during the summer of 1559. The grand Inquisitor, Fernando Valdés, edited his new *Index* of prohibited books. Teresa had to relinquish a good part of her library: the Bible in Spanish, works by Fr. Granada, Francis Borgia, and John of Avila.[29] This distressed her greatly, but she heard the Lord say to her: "Don't be sad, for I shall give you a living book." (L.26.5) Concerning these words she writes: "I was unable to understand why this was said to me, since I had not yet experienced any visions. Afterward, within only a few days, I understood very clearly, because I received so much to think about and such recollection in the presence of what I saw, and the Lord showed so much love for me by teaching me in many ways, that I had very little or almost no need for books. His Majesty had become the true book in which I saw the truths." (L.26.5)

The experience of the mystery of Christ intensified from the time when Teresa wrote her autobiography until it culminated in the grace of spiritual marriage in November of 1572. This grace, like many of the Christological graces she received, took place during the Eucharist. The spiritual marriage is profoundly Christological and ecclesial. It was the mystical experience of the union of Jesus Christ with the Church personalized in Teresa.[30] Now Teresa realized in a profound way that her life was Christ. "He also says: *For me to live is Christ, and to die is gain.* The soul as well, I think, can say these words now because this state is the place where the little butterfly we mentioned dies, and with the greatest joy because its life is now Christ" (C.7.2.5).

But this is not the end of Teresa's journey. As a result of this grace, she entered a very active period with her foundations, intense correspondence, and the writing of her books. She concretized her union with God through a life of love for neighbor and service to the

Church. In the seventh dwelling places, she reminds us that the purpose of the mystical marriage is to free us to carry on Jesus' salvific mission of compassion. "I want to tell you again lest someone think that the reason is solely for the sake of giving delight to these souls; that thought would be a serious error. His Majesty couldn't grant us a greater favor than to give us a life that would be an imitation of the life his beloved Son lived. Thus I hold for certain that these favors are meant to fortify our weakness, as I have said here at times, that we may be able to imitate him in his great suffering." (C.7.4.4)

2. The Humanity of Jesus Christ

St. Teresa's doctrine on the sacred humanity of Jesus Christ stands at the heart of her understanding of Christian life and arises from her personal experience of liberation by the Lord and from having erroneously left aside reflection on the person of Jesus in her prayer. Her teaching is charged with lived experience. "All my life I was devoted to Christ" (L.22.4); "I could only think of Christ as man." (L.9.6)

Although Teresa's doctrine on the humanity of Christ appears throughout her writings, she explicitly states her position on the subject with great vigor in chap. 22 of her *Life* and in chap. 7 of the sixth dwelling places in the *Interior Castle*. In both places she enters into a polemic with those spiritual writers of her time who advised serious Christians in pursuit of holiness to set aside all corporeal notions, representations, ideas, and thoughts in prayer, even those about the humanity of Jesus and the mysteries of his life, so as to remain in pure emptiness and immersed in the divinity.[31] Teresa knew that one cannot identify Jesus with images and representations; nevertheless, she was convinced through her own experience, as well as from Scripture and tradition, that we cannot at any point in the Christian life depart from the historical Christ, even less emphasize his divinity over his humanity. "Let us consider the glorious St. Paul: it doesn't seem that any other name fell from his lips than that of Jesus, as coming from one who kept the Lord close to his heart. Once I had come to understand this truth, I carefully considered the lives of some of the saints, the great contemplatives, and found that they hadn't taken any other path: St. Francis demonstrates this through the stigmata; St. Anthony of Padua, with the Infant; St. Bernard found his delight in the Humanity; St. Catherine of Siena and many others." (L.22.7)

What does Teresa actually mean by the sacred humanity of Jesus Christ? She means not simply his corporeal reality, but the Jesus of the Gospels, the Eternal Logos of the Father, who took flesh in time, lived, died, rose from the dead, and continues to live with the Father and with us in a new dynamic way. The Risen Lord Jesus, "God and man glorified," best expresses her understanding of the humanity of Jesus.[32] For Teresa, Jesus is not a mythological figure who lived in first century Palestine, but is now sunk into the incomprehensibility of God with no further relation to history. Rather, Jesus continues to have an abiding and significant presence with us. He is united to the Father but also lives among us in a new, permanent, and dynamic way.

What does Teresa teach us about the humanity of Jesus Christ and its importance for the personal and collective lives of Christians? First of all, Jesus is the "absolute and necessary mediator" in our encounter with God.[33] For Teresa, the experience of Christ is the experience of God. "It used to happen, when I represented Christ within me in order to place myself in his presence, or even while reading, that a feeling of God would come upon me unexpectedly so that I could in no way doubt that he was within me or I totally immersed in him." (L.10:1) In the person of Jesus Christ, "God has come absolutely close to us."[34] In him we meet God; he is the pledge of the Father's love for us. "As often as we think of Christ we should recall the love with which he bestowed on us so many favors and what great love God showed us in giving us a pledge like this of his love (L.22.14). . . . And I see clearly, and I saw afterward, that God desires that if we are going to please him and receive his great favors, we must do so through the most sacred humanity of Christ, in whom he takes his delight." (L.22.6) The God of Teresa is a God experienced in and through a relationship with Jesus of Nazareth. Her entire religious experience illustrates that any "personal absolute" of which we may speak or imagine we can attain by "mystical flight" can only be found in Jesus of Nazareth "in whom dwells the fullness of the Godhead in the earthly vessel of his humanity."[35]

Secondly, there is absolutely no growth in the Christian life apart from Jesus. Teresa assures us that if we hope to arrive at the fullness of Christian maturity, we do so only by traveling step by step in the company of Christ. "At least I assure them that they will not enter these last two dwelling places [the sixth and seventh dwelling places]. For if they lose the guide, who is the good Jesus, they will not hit upon the right road. . . . The Lord himself says that he is the Way; the Lord says also that he is the light and that no one can go to the Father but through him, and 'anyone who sees me sees my Father.'" (C.6.7.6)

In the seventh dwelling places, Teresa describes spiritual marriage, a favor given freely by God which reflects the highest stages of the spiritual life: a profound loving union between God and the individual. This grace comes through an imaginative vision of the sacred humanity of Jesus "so that the soul will understand and not be ignorant of receiving this sovereign gift." (C.7.2.1) It is in and through Christ that we penetrate deeper into the mystery of God and come to the fullness of who we are and the liberty of the children of God. Teresa tells us that many people do not reach deeper levels of personal liberty because they fail to focus their life and prayer on the person of Jesus. "In my opinion, this practice is why many souls, when they reach the prayer of union, do not advance further and attain a very great freedom of spirit." (L.22.5)

Human Nature

The necessity of the humanity of Jesus Christ for our encounter with God and for personal and spiritual growth becomes even clearer when we consider human nature. Teresa warns us against the temptation of striving to transcend our humanity in our efforts to reach God. She is one of the few spiritual writers of her time who affirmed without vacillation that matter is not opposed to the spirit and that the body has to be integrated within the plan of salvation.[36] Although propelled toward the infinite, we have bodies and live in a world where we must eat, sleep, and deal with material reality. We are not angels, but human beings who need human support no matter how spiritual we think we are. "It is an important thing that while we are living and are human we have human support." (L.22.9) Teresa speaks out emphatically on this point. "We are not angels but we have a body. To desire to be angels while on earth—and as much on earth as I was—is foolishness." (L.22.10)

Furthermore, Teresa reminds us that to be always withdrawn from corporeal things and enkindled in love is the trait of angelic spirits, not of human beings. Therefore, we need the company of those who have mortal bodies in order to learn how to please God and to work for him. How much more necessary is the sacred humanity of Jesus Christ from whom we learn about God and how to do God's will. "To be always withdrawn from corporeal things and enkindled in love is the trait of angelic spirits, not of those who live in mortal bodies. It's necessary that we speak to, think about, and become the companions of those who having had a mortal body accomplished great feats for God. How much more necessary is it not to withdraw through one's own efforts from all our good and help which is the most sacred humanity of our Lord Jesus Christ." (C.6.7.6)

There is another very functional reason for the necessity of the humanity of Jesus. Because life is hard, we need the example of one who has gone before us so as to better support our human weakness. Jesus is a model of how we are to live and he consoles us during the trials of life as we journey toward our heavenly homeland. Teresa has no illusions about life and our need for a faithful friend and companion to assist us along the way. "Life is long, and there are in it many trials, and we need to look at Christ our model, how he suffered them, and also at his apostles and saints, so as to bear these trials with perfection. Jesus is too good a companion for us to turn away from him." (C.6.7.13)

Jesus supports us because he is fully human. He entered our human condition completely and experienced human reality with all its brokenness, limitations, and weakness. "In sum, Lord, you are on earth and clothed with it. Since you possess our nature, it seems you have some reason to look to our gain." (W.27.3) For Teresa, Jesus is a God-Man who endured aloneness, rejection, neediness, weakness, and trials. She never tires of reminding us that he lived with trials during his entire life. (L.22.11) Jesus prayed, struggled with God's will, and was fully human.

This is what drew Teresa to him. "I strove to picture Christ within me, and it did me greater good—in my opinion—to picture him in those scenes where I saw him more alone. It seemed to me that being alone and afflicted, as a person in need, he had to accept me." (L.9.4) For Teresa, Jesus' solidarity with us in our human condition is the basis of our confidence and trust in him. This makes him our friend, brother, and companion in life. "A much greater love for and confidence in this Lord began to develop in me when I saw him as one with whom I could converse so continually. I saw that he was man, even though he was God; that he wasn't surprised by the weaknesses of men; that he understands our miserable make-up, subject to many falls on account of the first sin which he came to repair. I can speak with him as with a friend, even though he is Lord." (L.37.5)

Therefore, when we are in the midst of business matters, and in times of persecutions and trials, when we can't maintain so much quietude, and in times of dryness, "Christ is a very good friend because we behold him as man and see him with weaknesses and trials—and he is company for us." (L.22.10) With such a friend at our side, we are capable of everything for he is our best example and support. "Whoever lives in the presence of so good a friend and excellent a leader, who went ahead of us . . . strengthens us, and never fails; he is a true friend. . . . On this road you walk safely. This Lord of ours is the one through whom all blessings come to us. He will teach us these things. In beholding his life we find that he is the best example. What more do we desire than to have such a good friend at our side, who will not abandon us in our labors and tribulations, as friends in the world do." (L.22.6-7)

Jesus, A Living Book

Since Jesus exemplifies an authentic human life, we must constantly reflect upon the mysteries of his earthly life, death, and resurrection. For Teresa, Jesus is a "living book" in which we not only see and find God, but learn how to live and to discover the meaning of our own existence.[37] By entering fully into our human condition, he has transformed human life; in his life, death, and resurrection, we find a source of life and hope for all life's problems. Teresa has a dynamic understanding of the mysteries of Jesus' historical existence. The saving mysteries of his incarnation, birth and childhood, public ministry and miracles, passion, death, and resurrection, are not simply past events, but retain a perennial, dynamic reality.[38] They provide the means of relating to Jesus no matter what psychological or spiritual state we may find ourselves in. Furthermore, they have a sacramental character in that they bring about transformation and grace when we open ourselves to them. For instance, in chap. 26 of *The Way of Perfection,* Teresa instructs her nuns to look at the life of Jesus no matter what psychological state they experience. Every human emotion and situation, from pain and sorrow to joy and ecstasy, finds an echo in the historical life of Jesus. By relating our lives to the mysteries of his, we establish a relationship with Jesus, and will find renewed meaning, hope, and transformation.

> If you are joyful, look at him risen. Just imagining how he rose from the tomb will bring you joy. . . . Indeed, like one coming forth from a battle where he has gained a great kingdom! And all of that, plus himself, he desires for you. . . . If you are experiencing trials or are sad, behold him on the way to the garden: what great affliction he bore in his soul; for having become suffering itself, he tells us about it and complains of it. . . . Or behold him burdened with the cross, for they didn't even let him take a breath. He will look at you with those eyes so beautiful and compassionate, filled with tears; he will forget his sorrows so as to console you in yours, merely because you yourselves go to him to be consoled, and you turn your head to look at him. (W.26.4-5)

Furthermore, Teresa stresses that reflection on the historical Christ is the measure and source of any authentic Christian commitment, service, and relationship with him. He is the norm of all Christian action; "his humanity reflects Christian humanism, and his love for all people is the foundation for all charity."[39] If we do not consider his life, who he is, who his Father is, and strive to conform our lives to his, how can we hope to have a relationship with him? How can we truly know, love, and serve him if we never study his life? "Well, if we never look at him or reflect on what we owe him and the death he suffered for us, I don't know how we'll be able to know him or do works in his service. Or who will awaken us to love this Lord?" (C.2.1.11) The Gospels hold, therefore, a preeminent place in the Christian life for in and through them we encounter the living and transforming presence of the Risen Lord Jesus. "I have always been fond of the words of the Gospels (that have come from that most sacred mouth in the way they were said) and found more recollection in them than in very cleverly written books." (W.21.3)

Jesus as "the living book" who is the model of Christian life becomes master, teacher, and brother in *The Way of Perfection.* The heart of this work is Teresa's commentary on the Our Father. One by one, she explains the seven requests of the Our Father, and through each of them, we discover the sentiments of our master and brother, Jesus, which we must integrate into our lives so as to have a relationship with the Father. Jesus teaches us how to become authentic sons and daughters of so good a Father. For instance, Jesus knows the difficulty we meet in accomplishing the Father's will, so he prays on our behalf and teaches us what it means to surrender ourselves to the Father. "'Your will be done on earth as it is in heaven.' You did well, good Master of ours, to make this petition so that we might accomplish what you give on our behalf. For certainly, Lord, if you hadn't made the petition, the task would seem to me impossible." (W.32.2) For Teresa, the Lord's Prayer summarizes and contains the essence of the entire Christian life. It includes everything we need to know to reach the fullness of life. "We need to study no other book." (W.37.1)

What becomes evident in Teresa's commentary on the Our Father is Jesus' full solidarity with humanity. First of all, he is the Master who teaches us this prayer because he lived it fully. By entering into its meaning and making it our own, we catch a glimpse of the relationship between Jesus and his Father and learn what it means to love the Father as his adopted children. "Behold whether or not you are well paid and have a good Master; since he knows how the love of his Father can be obtained, he teaches us how and by what means we must serve him." (W.32.11)

Secondly, the incarnation makes Jesus our true brother. The Word of God, in taking on human nature, made himself the "Brother of creatures" who knows the brokenness and limitations of human existence. (W.27.2) He now joins us in prayer and prays on our behalf. He knows the "stuff" of which we are made because he is one of us. A marriage has taken place between heaven and earth which alters our relationship with the Father. "For once the earth has become heaven, the possibility is there for your will to be done in me." (W.32.2) Thus we share in that filial relationship Jesus has with the Father.

> Since you humble yourself to such an extreme in joining us in prayer making yourself the brother of creatures so lowly and wretched, how is it that you give us in the name of your Father everything that can be given? For you desire that he consider us his children, because your word cannot fail. You oblige him to be true to your word, which is no small burden since in being Father he must bear with us no matter how serious the offenses. If we return to him like the prodigal son, he has to pardon us. He has to console us in our trials. He has to sustain us in the way a father like this must. For, in effect, he must be

> better than all fathers. . . . And after all this, he must make us sharers and heirs with you. (W.27.2)

Jesus, therefore, is truly our Way to the Father. If we ask Teresa, "What is the way of perfection?" her answer is the person of Jesus Christ. He is "the Way, the Truth and the Life." (Jn 14:6)

Implications

Teresa's doctrine on Jesus Christ's humanity has several implications for our personal and collective lives as Christians. First of all, Teresa implicitly teaches a Christology from below. She begins with the man Jesus in his historical human reality, in the experience of his life, death, and resurrection. He is the one for whom we search and meet in our existential need and quest for salvation. Our personal encounter with Jesus of the Gospels opens us to the mystery of the Father. Teresa would be delighted with Rahner's assertion that the human starting point for Christology is the Christian's actual relationship with Jesus Christ.[40]

Secondly, by starting with the historical Jesus through whom we meet God, Teresa affirms that the fundamental characteristic of Christian life is incarnational. Her spirituality has no room for an evasion of the body, time, or the present world. She supports all that is human and thus breaks through the Neoplatonism of her time with its disdain for the body and material realities. In the Incarnation, God proved his unconditional and infinite love for created life. He performed a marriage between heaven and earth; therefore, we meet God in the human realm, in the heart of life and matter. In taking on human nature, Jesus elevated, gave dignity, and transformed our existence. Therefore, we have no need to transcend the human condition to meet God. "Well, come now, my daughters, don't be sad when obedience draws you to involvement in exterior matters. Know that if it is in the kitchen, the Lord walks among the pots and pans helping you both interiorly and exteriorly." (F. 5.8)

When we affirm the human, we affirm Christ and God. We must love everything created by God, not as something provisional which will one day dissolve into the infinite, "like clouds breaking up," but as something which has lasting validity before God.[41]

Furthermore, the humanity of Jesus helps us support and make sense out of the painful and difficult realities of life. Constant contact with the person of Jesus Christ, reflection on the mysteries of his life, death, and resurrection, enables us to stand in reality and joyfully embrace life as it is under God's conditions. Moreover, when God becomes more truly God for us, the rest of reality, which he loves and with which he has united himself through the Incarnation, becomes more real, valid, and true. Everything finds its real life in him and thus becomes a means of serving him. An experience of Teresa with life's arduous aspects illustrates this. "I was reflecting upon how arduous a life this is that deprives us of being always in that wonderful company, and I said to myself, 'Lord, give me some means by which I can put up with this life.' He replied: 'Think, daughter, of how after it is finished you will not be able to serve in ways you can now. Eat for me and sleep for me, and let everything you do be for me, as though you no longer lived but I; for this is what St. Paul was speaking of.'" (T. 51)

Teresa's doctrine on the humanity of Jesus Christ raises another important implication which Karl Rahner has addressed. Oftentimes when we think of the Man-Jesus as the absolute mediator of our salvation and encounter with God, we tend to think this in relationship to his past temporal existence. We often think of Jesus merely as the historical and moral mediator during his life on earth, but not now. We may conceive of his humanity as blessed and glorified in heaven, enjoying the beatific vision, and forget that he has an eternal and abiding significance for us in the present. Jesus' humanity did not cease to be with the end of his temporal history; rather, his human reality continues to exist and have soteriological significance for us two thousand years after his temporal existence.[42] He continues to offer healing, new life, and hope to all women and men. "I know a person with serious illnesses, who often experiences great pain. . . . But the Lord had given her such living faith that when she heard some persons saying they would have liked to have lived at the time Christ our Good walked in the world, she used to laugh to herself. She wondered what more they wanted since in the most Blessed Sacrament they had him just as truly present as he was then. . . . Now, then, if when he went about in the world the mere touch of his robes cured the sick, why doubt, if we have faith, that miracles will be worked while he is within us and that he will give what we ask of him, since he is in our house? His Majesty is not accustomed to paying poorly for his lodging if the hospitality is good." (W.34.6&8)

For Teresa, Jesus is the source of our salvation and the cause of all healing and sanctification in every age and historical situation. He is not only the model of Christian life, but the source of all health and human fulfillment. "Where have all my blessings come from but from you?" (L.22.4) This is why Teresa directs her readers to "look" at Jesus. To look at Jesus means to study with the heart all the movements and sentiments of his person.[43] In this way, the truth that he is will be imprinted in us. Furthermore, to look at Jesus means that we recognize the eternal significance his human reality has for our salvation and fulfillment as human beings. It is only in the light of this profound and mysterious truth that we arrive at an understanding of ourselves, of God, and come to experience the freedom of the children of God.

3. The Risen Lord Jesus

We turn now to St. Teresa's experience of the Risen Christ. What does Teresa's experience teach us in a systematic way about the meaning of resurrection and our participation in the resurrected life of Jesus?[44] We will discuss this question and then examine the relationship of the Risen Christ to her spirituality as a whole and its implications for our personal and collective lives as Christians.

Belief in the resurrection of Christ is central to Christian faith. If Jesus is not raised from the dead, then our faith is empty and meaningless. Furthermore, St. Paul tells us in his letter to the Romans, that through baptism we died and were buried with Christ in order to be raised to new life with him. Through baptism we are new creatures and have the possibility of living a new life "for God in Christ Jesus." (Rom 6:11) This new life is a participation, even now, in the risen life of the Lord Jesus. We often fail to realize that the resurrection is not simply a unique, finished event in the past, but a present reality which influences our present lives.[45] We are a people of the resurrection, a people who have the possibility of participating, although in a veiled and obscure way, in the life of the exalted Lord that we will share fully at some future time.

David M. Stanley, S.J., expresses a profound insight that can serve as an entrance into our study of St. Teresa's experience of the Risen Lord Jesus and what it teaches us about resurrected life. "Jesus Christ through his exaltation to the Father's right hand has not been removed to some mythical existence beyond the furthest galaxy, but is actually more dynamically present in the world than ever he was when he walked the hills of Galilee."[46]

Following Teresa's conversion in 1554, she began to experience the transforming and powerful presence of the Risen Jesus in ever deeper and decisive ways. She writes of these experiences beginning in chap. 27 of her *Life.* The first came to her by surprise.

> Being in prayer on the feast of the glorious St. Peter, I saw or, to put it better, I felt Christ beside me; I saw nothing with my bodily eyes or with my soul, but it seemed to me that Christ was at my side—I saw that it was he, in my opinion, who was speaking to me. Since I was completely unaware that there could be a vision like this one, it greatly frightened me in the beginning; I did nothing but weep. However, by speaking one word alone to assure me, the Lord left me feeling as I usually did: quiet, favored, and without any fear. It seemed to me that Jesus Christ was always present at my side; but since this wasn't an imaginative vision, I didn't see any form. Yet I felt clearly he was always at my right side and that he was the witness of everything I did. (L. 27.2)[47]

Teresa experienced this intellectual vision continually for several days. She strove to accomplish everything she did in such a way as to please the One who witnessed her every action. Then one day in prayer, she began to see different aspects of the Lord's humanity. First she saw only his hands, then his face, then his entire person. (L.28.1) She tells us that the Lord revealed himself "little by little" so as to adapt to her natural weakness. (L.28.1) Finally, on the Feast of the Conversion of St. Paul, 25 January 1561, Teresa had a vision of Jesus' sacred humanity in his risen form. "One feast day of St. Paul, while I was at Mass, this most sacred humanity in its risen form was represented to me completely, as it is in paintings, with such wonderful beauty and majesty." (L.28.3)

How are we to understand Teresa's Christological visions? Such experiences seem so far removed from the average Christian.

Nevertheless, we must not dismiss them as hysteria or mystical grace that has no relationship to the ordinary believer—to do so would be to overlook their underlying message and prophetic significance. The extraordinary phenomena of Teresa's visions of the Risen Lord were charismatic graces given to her for the benefit of her followers and the Church as a whole. It is best to view them in the biblical sense like the disciples' experiences of the Risen Lord. Teresa experienced within her the powerful and transforming presence of Jesus that increased her faith and love of God and set her free from fear. These encounters with the Risen Jesus are the foundation of her prophetic mission to God's people.[48] Like the apostles who left the upper room fearless and on fire with the love and presence of God in Jesus, Teresa experienced her exalted Lord within her and turned to those around her with this prophetic word: "Jesus is living within and among us; God is truly with us; we have nothing to fear!"

Interior Graces

A closer examination of Teresa's experiences of the Risen Lord and their effects in her life has much to teach us about the liberating power of Jesus and our participation in his resurrected life. First of all, these graces were deeply interior. Teresa did not see the Lord with the eyes of her body. Even the more imaginative ones were of a profound interior nature. (L.28.4) They took place in the sphere of the spirit rather than the senses. Teresa is often at a loss to explain how such visions happen. (L.28.6-7) What is at issue here is a real personal encounter with the Risen Lord Jesus who becomes present and initiates a person-to-person relationship on a new level of perception and communication. Teresa was "absorbed," possessed by the Lord present within her spirit.[49] In a powerful way, difficult to explain, the Lord Jesus revealed himself within her and awakened her to a faith and knowledge and love of God that transformed her entire life. In *The Interior Castle,* Teresa compares the Risen Lord's appearance in the center of the soul to the experience of the apostles. "The Lord appears in this center of the soul, not in an imaginative vision but in an intellectual one, although more delicate than those mentioned, as he appeared to the Apostles without entering through the door when he said to them *pax vobis.*" (C.7.2.3)

Secondly, and more important than the actual visions of the Risen Jesus, are the effects brought about by Christ's presence. Teresa experienced the heart of what resurrection means for all believers, that is, the experience that Jesus lives now for us in a dynamic and new way offering us renewed hope and liberation.[50] This led her to a new vision and knowledge of God, herself, others, and reality as a whole. It also brought changes. "All who knew me saw clearly that my soul was changed. . . . I saw clearly that by these experiences I was at once changed." (L.28.13) What are these changes that are pointers to resurrected life? What is this new vision?

The first is a new knowledge and love of God. Teresa's experience brought about a new knowledge of God's power and love which penetrates all reality. She learned in a deeper and experiential way that "God is powerful, that he can do all things, that he commands all and governs all, and that his love permeates all things." (L.28.9) Moreover, the vision of the Risen Jesus enlightened Teresa to the Lord's human condition and thus into the merciful and loving nature of God incarnated in the Man-Jesus. "I saw that he was man, even though he was God; that he wasn't surprised by the weaknesses of men; that he understands our miserable makeup, subject to many falls on account of the first sin which he came to repair. I can speak with him as with a friend, even though he is Lord." (L.37.5)

Furthermore, as an indication that it was truly he, the Risen Lord, Jesus increased within her the love of God to such a degree that Teresa didn't know where it came from. (L.29.8) A new, living, elevated love began in her and became the foundation of a deep faith whereby God became the real basis and purpose of all life for her. In the words of St. Paul, Teresa desired to "live for God in Christ Jesus." (Rom 6:11) The effects of Teresa's encounter with the Risen Lord illustrate Paul's statement: an habitual remembrance of God, a deep concern to avoid displeasing him, a continual awareness of his companionship which gave rise to a tender love for him and desire to serve him totally, and an increase in humility. (C.6.8) As a result of this experience, Jesus Christ dominated the rest of Teresa's existence. She saw the reality of things from the light of Jesus with a new and profound intensification extending from the smallest details of life to the most significant. Everything became Christological—her prayer, her actions and apostolic trips, her interpretation of the mystical life, her way of understanding love, truth, strength, poverty, grace, sin, the liturgy, and the Church.[51]

Liberation

The second effect of Teresa's experience of the Risen Jesus is liberation. Expressions of freedom abound on almost every page of her autobiography where she describes her experience of her resurrected Lord. Jesus told her: "Do not fear, daughter; for I am, and I will not abandon you; do not fear." (L.25.18) Teresa found in Jesus a love and power which liberated her from the slavery of sin and anxiety, the fear of death, and in turn enabled her to embrace reality with a firm hope and confidence amidst life's trials and sorrows.

First of all, Jesus freed Teresa's affectivity and thus empowered her to love others with a mature, less dependent, and selfless love rooted in God. No longer would her inordinate need for human love rob her of her personal freedom to focus her love and energies on him alone who is the source of all true love.

> The benefit I received was most advantageous, and this is what it consisted of: I had a serious fault that did me much harm; it was when I began to know that certain persons liked me, and I found them attractive, I became so attached that my memory was bound strongly by the thought of them. There was no intention to offend God, but I was happy to see these persons and think about the good things I saw in them. This was something so harmful it was leading my soul seriously astray. After I beheld the extraordinary beauty of the Lord, I didn't see anyone who in comparison with him seemed to attract me or occupy my thoughts. . . . I hold that it would be impossible for me (provided the Lord would not permit that, on account of my sins, this impression be erased from my memory) to be so occupied with the thought of anyone that I couldn't free myself from it by only a slight effort to remember this Lord. (L.37.4)

Teresa's renewed capacity to love reflects a deeper liberation from sin. She tells us that the presence of Jesus purified her soul. (L.38.18) It also increased within her sorrow at having offended God, concern about avoiding anything displeasing to him, and a contempt for everything that did not bring her to him. (C.6.8) In the midst of temptations, and when Teresa sensed her own poverty and sinfulness, she could no longer think about God, and felt so angry toward others that she could "eat everyone up," she would hear the words, "Don't grow weary; don't be afraid." (L.30.12-19) Teresa truly sought the glory of God alone in all things with greater liberty.

Secondly, Teresa was freed from the fear of physical death and death in the sense of that negative "power and fate" which seek to undercut the trustworthiness of reality.[52] Little of Teresa's earlier fear of death remained in the presence of the Risen Jesus. Death seemed to her to be the easiest thing for anyone who serves God, "for in a moment the soul finds it is freed from this prison and brought to rest." (L.38.5) Not only does the fear of death and the mysterious unknown beyond this side of the grave evaporate in the light of Christ, but the terror of evil forces which threaten to extinguish life dissolves in his presence. Because Jesus Christ has conquered all the powers of evil, Teresa realized that she had nothing to fear. "In this vision the powerlessness of all the devils in comparison with your power is clearly seen, my Jesus, and it is seen how whoever is pleasing to you can trample all hell under foot . . . I see that You want the soul to know how tremendous this Majesty is and the power that this most sacred humanity joined with the divinity has." (L.28.9)

Teresa's encounter with the Risen Lord did not exempt her from the exigencies and limitations of human existence. Jesus did not release Teresa from the trials, pains, and labors which often stigmatize human life; rather, he plunged her deeper into this world of flesh and blood, life and death, joys and sorrows. There he empowered her to embrace reality with confidence and trust in his faithful and enduring love which accompanied her in the midst of all life's complexities and difficulties. The period of Teresa's intense activity of founding her reform movement throughout Spain began with her experiences of the Risen Lord.[53] Walter Kasper states: "Easter hope sets a Christian on the way of the cross, which is none other than the way of actual, bodily obedience in everyday life."[54] Christian hope holds no contempt for the world or reality as it is under God's conditions; rather, it stands in life, remains loyal to the world created by God, knowing that God is trustworthy and faithful despite all appearances to the contrary. Easter hope knows that nothing can separate us from the love of Jesus. We find this hope in a striking way in Teresa's life. It helped her to accept her body and its limitations and to serve the Lord as best she could, despite her personal deficiencies.

> Sometimes I worry because I see I do so little in his service and that I must necessarily take time for a body as weak and wretched as mine, more than I would want. Once I was in prayer, and the hour for going to bed came; I was feeling many pains and had to induce the usual vomiting. Since I was so bound to myself and that my spirit on the other hand wanted more time, I got so wearied I began to weep freely and grow distressed. (This happened not only once, but, as I say, often.) It seems to me I became angry with myself in such a way that I then truly hated myself. But usually I know I don't hold myself in abhorrence, nor do I fail to do what I see is necessary for myself. . . . This time of which I'm speaking, the Lord appeared to me and greatly comforted me and told me that I should suffer and do these thing for love of him because they were now necessary for my life. So, I think I was never afflicted afterward, because I'm determined to serve this Lord and my comforter with all my strength; even though he allowed me to suffer a little, He consoled me in such a way that I don't do anything in desiring trials. (L.40.20)

The Risen Lord also helped Teresa accept the unstable conditions of life with its alternating patterns of light and darkness, joy and sadness, consolation and desolation. For instance, once while very disturbed and troubled, powerless to recollect herself and struggling with her thoughts which were turning "to imperfect matters," Teresa thought all the favors she had received from the Lord had been illusions. The Lord spoke to her and told her not to be anxious in seeing herself in such a condition. What should she expect? He reminded her that there is no security in this life and the experience of her weakness only underscored her dependence on him. He had not forgotten her; nor would he abandon her. It was necessary to do what she could and leave the rest to him. (L.39.20).

On another occasion, Jesus told Teresa "with much love" that she shouldn't be anxious because in this life we cannot always live in a stable condition. Sometimes the soul will experience fervor and, at other times, it will feel disturbances or temptations, or even quiet. But in the midst of all this it should hope in him and not be afraid. (L.40.18) These experiences clearly illustrate that Teresa knew the Risen Lord Jesus as an empowering presence which dispelled her fear and anxiety, enabling her to stand in reality with courage, confidence, and faith despite hardships. She could say "yes" to life because God, the Ground of all reality, is trustworthy and faithful. She could rely totally on God in life and death.

The Eucharist

A discussion of Teresa's experience of the Risen Christ would be incomplete without reference to the Eucharist, for most of her experiences took place within the context of the Eucharist. "The Lord almost always showed himself to me as risen, also when he appeared in the Host." (L.29.4) Elsewhere in her *Life,* she writes: "He makes it known that he is both man and God, not as he was in the tomb but as he was when he came out of the tomb after his resurrection. Sometimes he comes with such great majesty that no one could doubt but that it is the Lord himself. Especially after receiving

Communion—for we know that he is present, since our faith tells us this—he reveals himself as so much the lord of this dwelling that it seems the soul is completely dissolved." (L.28.8)

In speaking of resurrection corporeality, Walter Kasper writes that Jesus is permanently with God with all his person and is also with us in a new divine way. This is the meaning of resurrection corporeality. Jesus lives to God, but also lives with us in a new, permanent, and divine manner.[55] The Eucharist most clearly expresses Jesus' permanent and new way of being with us. "The Eucharist is the symbolic expression of the new redemptive presence of Jesus in and among his own."[56] It is there, in addition to the Word, where we meet the Risen Lord. This corresponds to Teresa's experience. For her, the Eucharist is the means that Jesus chose to remain with us sustaining, healing, and loving us on our journey through life. "Since the Father has already given us his Son and, just because he wanted to, sent him into the world, the Son, just because he wants to, desires not to abandon us but to remain here with us, to the greater glory of his friends and the affliction of his enemies. He asks again for no more than to be with us this day only, because it is a fact that he has given us this most sacred bread forever." (W.34.2)

Jesus becomes our servant and slave in the Eucharist (W.33.4; 34.2). There he wishes to remain with us and not abandon us until the end of time. The Eucharist is the "manna and nourishment of his humanity, that we might find him at will and not die of hunger." (W.34.2) Furthermore, "there is no need or trial or persecution that is not easy to suffer if we begin to enjoy the delight and consolation of this sacred bread." (W.34.2) This heavenly food provides both spiritual and bodily sustenance. It is a great "medicine" even for bodily ills. (W.34.6) Moreover, Teresa tells us that if our health doesn't allow us to think always about the passion of Jesus, who can prevent us from being with him in his risen state present in the Eucharist? "We have him so near in the Blessed Sacrament, where he is already glorified and where we don't have to gaze upon him as being so tired and worn out, bleeding, wearied by his journeys, persecuted by those for whom he did so much good, and not believed in by the Apostles. Certainly there is no one who can endure thinking all the time about the many trials he suffered. Behold him here without suffering, full of glory, strengthening some, encouraging others, our companion in the most Blessed Sacrament." (L.22.6)

The Risen Christ and Teresian Spirituality

Now that we have examined Teresa's experience of the Risen Lord Jesus and its effects on her life, we turn to the relationship of the Risen Christ to her spirituality as a whole and its implications for our personal and collective lives as Christians.

We rightly think of Teresa of Jesus as a teacher of prayer. Her doctrine on prayer has one purpose—to lead us to an ever deeper awareness of the presence of the living Lord Jesus within our hearts and in one another. The relationship of the exalted Lord to Teresa's spirituality is extremely important; in fact, the mystery of the Risen Lord Jesus is the very source of Teresa's life and charism. For Teresa, Jesus Christ is not a mythological being who lives remote from our world, but he is a living Person who is as present to us as when he walked this earth. (W.34.6) "The difference lies in that which there is between a living person and a painting of him—no more nor less. For if what is seen is an image, it is a living image—not a dead man, but the living Christ. And he makes it known he is both man and God, not as he was in the tomb but as he was when he came out of the tomb after his resurrection." (L.28.8) Teresa witnesses to the reality of this living Lord like Mary Magdalene in the Gospel of St. John. "'I have seen the Lord,' she announced. Then she reported what he had said to her." (Jn 20:18) Having experienced the Risen Jesus within her heart,

Teresa comes to each of us with the good news that Jesus lives within us, and in one another, offering his friendship and love if only we will open ourselves to him in faith and trust.

Teresa's encounter with the Risen Christ profoundly shaped her particular vision of the Christian life, primarily her view of prayer. The Teresian charism is above all a charism of prayer. For Teresa, it is in prayer that we make contact with Christ. In the depths of silent prayer, Teresa experienced the liberating power of the Risen Jesus[57] freeing her from fear and awakening her to a deeper faith, knowledge, and love of God. This was an inbreaking of the Kingdom of God within her, an experience of being "absorbed," possessed by the Spirit of the Risen Lord Jesus. Teresa challenges us: are we going to allow ourselves to be possessed by the Risen Christ? Are we going to give ourselves over to his liberating and transforming presence through prayer, the Eucharist, meditation on the word of God, relationships with one another, and service to those in need? Teresa stands as staunch witness to the transforming power of a life of prayer as the means for a personal encounter with Jesus Christ. She would agree wholeheartedly with Rahner's assertion about the real possibility of an immediate and concrete loving relationship with the living Jesus. Rahner maintains that we are really only dealing with Jesus when we "throw our arms around him and realize right down to the bottom of our being that this is something we can still do today."[58] For Teresa, the primary means for this to take place is prayer.

The Risen Christ also freed Teresa from fear, empowered her to love freely, and enabled her to espouse reality with trust and confidence in the fidelity and love of God. This experience of liberation has left its mark on Teresian spirituality. The presence of the Risen Jesus thrust Teresa into the heart of life. He freed her to live more fully in the here and now. In no way does the Teresian charism evade reality nor encourage flight from the hardships and trials of everyday bodily existence. Rather, it involves obedience to life under God's conditions. It is thoroughly incarnational. It accepts the concrete world of flesh and blood, life and death, joy and sorrow, with undaunted trust and confidence in the creative and faithful love of God whose power and care over us abides with us in life and death.

Furthermore, the freedom Teresa received from the Risen Christ led to proclamation and service. This, too, influenced the way of life Teresa envisioned for her friars, nuns, and all Christians. Beginning with the period of these experiences, Teresa traveled throughout Spain founding her monasteries and writing her works. She wanted to spread far and wide the message of freedom, love, and friendship she found in Jesus. She desired to proclaim to the people of her time the difference he makes in their lives when they surrender to him and place all their trust in his love and power.

> O my Lord, how you are the true friend; and how powerful! When you desire you can love, and you never stop loving those who love you! All things praise you, Lord of the world! Oh, who will cry out for you, to tell everyone how faithful you are to your friends! All things fail; you, Lord of all, never fail! . . . Oh my God, who has the understanding and learning, and the new words with which to extol your works as my soul understands them? All fails me, my Lord; but if you do not abandon me, I will not fail you. Let all learned men rise against me, let all created things persecute me, let the devils torment me; do not fail me, Lord, for I already have experience of the gain that comes from the way you rescue the one who trusts in you alone. (L.25.17)

Finally, her Risen Lord freed Teresa for selfless and loving service of her neighbor. She is quite clear in her teaching that the freedom we receive from prayer is not for our own selfish benefit; rather, it equips us for selfless service in imitation of Jesus Crucified. "I want to tell you again here lest someone think that the reason is solely for the sake of giving delight to these souls; that thought would be a serious error. His Majesty couldn't grant us a greater favor than to give us a life that would be an imitation of the life his beloved Son lived. Thus I hold for certain that these favors are meant to fortify our weakness, as I have said here at times, that we may be able to imitate him in his great sufferings. (C.7.4.4)

Here the cross and resurrection are one. The greater the freedom, the more we are summoned to help Jesus carry out his ongoing redemptive mission of compassion and love by a life of humble and loving service. For Teresa, the cross means "love and service"; her spirituality, which springs from an encounter with the Risen Lord Jesus, is truly apostolic as well as contemplative.[59] Its thrust is toward the building up of the Kingdom of God. "Fix your eyes on the Crucified and everything will become small for you. . . . Do you know what it means to be truly spiritual? It means becoming the slaves of God. Marked with his brand, which is that of the cross, spiritual persons, because now they have given him their liberty, can be sold by him as slaves of everyone, as he was." (C.7.4.8)

4. Conclusion

As I stated in my introduction, this essay purposes to have St. Teresa of Jesus answer that great Christological question that has haunted Christians down through the centuries: "And you, who do you say that I am?" (Mk 8:29) Having now examined Teresa's life, her struggles and conflicts that led to her encounter with Jesus Christ, her doctrine on his sacred humanity, and her experiences of his risen presence, we are in a position to answer Jesus' query. For Teresa, Jesus is above all friend and liberator. Her life was indeed a mystery in search of love, wholeness, and God. She longed for a love that would satisfy her restless heart. Her search for love compelled her toward God. She sought him through prayer, solitude, reading, and in struggling to do his will.

Although propelled toward the infinite, Teresa's human heart was also made of flesh and blood. She was firmly planted on this earth no matter how much she desired to take mystical flight into God. There was no denying or escaping her humanity. Thus, Teresa's thirst for love also thrust her toward the earth with its joys, vanities, human loves and friendships, and sensuous pleasures. It drove her repeatedly to pour herself out in the finite, in other people, hoping they, in some way, could fill the void of her spirit created for infinite love and divine union. Torn between her quest for God on the one hand, and her longing for the earth on the other, Teresa found herself in a state of inner conflict and captivity. Love held her prisoner and she could find no escape or solution to the tension existing within her. Suspended between heaven and earth, Teresa felt life ebb away; a shadow of death encompassed her. Yet, when all other human possibilities had failed her, when she had exhausted all her energies in helping herself, she found an answer to the mystery of her life. She discovered the God-Man, Jesus of Nazareth, the "real symbol" of the union that exists between heaven and earth.[60] In Jesus, Teresa found a friend who alone could appease her restless heart that hungered for love and union. He provided the solution to her divided heart, for he reconciled in himself the polarity between her spirit that longed for mystical union with God, and her earthy nature that tenaciously clung to human life.

Jesus became Teresa's "friend par excellence," not in some ethereal manner, but in a real way. (L.37.6) For Teresa, the possibility of entering into a dynamic and personal relationship with Jesus exists, not as an abstract idea, but as a reality. Jesus is as real and living as the person nearest us, and he offers his friendship if we open ourselves to him. "In the measure he sees that they receive him, so he gives and is given. He loves whoever loves him; how good a beloved! How good a friend! O Lord of my soul, who has the words to explain what you give to those who trust in you. . .!" (L.22.17)

Just as Teresa's relationship with Jesus was no abstract concept, but a reality, neither were the effects of their friendship something out of the ordinary or esoteric. Jesus was Teresa's liberator. Her relationship with her risen Lord brought about freedom in very concrete ways. He liberated her from her crippling dependency on others. In a moment, her compulsion to seek in others a love that no human being can possibly give to another dissolved. As a result, Teresa loved more freely, generously, without making excessive demands on others, realizing that ultimate satisfaction of heart is found only in God. The Risen Lord also liberated Teresa from the selfishness and sinfulness deeply rooted in her heart and replaced it with a new love and knowledge of God. The love of God became the basis of her entire life and perception of reality. Furthermore, Jesus freed her from her fears and doubts about the trustworthiness of reality and empowered her to embrace life under God's conditions with greater trust and confidence in his providential and loving care over her. However, far from removing her from the hardships and trials of life, Jesus plunged Teresa into the thicket of human existence with its ups and downs, joys and sorrows, certainties and doubts, light and darkness. She became courageous and desired to go out and proclaim the compassion, mercy, and love of her friend and liberator to the whole world.

Teresa of Jesus invites us in the twenty-first century to open ourselves to Jesus' liberating love and to make him our friend and companion in life. She challenges us to take the risk of bringing our struggles, conflicts, and aspirations before our Risen Lord, and with confidence and trust, to surrender to his transforming and liberating power. If we have the courage, and take the time, to accept Teresa's challenge, we, too, will be able to reply in our own unique and personal way to Jesus' inquiry: "And you, who do you say that I am?" (Mk 8:29)

Notes

1 Walter Kasper, *Jesus The Christ* (New York: Paulist Press, 1976), 151.

2 Secundino Castro, *Cristología teresiana* (Madrid: Editorial de Espiritualidad, 1978), 110.

3 By "encounter" I mean an interior faith experience which brought about a change in Teresa's life. I will use the term "encounter" more than once in this essay to describe Teresa's experience of the Lord. Each time it refers to a faith experience; however, Teresa's experience of Jesus became more profound as she grew in the spiritual life. Therefore, her encounter with Jesus became deeper.

4 Schillebeeckx, *Interim Report on the Books Jesus & Christ* (New York: Crossroad, 1982), 12.

5 Maximiliano Herraiz García, *Solo Dios basta* (Madrid: Editorial de Espiritualidad, 1981), 265.

6 Tomás Alvarez, "Jesucristo en la experiencia de Santa Teresa," in *Experiencia de Dios* (Burgos: Editorial Monte Carmelo, 1980), 101.

7 Herraiz García, *Solo Dios basta,* 272. I want to stress here that I in no way intend to undermine the value and importance of friendship for Teresa of Jesus. Her spiritual life flowered and grew within the context of relationship, and neither she nor her charism can be understood without realizing her great capacity for friendship and its place in her life. However, there was an aspect of her ability to establish warm and caring relationships that needed healing and integration. This will become clearer as our study develops. I would refer the reader to the precious article of Luigi Boriello, "Amore, amicizia e Dio in S. Teresa," *Teresianum/ Ephemerides Carmeliticae* 33 (1982): 283-330.

8 Otger Steggink, *Experencia y realismo en Santa Teresa y San Juan de la Cruz* (Madrid: Editorial de Espiritualidad, 1974), 138. See also Angel Garcia Ordás, "Expresión cristiana de la afectividad," *Revista de espiritualidad* 31(1972):183-97.

9 Steggink. *Experiencia y realismo en Santa Teresa y San Juan de la Cruz,* 137-38. For further study of Teresa's concept of the world, see Adolfo Muñoz Alonso, "Concepto del mundo y de las cosas en Teresa de Jesus," *Revista de Espiritualidad* 22 (1963): 489-98.

10 Ibid., 135.

11 Secundino Castro, *Ser cristiano según Santa Teresa* (Madrid: Editorial de Espiritualidad, 1981), 26.

12 It would take us far afield to discuss the nature and content of these books on chivalry. I would refer the reader to the discussion of Efrén J. M. Montalva, *Santa Teresa por dentro* (Madrid: Editorial de Espiritualidad, 1982), 64-67.

13 When we read Teresa's account of this period of her life, we must remember that she wrote these remembrances after she had advanced far along in the mystical life. Therefore, her perception may be different from ours. It seems to me that, although her behavior at this time was probably normal for her age and natural disposition, her interests could lead her into a shallow existence later on where the question of God would finally recede into the background.

14 Montalva, *Santa Teresa por dentro,* 93.

15 It would take us beyond the scope of this study to discuss Teresa's vocational crisis. I refer the reader to the fine discussion of Daniel de Pablo Moroto, *Santa Teresa de Jesús, doctora para una Iglesia en crisis* (Burgos: Editorial Monte Carmelo, 1981), 47-52. Moroto understands Teresa's crisis as a split between her reasoning and her affectivity. Her heart was divided between God and the world (her family, friends of childhood, and father). Moroto maintains that Teresa lived under the illusion that her entrance into Carmel would bring some harmony to her affectivity and resolve her problem. However, she was mistaken as her later experience in religious life proves. This vocational crisis was the beginning of the battle she would endure later on in religious life.

16 On Teresa's illnesses see Efrén de la Madre de Dios y Otger Steggink, *Tiempo y vida de Santa Teresa* (Madrid: Biblioteca de Autores Cristianos, 1968), 108-34. See also Montalva, *Santa Teresa por dentro,* 136-47. Teresa's illness has been the subject of much speculation by scholars. Some are of the opinion that she underwent a kind of nervous breakdown from the strain and

tension brought on by her great desire to please God on the one hand, and the awareness of her faults on the other. Still others believe that she had not resolved the conflict between her hunger for God and her inability to separate from father, family, and friends. Another theory is that it was caused by goats' milk. Regardless of its nature, Teresa's illness played an important and providential role in her life. It forced her to go within herself and find her way. See Donazar Augusto, *Meditaciones teresianas* (Barcelona: Juan Flors, 1957), 86.

17 Moroto, *Santa Teresa de Jesús, doctora para una Iglesia en crisis,* 51.

18 Montalva, *Santa Teresa por dentro,* 189-93. This vision has been the subject of much speculation. It may have been something of a hallucination caused by the anxiety Teresa experienced due to her conflict. In the above work, Montalva writes: "Era el producto de una ansiedad que le devoraba todo el ser, desde el subconsciente, como los rugidos de un volcan." (191)

19 Herraiz García, *Solo Dios basta,* 276.

20 Ibid., 276.

21 Moroto, *Santa Teresa de Jesús, doctora para una Iglesia en crisis,* 62.

22 Again, I refer the reader to the article by Borriello, "Amore, amicizia e Dio in S. Teresa," 319-26. Friendship was very important for Teresa. Her communities were based upon friendship. "In this house . . . all must be friends, all must be loved, all must be held dear, all must be helped." (W.4.7) See also the quote from her *Life,* 40.19.

23 Ordás, "Expresión cristiana de la afectividad," 195.

24 Maximiliano Herraiz García, "Donación de dios y compromiso del hombre," *Teresianum/ Ephemerides Carmeliticae* 33 (1982): 358.

25 Montalva, *Santa Teresa por dentro,* 280.

26 Alvarez, "Jesucristo en la experiencia de Santa Teresa," 81-86.

27 Ibid., 80.

28 Karl Rahner, *Foundations of Christian Faith* (New York: Seabury, Crossroad Book, 1978), 309.

29 Alvarez, "Jesucristo en la experiencia de Santa Teresa," 85.

30 Jesús Castellano, "Espiritualidad Teresiana," *Introducción a la lectura de Santa Teresa* (Madrid: Editorial de Espiritualidad, 1978), 156.

31 Secundino Castro, "L'humanité du Christ selon Ste. Thérèse d'Avila," *Carmel* 33 (1984): 32-33.

32 Secundino Castro, "Aproximación al pensamiento religioso de Teresa," *Revista de Espiritualidad* 41 (1982): 73.

33 Castro, *Cristología Teresiana,* 13.

34 Karl Rahner, *The Love of Jesus and the Love of Neighbor* (New York: Crossroad, 1983), 37.

35 Karl Rahner, "The Eternal Significance of the Humanity of Jesus for Our Relationship with God," *Theological Investigations,* vol. 3 (Baltimore: Helicon, 1967), 43.

36 Castro, *Ser cristiano según Santa Teresa,* 105.

37 Ibid., 125.

38 David M. Stanley, "Contemplation of the Gospels, Ignatius Loyola, and the Contemporary Christian," *Theological Studies* 29 (1968): 430.

39 Castellano, "Espiritualidad Teresiana," 155.

40 Rahner, *Foundations of Christian Faith,* 203.

41 Rahner, "The Eternal Significance of the Humanity of Jesus for Our Relationship with God," 41.

42 Rahner, *Foundations of Christian Faith,* 308.

43 Castro, "L'humanité du Christ selon Ste. Thérèse d'Avila," 41.

44 As a framework to study Teresa's experience of the Risen Christ, I have relied upon Walter Kasper's discussion on the resurrection which helped me to situate and examine Teresa's encounter with the Risen Christ in light of the apostle's experience of the Risen Lord. Kasper, *Jesus the Christ,* 124-59.

45 Ibid., 129.

46 Stanley, "Contemplation of the Gospels, Ignatius Loyola, and the Contemporary Christian," 425.

47 Teresa distinguishes three kinds of visions: intellectual, imaginative, and corporeal. Her experiences of the Risen Lord were not experienced through the senses. She did not see Christ with the eyes of the body, nor of the soul. They were intellectual visions. She explains the intellectual vision as ". . . represented through knowledge given to the soul that is clearer than sunlight. I don't mean that you see the sun or brightness, but that light, without your seeing light, illumines the intellect so that the soul may enjoy such a great good." (L.27.3)

48 Alvarez, "Jesucristo en la experiencia de Santa Teresa," 88.

49 Kasper, *Jesus the Christ,* 139.

50 Ibid., 155.

51 Alvarez, "Jesucristo en la experiencia de Santa Teresa," 89.

52 Kasper, *Jesus the Christ,* 157.

53 Castellano, "Espiritualidad Teresiana," 158.

54 Kasper, *Jesus the Christ,* 155.

55 Ibid., 151.

56 Ibid., 159.

57 Ibid., 140.

58 Rahner, *The Love of Jesus and the Love of Neighbor,* 23.

59 Maximiliano Herraiz Garcia, *La oración historia de amistad* (Madrid: Editorial de Espiritualidad, 1982), 117.

60 Karl Rahner, "The Theology of Symbol," *Theological Investigations*, vol. 4 (Baltimore: Helicon, 1966), 237. By saying that Jesus is the "real symbol" of the union that exists between heaven and earth, I mean this in the way Rahner uses it. Jesus is truly the expression and revelation of that union between God and the world which has now taken place in and through the incarnation. Rahner writes: "The incarnate word is the absolute symbol of God in the world, filled as nothing else can be with what is symbolized. He is not merely the presence and revelation of what God is in himself. He is also the expressive presence of what—or rather, who—God wished to be, in free grace, to the world, in such a way that this divine attitude, once so expressed, can never be reversed, but is and remains final and unsurpassable." (237)

Fair is Foul and Foul is Fair: *An Interpretation of Chapter Fourteen of Book One of* **The Dark Night** *by St. John of the Cross*

Marc Foley, O.C.D.
Institute of Carmelite Studies
Washington, DC

Introduction

Our interpretations of our experiences are often based upon erroneous presuppositions. Perhaps the most pervasive of these presuppositions is the belief that if something feels good it must be good, and if something feels bad it must be bad. However, this is not always true, for what *feels* fair can *be* foul and what *feels* foul can *be* fair. For example, we can believe that when we feel good about ourselves we are in a good place, and when we feel bad about ourselves we are in a bad place. But this is not always the case as the parable of the Pharisee and the Tax Collector teaches. The pharisee felt good about himself but was blind to his spiritual condition before God; whereas, the tax collector felt wretched about himself, but he was facing the truth about his life.

As the parable indicates, our feelings are often not the best judges of the state of our spiritual lives. We need to judge spiritual things spiritually, but this is not an easy task, for the graces we receive from God do not carry with them their own interpretations. We need to be enlightened in order to unlock their meaning. St. Teresa wrote, "it is one grace to *receive* the Lord's favor; another, to *understand* which favor and grace it is." (L.17.5) (italics added)

St. John of the Cross possessed both graces to a high degree; not only was he the recipient of various mystical graces, but he was also endowed with the spiritual genius which enabled him to interpret them. In consequence, we have in his writings a wise and experienced guide who can help us to understand the workings of God in our lives.

Perhaps the single most valuable insight that John imparts to us is that our feelings are not always a reliable guide for interpreting spiritual experience. Throughout his writings, John tells us, in various ways, that "Neither the sublime communications nor sensible awareness of [God's] nearness is a sure testimony of his gracious presence, nor are dryness and the lack of these a reflection of his absence." (C.1.3) For example, the depth of our prayer cannot be judged by sensible consolation or the lack of it; "many individuals think they are not praying when, indeed, their prayer is very deep. Others place high value on their prayer while it amounts to little more than nothing. (A.Prol.6) Likewise, John tells us that often our longing for God is an experience of the God for whom we long; what we label as the absence of God is actually an experience of God's *presence.*

In the same vein, a soul has many experiences during the process of spiritual transformation that can be easily misinterpreted as symptoms of regression but which are actually signs of growth.[1] In this essay we will explore three such experiences that John describes in chap. 14 of book 1 of *The Dark Night.* Here he lists three trials that souls who take the spiritual journey seriously and whom God is calling to a deeper process of transformation will often have to endure: intense sexual temptations, anger toward God (temptations to blaspheme), and mental confusion regarding coming to peace with determining God's will (scrupulosity).

John does not say why these trials are archetypical for these souls (and neither should they be taken as an exhaustive list), but I believe that if we read chap. 14 in the light of John's overall teaching on the dark night, keep in mind the particular type of soul that he is writing about, and consider where the chapter is situated in the text, we can come to some understanding of why these trials occur. However, I caution the reader not to expect any simple answers, for our psychic life is extremely complex, and the process of spiritual transformation is truly a mystery.

Intense Sexual Temptations: The Spirit of Fornication

> For those who must afterward enter into the other more oppressive night of the spirit in order to reach the divine union of love—because not everyone but only a few usually reach this union—this night [the sensory night] is ordinarily accompanied by burdensome trials and sensory temptations that last a long time, and with some longer than with others. An angel of Satan (2 Cor 12:7), which is the spirit of fornication, is given to some to buffet their senses with strong and abominable temptations, and afflict their spirit with foul thoughts and very vivid images, which sometimes is a pain worse than death for them. (N.1.14.1)

In order to understand both the psychological and spiritual reasons for these temptations of lust, we need first to locate them *where* they emerge on the spiritual path. John mentions them in the *last* chapter of book 1 of *The Dark Night,* which is a transition chapter that bridges his treatment of the night of the senses and the night of the spirit. In other words, he is writing of people who have been on the spiritual path for many years and who "have more considerable capacity and strength for suffering" in contrast to souls that "are never wholly in the night or wholly out of it." (N.1.14.5) Thus, John is indicating that these temptations are often more intense in souls who have fully embraced the first stage of transformation that he calls the night of the senses and are open to being led by God into deeper transformation. To give an answer why these souls are often bombarded with sexual temptations is not an easy task, for such temptations may be the result of any number of different causes or a combination of causes. Let us explore some possibilities.

Seeking Relief. When a soul chooses to enter into the night of the senses in earnest, as is outlined by John in chap. 13 of book 1 of *The Ascent of Mount Carmel,* it chooses a lifestyle which bridles the pleasure principle by mortifying its inordinate appetites. Human nature naturally rebels against such restrictions and presents its cravings to the conscious mind in the form of images. Perhaps the most basic reason why the sexual images are "foul" (*feas* in Spanish can connote brutality and moral depravity) has to do with the brute strength of pent up sexual tension that seeks relief in discharge.

Assuaging Anxiety. "He started thinking about Woman again. He let pictures rise in the dark, all kinds; clothed, naked, asleep, awake, drinking, dancing. . . . A little spark of desire began to glow. . . . He blew on it deliberately. Nothing like lust for keeping fear at a distance."[2] This observation by C. S. Lewis regarding the relationship between lust and fear is relevant to our topic because there is much anxiety in the dark night. One source of anxiety that is native to the dark night is the result of relinquishing control over one's life and allowing oneself to be led by God down dark and unfamiliar paths. "As regards this road to union, entering on the road means leaving one's own road" and passing "beyond the interior and exterior limits of [one's] own nature." (A.2.4.5)

Who hasn't known the cold fear and trembling anxiety that ensues from being confronted by God's call to venture into an untried territory of life? Such experiences can trigger our deepest insecurities and inadequacies, make us feel defective and unfit for life, and resurrect our self-doubts that feed our deepest suspicions that we are nothing but frightened children masquerading as adults. The psyche instinctively attempts to anesthetize this devouring anxiety by calling to mind sexual images (among other types of images) that are equally as savage as the anxiety that it tries to assuage. Therefore, we should neither be shocked nor frightened at the foulness, the rawness, the pure animality, or even the perversity of the images that come to our minds during times of severe anxiety, because the intensity of the sexual passion that is evoked by the image is an attempt on the part of the psyche to override the feeling of fragmentation and restore psychic equilibrium.

Also, we need to keep in mind that the spiritual life is not a cubicle isolated from the rest of life; it is God's grace operating in us *as we are.* If, for example, we have a history of emotional abandonment, we have probably learned to narcotize our high degree of separation anxiety by some means, be it food, alcohol, drugs, work, or sex. Therefore, it should not be surprising that when a soul is being led by God to journey deeper into the thicket of transformation, beyond the rim of the familiar into the hinterland of the unknown, those old and deeply ingrained patterns of self-soothing will reassert themselves with a vengeance. John says as much in stanza 3 of *The Spiritual Canticle* where the Bride, as she begins to seek her Beloved by practicing the virtues and entering into a deeper process of detachment, encounters "wild beasts" that attempt to block her path. One of these beasts is "the natural rebellions of the flesh. . . . [that] sets itself up as though on the frontier to oppose the spiritual journey." (C.3.10)

This is a natural reaction to both the fear that is engendered by venturing outside our emotional comfort zone and the deep inertia embedded in our sensual nature. Whenever we try to "get up from the bed of [our] own satisfaction and delight," (C.3.3) our ingrained lethargy and addiction to comfort combine forces and attempt to drive us back again. This dynamic is symbolized at the beginning of Dante's *Divine Comedy* when Dante attempts to leave the dark wood of sin and ignorance. As he starts to climb out of the dark wood, his path is blocked immediately by the Leopard of Lust and two other beasts. They will not allow him to pass because he cannot bypass human nature on his way to God.

We cannot do an end run around ourselves in the dark night because the night brings to light, that is, brings to consciousness, all that is within us that needs to be healed and redeemed, for the "dark night is an inflow of God into the soul which purges it of its habitual ignorances and imperfections, natural and spiritual" (N.2.5.1) that "the soul has contracted throughout its life." (N.2.6.5) In psychological terms, there is a lifting of repression; things that have been pushed down into the unconscious begin to surface in order to be transformed.

The Emergence of Regressive Longings. Lust or any form of sensuality can also be compensatory. It offers the committed soul relief from the monotony that accompanies steadfast fidelity to the nitty-gritty of daily life and attempts to compensate for the many losses that a soul incurs as the result of choosing to do God's will. Here is an example.

Ann is thirty-eight, married, and has two children ages two and four. Last year she made a difficult decision to curtail her work as an English teacher at a nearby state university in order to spend more time at home with her children. Even though Ann believes that she has made the right decision, she misses teaching and the intellectual stimulation of her colleagues. Also, the monotony of being a full-time mom is beginning to take its toll.

Recently she has found herself daydreaming about an old boyfriend named Bob with whom she used to go steady in college. At first, these daydreams were intermittent, but recently Bob has been on her mind constantly, and sometimes Ann feels that he is with her. Bob's "presence" produces a bittersweet mood in Ann that is so poignant at times that it makes her cry. At other times, his image creates a strange melancholic mood within her, a nostalgia for something that she cannot name, a kind of paradise-lost yearning for something she cannot fully grasp.

Ann feels guilty because she believes that she is being unfaithful to her husband. She is also confused, for she does not understand what is happening to her. She is too ashamed to talk to anyone about her romantic/sexual feelings toward a man she hasn't seen for nearly twenty years, and she is beginning to wonder if she is doing something wrong. "Am I becoming lax in my spiritual life? Maybe if I prayed more or was more attentive to doing God's will, these fantasies and feelings would not be plaguing me." But Ann has been faithful to her spiritual life and has taken the following of God's will seriously. Paradoxically, Ann's faithfulness may be the catalyst that is triggering her "very vivid images" (N.1.14.1) of Bob.

Ann's choice to curtail her career and spend more time with her children has exacted sacrifices from her, the depth of which she is not fully conscious. Even though Ann is still teaching as an adjunct, she is unconsciously mourning her lifelong dream of becoming a full professor with a brilliant academic career. The mourning of her dream, coupled with the loss of intellectual stimulation and the burden of a thousand-and-one thankless tasks of being a mom, is wearing on Ann. Within this context we can begin to understand Ann's daydreams about Bob.

To comprehend the reasons for Ann's fantasies, we must not focus too narrowly on her romantic/sexual feelings toward Bob, but rather interpret the emotional atmosphere surrounding her memories of Bob. Proust once compared the recesses of memory to thousands of vases, situated on the various layers of our past, each filled with an atmosphere reminiscent of a particular period of our life. Using this image, we can view the atmosphere or emotional tonality permeating Ann's memory of Bob as everything that was going on in her life during her college days; in short, *who she was,* her philosophy of life, her dreams for her future, etc.

The atmosphere of Ann's college days was full of excitement. Living in a college dorm away from home for the first time in her life during the sexual revolution and drug culture of the sixties made her feel alive. In addition, Ann was free of the worries and adult responsibilities of being a breadwinner, wife, and mother, and she dreamed of becoming an English professor. Bob was an integral part of Ann's dream. They talked about marriage and fantasized about their future life together. Both were academically orientated and aspired to careers in teaching English.

Considering the compensatory nature of the psyche, it is understandable that it would choose this period in Ann's life as a means of trying to offset the losses of her present situation. However, we must continue to dig deeper to completely understand the strength of Ann's "very vivid images." Because our psychic life is an organic unity (or one *suppositum* as John would put it), the longings and dreams of Ann's college days are rooted in all the unconscious desires, unmourned dreams of her childhood, and the deep regressive "longings for mother, the nostalgia for the source from which we came."[3]

When the tasks or challenges of life become too heavy for us to bear the deep regressive longings of our psyche come to the surface. All we want is to return to the womb, to a place of complete security and peace; to be free of all worries, concerns, responsibilities, and to be relieved of the anguish of conscience and choice. We pine for absolute freedom to do whatever we choose and simply to be left alone.

Our regressive longings beckon us to flee life by either numbing ourselves with food, drink, drugs, sex, sleep, etc., by hurling ourselves headlong into various forms of frantic activity, or by escaping into fantasy. All are forms of escape that attempt to compensate for the monotony of life. Ann's fantasies about Bob fall into this category; they present to her an idealized life that is in stark contrast to her present situation. So how should we assess Ann's fantasies?

From a psychological perspective we can view Ann's fantasies as a natural phenomenon of the psyche. They are the psyche's attempt to sooth pain; they are expressive of the pleasure principle that is embedded in our nature. However, from a spiritual viewpoint, Ann's fantasies are part of the cross that follows upon her choice to do God's will. Her choice to endure her fantasies as she chooses to remain faithful to God's will is an example of what John calls the "passive night." Passive purification consists in accepting her regressive longings without giving into them.

We find an archetypical image of this purification in Odysseus's encounter with the Sirens. The Sirens were nymphs that lived on an island and who lured unexpecting sailors to a watery grave. They did so by singing so sweetly of a sailor's past that it evoked in any sailor who listened to their song such an irresistible longing that it made him abandon his journey and swim toward the island.

As Odysseus sailed by the island of the Sirens on his way home to Ithaca to his family and to resume his role as king, he protected his men from hearing the enchanting voices of the Sirens by filling their ears with wax, while with ears unplugged, he had his men bind him to the mast of the ship. This image of Odysseus enduring the Sirens' song as his men faithfully plied their oars and rowed toward home symbolizes an important transforming aspect of the passive night: the soul remains steadfast in doing God's will while enduring all the forces and enticing allurements that war against it. Like the fish that jumped out of the river and attempted to devour Tobias, the regressive longings and inordinate appetites that threaten to swallow us up, once wrestled with, become food and medicine for the journey. As John puts it, our imperfections and inordinate appetites are the "fuel" of transformation. (N.2.10.5) Ann's fantasies can be understood within this context. They are deep tendencies of her soul that must come to the surface and be endured in order to be transformed. Let us explore this from another perspective.

The Return of the Repressed. The Christological principle—"that which is not assumed is not healed," that is, any part of human nature not incarnated by the Word is not redeemed—may also be applied to the spiritual life. Any part of ourselves that is not consciously incorporated into our life is not transformed. This is why in the dark night, the repressed parts of ourselves that have been sent into exile in the unconscious begin their long journey home; they need to be brought to consciousness in order to be redeemed and transformed. However, when they finally do show up at the door of our conscious mind, they evoke fear in us because they are so strong.

There are two reasons why they are so powerful. First, the repressed gathers energy in the unconscious. Like an exiled king who raises an army to return to his realm, so too, the banished parts of ourselves gather strength to break through the wall of repression in order to reunite themselves to consciousness. Second, because the repressed elements of our psyche have been denied the civilizing influence of conscious choice, they regress to a primitive state; they are like feral children. For example, in Ann's case, the regressive longings that usually take the form of romantic fantasies will often become so intense that they convert themselves into highly sexually charged images. It is precisely because of the repressed nature of what emerges during the dark night that the sexual images assailing the soul are often so strong, foul, and abominable. So why do they emerge at this point on the spiritual path? To answer this question I would like to make an analogy between Freud's latency stage of psychosexual development and the subsequent onset of puberty, and the relationship between the night of the senses and the night of the spirit.

First, during the latency period when sexual energy is dormant and the forbidden impulses associated with the oedipal period repressed, the ego grows in strength as it differentiates itself from the id. During this time, sexual energy begins to undergo a process of transformation; it is channeled into various cultural activities (e.g., friendships, sports, hobbies, etc.). In a similar way, because of the mortification that is exercised during the night of the senses, the sensual appetites are "lulled to sleep," (A.1.15.2) during which time the soul gathers strength by growing in the virtues. (N.2.1.1)

Secondly, just as at the onset of puberty, there is a resurgence of sexual energy that resurrects old oedipal themes and conflicts, so too does the soul that begins to enter the dark night of the spirit reencounter temptations that it previously struggled with during the night of the senses. Just as the issues that emerge during the oedipal period are not completely resolved but temporarily negotiated, so it is with the sensual appetites that are mortified during the night of the senses; they are reformed but not completely transformed, they are bridled but not tamed. "This sensitive purgation . . . serves more for the accommodation of the senses to the spirit than for the union of the spirit with God." (N.2.2.1) "Hence the night of the senses . . . should be called a certain reformation and bridling of the appetite rather than a purgation." (N.2.3.1)

This is an important perspective that John offers his readers. It is very easy to naively believe that because the first *battle* with sensuality has been waged, the *war* is won. But John tells us that it has only just begun. This is because the "real purgation of the senses *begins* with the spirit" for "all the imperfections and disorders of the sensory part are rooted in the spirit." (N.2.3.1) (italics added) The night of the senses prunes the behavioral "branches" of our sensuality; but the night of the spirit pulls up its psychic "roots" (N.2.2.1). John's use of the images of "pruning" and "bridling" to describe what happens during the night of the senses symbolizes the two virtues (temperance and fortitude) that are needed in order to endure the trials of the dark night of the spirit.

Greek philosophers and medieval theologians made a strong connection between the virtue of temperance and beauty, for temperance brings order, harmony, symmetry, and peace into the soul. "The purpose and goal of *temperantia,*" writes Josep Pieper, "is man's inner order, from which alone 'serenity of spirit' can flow forth."[4] According to John, this "serenity of spirit" or emotional stability, which temperance provides, is a foundation for the fortitude needed in the night of the spirit. "This was the *purpose* of the reformation of the first night and the *calm* that resulted from it; that the sensory part, united in a certain way with the spirit, *might undergo* purgation and suffering [in the passive night] *with greater fortitude.*" (N.2.3.2) (italics added) The fortitude that is needed in the passive night is the strength of endurance. Two things must be endured, the first being the untransformed part of our nature. Fortitude keeps a firm grip on the bridle of impulse and a steady hand on the rudder of emotion during storms of passion. Without the strength of will engendered by fortitude and the serenity of spirit that flows from temperance, a person's spiritual house is built on sand and will collapse when buffeted by "strong and abominable temptations." (N.1.14.1) The second thing that needs to be endured in the passive night is the presence of God, which is the root cause of the increase of sexual desire and its consequent temptations.

The Nature of God and Human Nature. Because God is infinite, God is Ultimate Mystery and will remain so for all eternity; even in the beatific vision, God will remain incomprehensible. John writes: "One of the outstanding favors God grants briefly in this life is an understanding and experience of himself so lucid and lofty that one comes to know clearly that God cannot be completely understood or experienced. This understanding is somewhat like that of the blessed in heaven: Those who understand God more understand more distinctly the infinitude that remains to be understood; those who see less of him do not realize so clearly what remains to be seen." (C.7.9) "It is no wonder that God is strange to humans who have not seen him, since he is also strange to the holy angels and to the blessed. For the angels and the blessed are incapable of seeing him fully, nor will they ever be capable of doing so." (C.14&15.8)

These passages express more than the doctrine of divine incomprehensibility; they also point to the basic way that we experience God. For if God is a presence who is simultaneously *already here* and *still yet to come,* then desire, which is the tension between the two, is the fundamental way that we experience God. This is one of John's main teachings in *The Spiritual Canticle:* the tension between what is revealed and what is still hidden "wounds" the Bride with desire for her Beloved. She experiences this wound in the beauty of creation and the loveliness of rational creatures (angels and humans) because, as handiworks of her Beloved, she sees in them "a trace of the beauty of her Beloved" (C.6.1) that "awakens her appetite" (C.6.4) for a clear vision of her heart's desire. The experience of the wound reveals to the soul not just the nature of God but also what it means to be human.

To be human in the deepest sense of the word is to be made in the image and likeness of God. This means that we are a reflection of God's nature. This is how the early Christian writers understood "image and likeness." They saw *image* as our capacity and drive toward God and *likeness* as the fulfillment of this desire. Thus, our desire and longing for God, who is simultaneously *already present* and *still yet to come,* is also an experience of our deepest self, which exists in the creative tension between being and becoming. However, because of the anesthetizing effects of sin, which results in a blunting and numbing of our desire for God, we are alienated from our deepest self. But as we are purified and transformed by God's presence our desire to be united to God is awakened, and since all the levels of our being are interconnected, or, as John puts it, are parts of one *suppositum,* (N.1.4.2; 2.1.1; 3.1; C.13.4) our thirst for union on the deepest level of our being reverberates on every other level.

John gives an example of this phenomenon in dealing with what he calls spiritual lust, which is called spiritual "because it *proceeds from* spiritual things." (N.1.4.1) (italics added) When a person is absorbed in prayer and is experiencing spiritual consolations, "without the person being able to avoid it, impure movements will be experienced in the sensory part of the soul" (N.1.4.1) because each level of our nature "shares according to its mode in what the other receives." (N.1.4.2) In short, any experience on one level of our nature will tend to trigger kindred experiences on other levels. This is the spiritual reason why strong temptations to lust emerge at this point on the spiritual path. For as we draw closer to God and grow in our desire to be united to God, so our desire for union on every other level of our being also grows.

When two people are growing in true love—which cannot be separated from growing in union with God—sexual desire becomes more numinous because it becomes more sacramental. As love discloses deeper and deeper levels of our beloved's being, our desire to be united to him or her physically, emotionally, psychologically, and spiritually increases and also discloses a mysterious Other that we cannot touch, who is both *within* and *beyond* our beloved: the God who is *always present* and *still yet to come.* This is an experience of the growth dimension of the transformation of our sexuality, but "when the crop began to mature and yield grain the weeds made their *appearance as well.*" (Mt 13:26) (italics added)

The "weeds" of our sexuality that come to light as we grow spiritually are the untransformed and unintegrated tendencies and inclinations of our sexual nature that we call lust. The transformation of these tendencies is like the purging in homoeopathic healing; it brings to the surface all the deeply embedded toxins of a lifetime in order to expel them.[5] John's metaphor of the log (soul) being transformed by fire (God) captures this purifying aspect of transformation. "The soul is purged and prepared for union with the divine light just as the wood is prepared for transformation into the fire. . . . [T]he fire brings to light and expels all those ugly accidents that are contrary to fire." (N.2.10.1) So what should we do when all these untransformed parts of our nature begin to surface? What should be our response when the capital sin of lust emerges? First, we need to understand the nature of the capital sins.

The Capital Sins. In scholastic theology the seven capital sins are not deeds but the *tendencies* that incline our will toward sinful actions. There is no personal guilt associated with the capital sins because guilt is the result of choice, even though a person may *feel* guilty because she is plagued by one of these tendencies. In fact, what people often label as sinful may actually be virtuous. For example, in the confessional I frequently hear people confessing the sin of anger, but as I explore with them "what happened," it often becomes evident that they were actually being very virtuous by exercising great restraint as they were feeling the emotion of anger. "Yesterday my seven year old, wanting to be mommy's little helper, polished all of my good silverware with Comet and a Brillo pad. He did a very, very thorough job! I was furious with him. Even though I didn't yell at him, I felt so guilty because I thought he knew that I wasn't happy with him. If I really loved my son, I wouldn't have felt that way."

Here is an example of what *feels* foul *is* fair. The woman's anger was a natural *reaction* in the face of having her silverware ruined; it had nothing to do with her *relationship* with her son. In fact, her anger was actually the context in which her love for her son was manifested in her act of self-restraint. The same is true with the other capital sins, even lust; "without the person *being able to avoid it*, impure movements will be experienced in the sensory part of the soul." (N.1.4.1) (italics added)

Even though John is specifically writing about spiritual lust in the above passage, he is also talking about the human condition in general. In many ways, we inadvertently become sexually aroused as we go through our day, whether it's when someone sees a seductively dressed person walking down the street, or when a lustful memory arises in the mind, or when we see an erotic image on television or in a magazine. However, just as with the passion of anger, so too the passion of lust provides a context for transformation.

The Threshold of Assent. The context of the transformation of all the capital sins is choice: the choice to endure the tension between the inclination of the passion and the action it provokes. By consciously choosing to suffer this tension, not only do we prevent our consciousness from being further swallowed up by our compulsiveness, but we begin to reverse the process. Orpheus, for example, succeeded in rescuing Eurydice only as long as he endured the tension of not turning around to look at her as he was bringing her up from the underworld. Similarly, we rescue a part of ourselves from the blind cavern of impulse and begin to transform and integrate its vital energy into our response to God as long as we choose to endure the tension of any temptation. The energy that our inordinate appetites consume is the "fuel that catches on fire" (N.2.10.5) in the process of transformation. This process occurs at the threshold of assent.

The threshold of assent is that moment of consciousness when we become aware of the "first movements" of the subliminal urges of the capital sins. A person should not think that as they grow in God's grace that the urges that show up at the threshold of consciousness decrease, for as John indicates in chap. 14 of the 1st book of *The Dark Night* and elsewhere in his writing, they will often increase in intensity. However, as long as we do not give our willful consent to them, they can only harass us; they cannot harm us. "Clearly, for a soul to reach union with God through its will and love . . . one must not give consent of the will advertently and knowingly to an imperfection. . . . I say 'knowingly' . . . because one will fall into the above-mentioned natural appetites without having advertence or knowledge or control in the matter. It is written of these semivoluntary and inadvertent sins that the just will fall seven times a day and rise up again." (Prv 24:16) (A.1.11.3)

John is making a vital distinction in this passage between *experiencing* the passions, which are outside of our control (e.g., feeling the emotion of anger or feeling sexually aroused), and *adverting* to the experience (*advertir* to take notice of or observe), that is, choosing to focus on it, or what we commonly call "entertaining a temptation." Merely experiencing the passions cannot *harm* us; in fact, John indicates that choosing to suffer the tension that they create is one of the trials that *heals* us. "People . . . should live with great patience and constancy in all the tribulations and trials God places on them, whether they be exterior or interior, spiritual or bodily, great or small, and they should accept them all from God's hand as a good remedy . . . for they bring health. . . . [They] will cut off the roots of your sins and imperfections." (F.2.30)

This is the perspective that we should have regarding the temptations toward fornication that John mentions in chap. 14 of book 1 of *The Dark Night:* the "strong and abominable temptations" may indicate that the roots of our disordered sexuality are being severed so that we can be healed and transformed, and when our sexuality is transformed, all of our relationships are healed and transformed. (cf. F.1.21)

Before ending this section two issues ought to be considered. The first is whether there is something peculiar about temptations of lust, as distinct from the other capital sins, that brings them to the fore at this juncture on the spiritual path. This is not to say that the other capital sins such as pride and sloth, for example, don't appear at this time, but since John seems to single out lust (along with the passion of anger-blasphemy) the question arises, Why? Is it a biographically colored issue or the distilled experience of a seasoned spiritual director?

While I believe that both elements underlie John's choice, I also think that John's mystical soul intuitively grasped the strong kinship between the sexual instinct and the religious instinct. Both instincts strive for union and are relational. As Catherine LaCugna writes: "Sexuality broadly defined is the capacity for relationship. . . . [It] is a clue that our existence is grounded in a being whose To-Be is To-Be-For."[6] Therefore, as a soul is being called into a deeper relationship with God, it would follow that the untransformed aspects of its sexuality (relationality) would come to the surface to be purified.

Secondly, since our sexuality is interwoven with other major issues in our lives (e.g., power, the need to be loved or to dominate, self-esteem, dependency, acceptance, exploitation, manipulation, etc.), we should not interpret the temptations to fornication too narrowly. Even though the erotic element of a particular temptation is in the foreground, it may nevertheless be secondary to another part of our sexuality (relationality) that is being called forth to be purified and transformed.

The psychologist Edward C. Whitmont gives an example of this in his book *The Symbolic Quest.*[7] During the course of analysis, one of his clients, a very chauvinistic man who demeaned women and looked down upon them with supercilious disdain, began having a recurring fantasy that he could not make love to a woman until he kissed her feet. This "foul thought" as John might label it, or this "foot fetish" as Freud might diagnose it, symbolized the healing that the man was being called to undergo; it represented what he had to do psychologically in order to correct his egotism. Debasing himself before what he demeaned was the psyche's attempt to compensate and correct his conscious attitude toward women. Considering his haughtiness and disdain of women, the man's "perverse" fantasy was an apt image of humility, the virtue that he needed to grow in, in order to heal his pride.

Anger Toward God: A Blasphemous Spirit

> At other times a blasphemous spirit is added; it commingles intolerable blasphemies with all one's thoughts and ideas. Sometimes these blasphemies are so strongly suggested to the imagination that the soul is almost made to pronounce them, which is a grave torment to it. (N.1.14.2)

What does John mean by a blasphemous spirit? To answer this question let us recall the type of soul that he is writing about and where it is situated on the spiritual path. He is referring to souls who *have said yes* to God and are standing on a threshold of being asked to say *yes again* on a deeper level. The blasphemous spirit that is experienced at this juncture is the soul's *resistance* to change. This resistance reflects the unconverted part of the soul that the divine fire of contemplation brings to consciousness for the sake of transformation. It is part of the "natural and vicious darknesses" that arise out of the inner recesses of the soul that must be expelled. "This divine purge stirs up all the foul and vicious humors of which the soul was never before aware." (N.2.10.2) "When this flame shines on the soul, since its light is excessively brilliant, it shines within the darknesses of the soul, which are also excessive. Persons then feel their natural and vicious darknesses that are contrary to the supernatural light." (F.1.22) The soul's natural darkness can be called "vicious" because when God's supernatural light shines on its resistance, it reacts like a fearful animal that has been cornered; it feels threatened and trapped and is fighting for its life.

The souls that John describes in chap. 14 of book 1 of *The Dark Night* feel trapped. As a result of their spiritual growth, they find it increasingly more painful to say no to God. Because God has become more and more the center of their lives, they experience a refusal to do God's will as an act of self-betrayal. Put simply, when they say no to God, they find it more difficult to live with themselves. They feel deeply the truth of John's admonition: "Since a double measure of bitterness must follow the doing of your own will, do not do it even though you remain in single bitterness." (S.17)

As God beckons them to a deeper conversion of heart, they feel trapped; their inner resistance balks at saying yes, but they can't live with themselves if they say *no*. The soul is torn between its biddings and forbiddings. Psychologist Marie-Louise von Franz captures this conflict that arises when God breaks into our lives. She writes: "The ego . . . is wounded because something greater [the Self] breaks into its life. Which is why Dr. Jung says that it means tremendous suffering to get in touch with the process of individuation. It causes a tremendous wound because, put simply, we are robbed of the capacity for arranging our own lives according to our own wishes. . . . To be deprived of an evening out, or a trip, is not so bad, but there are more serious matters where we greatly want something that is suddenly vetoed by the unconscious. We feel broken and crucified, caught in a trap or imprisoned, nailed against the cross. With your whole heart and mind you want to do something, and the unconscious vetoes it."[8]

The blasphemous spirit engendered by *feeling trapped* and *being robbed* of the capacity to arrange one's life according to one's wishes is fanned into resentment when we believe that those around us are not in this situation. Céline, the sister of St. Thérèse, once felt that God was asking her "to renounce some legitimate pleasures which other sisters could enjoy in peace."[9] The resentment that Céline felt was not due solely to the fact that God was asking *her* to renounce some legitimate pleasures but was the result of her perception that *others* were not being asked. Her anger belonged to the same species of anger that Elizabeth Kübler-Ross describes in her stages of death and dying; it is a reaction of "Why Me?" "Why is God picking on me? It isn't fair that I'm asked to do something that others don't have to do!" The reaction is similar to St. Peter's response to Jesus after Jesus indicated to Peter the sort of death that he would have to endure. Peter looked around, and when he saw the disciple whom Jesus loved, he said, "But Lord, what about him?" (Jn 21:21) We can all identify with this. We felt it when our mother asked us to do an extra chore that our siblings were not asked to do. "But, ma, what about Frank? Why can he go out and play when I have to stay in and mop the kitchen floor? It's not fair!" Feeling singled out by God to do something that others are not called to do, I believe, is at the core of the resentment of the blasphemous spirit of which John writes. But the question arises, "Does this feeling of being singled out by God have any validity to it?"

We need to answer this question carefully. It involves more than how we interpret our feelings; it touches upon how we image God. Lurking behind the temptation to blasphemy can be an image of a god who is lying in wait for an opening to "send us sufferings." Perhaps it would be more accurate to say that because the souls that John is talking about have entered deeply into the purification of the dark night and "have more considerable capacity and strength for suffering," (N.1.14.5) they are more conscious, attentive, and open to responding to life's opportunities to love than many other souls around them.

The temptations to blasphemy that these souls experience are usually not directed toward God, but are displaced upon people in their environment; what is displaced is often a combination of anger and envy. For example, an individual may create in a community or the work place a situation that should be dealt with for the good of the group, but everyone is tiptoeing around it. After prayer and counsel you conclude that God is asking you to confront this individual. You are furious with others for what you label as their obtuseness, apathy, or a lack of nerve; yet, you are also envious of them and wish that you were not burdened with a heightened conscience.

Whenever love bids us to restructure our lives, we resist, and when we feel that what is being asked of us isn't being asked of others, we resent it. These dynamics play themselves out in a thousand ways in daily life. Like Céline, we are sometimes asked to renounce a legitimate pleasure that others can enjoy in peace, not because God is singling us out but rather because something in our makeup needs attention.

For example, over the past couple of years a friend had to face the fact that alcohol was becoming a problem in his life. Not only was he drinking too much wine with his evening meal, but he was beginning to drink alone in his room after supper. When he finally came to grips with his problem and chose to curtail his drinking, he felt resentful that others could freely enjoy this legitimate pleasure in peace. His resentment was irrational because the appetite that God was calling him to restrict was inordinate. This is an example of how a "blasphemous spirit" is projected as resentment upon others.

The resentment was easy to deal with for three reasons. First, restricting the consumption of alcohol did not cause a major crisis in his life; second, his consumption of wine was clearly inordinate; and third, even though his choice demanded a sacrifice, he was more than compensated by the positive effects that it produced in his life (e.g., no guilt, no hangovers, etc.). However, sometimes, as in Ann's case, God asks us to relinquish something of great weight. In these situations, a blasphemous spirit has the potential of becoming a corrosive force in our lives. We are in danger of growing embittered toward people who seem free to do what we have been asked to relinquish. Even after we have made the choice to let go of something, we are still not completely detached from it. Cutting off a branch does not mean that we have dug out the roots. St. Teresa says that while external detachment is a necessary condition of transformation, it is not sufficient. It must also be accompanied by internal detachment; otherwise, we are like a person who "after having locked his doors for fear of thieves. . . [allows] the thieves to remain inside the house." (W.10.1)

Teresa is warning us that unless we do the necessary inner work regarding a choice that we have made in the outer world, we can be robbed of the fruit that we have gained so far. What can rob us is the bitterness that often attends the choice to make a major sacrifice. If we are not attentive, we can begin to ruminate and seethe inwardly with resentment as we mentally compare our lot with those around us.

Even though this is a danger, we should not see the bitterness as the enemy. The *choices* we make in face of our bitterness are the issue. For just as the bitterness that often follows in the wake of saying yes to God can fester resentment, it can also be the context for growth. John says that the two chief characteristics of our inordinate attachments are that they make us "dissatisfied and bitter." (A.1.6.3) We can consider bitterness or the "blasphemous spirit" as one experience of the "roots" of our inordinate attachments that need to be exposed and endured in order to be healed.

Perhaps the greatest area of our inner healing, as we remain steadfast in doing what God asks of us while enduring the feelings that "it's not fair," is envy and resentment rooted in comparing our lives with the lives of others. As this healing takes place, we grow in the capacity to "live in the monastery as though no one else were in it." (Counsels to a Religious.2) We grow in what John calls "spiritual solitude" which is soul's capacity to rest in God's presence.

The Spirit of Confusion

> Sometimes another loathsome spirit, which Isaiah calls *spiritus vertiginis* (Is 19:14), is sent to these souls, not for their downfall but to try them. This spirit so darkens the senses that such souls are filled with a thousand scruples and perplexities, so intricate that such persons can never be content with anything, nor can their judgment receive the support of any counsel or idea. This is one of the most burdensome goads and horrors of this night—similar to what occurs in the spiritual night. (N.1.14.3)

To understand this trial, we must first comprehend the state of mind that John is describing. He tells us that at the core of this trial lies the fact that the "senses" (*sentido*) of these souls are darkened. Within the context of this passage *sentido* is best rendered as judgment. These souls cannot come to any resolution regarding a decision in their lives because their judgment is "darkened" (*oscurece*). What they should do is not clear; it is obscure.

What is the cause of the obscurity? As with the other two trials, we should not try to pinpoint a *single* reason because there may be several. However, for the sake of brevity, we will explore one possible scenario. Before we do so, it is important to situate this scenario within John's teaching on faith, because the further these souls travel on the spiritual path, the more faith becomes the means by which God guides them.

The Experience of Faith. It is common to speak of faith as a type of knowledge that is the result of grace. While this statement is true, it nevertheless tends to reify faith, that is, to speak of faith as "an object" or a "thing." However, faith may more accurately be spoken of in personal terms. It is a mode of experiencing God's presence, for faith "gives and communicates God himself to us." (C.12.4) Even though how we experience God's guidance through faith varies, John seems to indicate that it is often similar to our experience of intuition or instinct. It is a mode of apprehension, a "felt sense" rather than clear distinct ideas. Or as John puts it, knowledge that faith imparts "brings *certitude* . . . [but] it does not produce *clarity.*" (A.2.6.2) (italics added) This knowledge may be compared to peripheral vision; we are *certain* that we see things out of the corner of our eye, but we do not see them *clearly.*

I would like to suggest that experiencing the certain though obscure knowledge that faith provides is the *precondition* of the spirit of confusion, because part of the experience of the unfocused certainty of faith is doubt. Doubt is inherent in the very structure of faith.

As Paul Tillich writes regarding the experience of faith, "if doubt appears, it should not be considered as a negation of faith, but as an intrinsic element which always and will always be present in active faith."[10] Doubt is always present in *active faith,* that is, in a soul that is choosing to trust in the guidance of a Presence that it cannot see. This is for two reasons. First, the fear engendered in a soul that takes the risk of stepping out into the unknown provides the soul with a thousand logical reasons why it should not venture forth (e.g., it's too rash, it's presumptuous, etc.). Second, the light that faith imparts will often overwhelm the light of reason. One of the changes that will happen to the soul that is growing in faith is that because it is now seeing things in God's light, its whole worldview and way of interpreting reality is called into question. This will throw the soul into confusion, because at times, it will no longer know what is right and what is wrong. Let us explore an example.

Developmental Scrupulosity. There is an incident in Mark Twain's novel, *The Adventures of Huckleberry Finn,* that illustrates God's light breaking into a person's life. In Twain's story, Huck is helping Jim, a runaway slave, to escape into freedom. However, the night before they anticipate that their raft will arrive at Cairo, Illinois, where they plan to board a steamboat up the Ohio to the Free States, Huck has qualms of conscience. He feels guilty because it finally dawns on him that what he is doing is wrong. "I begun to get it through my head that he *was* most free and who was to blame for it? Why *me*. I couldn't get that out of my conscience, no how nor no way. It got to troubling me so I couldn't rest; I couldn't stay still in one place . . . tried to make out to myself that *I* warn't to blame, because *I* didn't run Jim off from his rightful owner to blame; but it warn't no use, conscience up and says, every time, 'But you knowed he was running for his freedom, and you could 'a' paddled ashore and told somebody.'"[11]

Yet there is still time to right this wrong. So Huck climbs into the canoe to turn Jim in, telling Jim that he is just going up the river a piece to ascertain their location. Once on the river, Huck encounters two men in a skiff looking for runaway slaves. When they ask Huck if he has seen any runaway slaves, he lies to the men. Something inside of Huck tells him that it would be wrong to hand over a friend. It is beginning to dawn on Huck that Jim is more than what his culture has told him; he's not just a slave, but a human being. However, his decision not to hand Jim over doesn't bring peace to Huck. He feels guilty because he hasn't done the "right thing," but he also knows that he would feel guilty if he did. "They went off and I got abroad the raft, feeling bad and low, because I knowed very well I had done wrong. . . . Then I thought for a minute, and says to myself, hold on; s'pose you'd 'a' done right and give Jim up, would you felt better than what you do now? No, says I, I'd feel bad—I'd feel just the same way I do now. . . . I was stuck."[12]

Huck's anguished dialogue with himself mirrors the state of souls that John describes as "filled with a thousand scruples and perplexities so intricate that [they] can never be content with anything, nor can their judgment receive the support of any counsel or idea." (N.1.14.3) Huck cannot find peace with either decision; no matter what he does, he isn't at home with himself, or as John puts it, "[t]here is no room for it within itself." (N.2.11.6) Huck's dilemma may best be labeled as what psychologist Joseph Ciarrocchi calls *developmental scrupulosity* which is the result of a "newly emerging sense of conscience."[13] Since Huck grew up in a culture that told him that slavery was not evil and that people had a right to own slaves, he would naturally feel guilty when he believed that he was violating the rights of a slave owner. However, when this ingested belief clashes with his growing conscience, Huck is thrown into confusion; he is torn and suspended between two worlds, one dying and the other laboring to be born. What makes Huck's struggle so painful is that all he wants is to do the right thing, but he isn't sure what that is. This is often the situation in which the souls whom John is referring to in chap. 14 find themselves. Let's take another example.

Jeff is forty-five and is employed as a proofreader and copy editor at a leading publishing house. Besides being professional in his work, Jeff is good-natured, generous with his time, affable, and super-dependable. His coworkers have come to depend upon him greatly. He's always on top of things, takes up the slack whenever needed, and is the only one in the office who has both the patience and willingness to mentor the greenhorns.

Jeff was raised Catholic, a faith that has always meant a great deal to him. He attends daily Mass before going to work, and five years ago he joined the Secular Order of Discalced Carmelites. His fidelity to daily meditation, which is a part of the Carmelite Rule, has made him grow in self-knowledge. In consequence, Jeff has become increasingly aware that the underlying motive of his generosity is not purely altruistic but is mingled with fear.

He discovered this in following what he believes is God's call in his life, namely, to deepen his prayer life and become more involved in both the Secular Order (doing formation work) and his neighborhood parish (teaching CCD and being on the parish council). As a result of these new commitments, Jeff has less time and energy to give to colleagues at work. He is still both diligent in his work and generous with his time but is no longer available to jump into the breach and take up the slack as he used to.

These changes have been difficult for Jeff because of his fear of disapproval. Sometimes he can't get to sleep at night because he is afraid that his colleagues think he is becoming selfish. But this isn't his greatest fear. He wonders if he *really* is becoming selfish. Even though Jeff has come to recognize that his indiscriminate generosity is rooted in his wish to please others and allay his fear of their disapproval, and even though his spiritual director has pointed out to him that bearing the fear of what other people think of him, as he continues to do what he believes is God's calling in his life, is part of the cross that he must bear, and even though Jeff believes what his director says is true, and even though Jeff knows that the guilt that he feels when he says "no" to a request made by one of his colleagues is not the guilt that is the result of not heeding God's voice but is a reaction of his punishing superego, in spite of all this, Jeff is still *not sure* that what he is doing is the right thing.

He is "filled with a thousand scruples" (*escrúpulos*). *Escrúpulos,* derived from the Latin *scrupus* (*scrupulus* is its diminutive), is a small stone weighing one twenty-fourth of an ounce (the smallest unit of weight in the Roman Empire). Someone with a scruple is like a very sensitive person who has an extremely small stone in his shoe which he feels whenever he takes a step. No matter the direction in which his choice leads him, he feels a pang or qualm of conscience. Because the souls that John is dealing with in chap. 14 are intent on doing God's will, they scrutinize their scruple. This condition of soul should not be confused with what moral theology calls scrupulosity or psychology categorizes as an obsessive-compulsive disorder, despite the descriptive similarities between them. Rather, it is more akin to what is called a "delicate" or "tender" conscience. Under the influence of grace, the soul is becoming sensitive and highly attuned to what is and what is not of God's will. A similar condition is found in David Fleming's interpretation of St. Ignatius's notes concerning scruples in *The Spiritual Exercises.* Fleming writes: "In the spiritual life, there can be a true awakening of conscience to a wholly new delicacy of conscience. . . . Properly speaking, the temporary lack of certitude and firmness of judgment aroused by this experience is not scrupulosity. Instead, this is recognized traditionally as a symptom of growth. . . . We desire to move beyond the now-recognized dullness or obtuseness of our conscience because we are roused by a new sensitivity of love."[14]

In spite of, or maybe because of, such growth, souls find themselves in periods of transition, similar to Jeff's situation, in which there is great confusion. They are plagued by inner doubts that always seem to be whispering "but are you *really* sure?" They cannot come to peace with either choice. So what does a person do at this time?

First, the soul should keep in mind that God is leading it in the darkness. This trial, like the other two trials (temptations to fornication and blasphemy), is not for its downfall, but for its advancement, "so that thus chastised and buffeted, the senses and faculties may gradually be exercised, prepared, and inured for the union with wisdom." (N.1.14.4) Specifically, regarding the trial of confusion, the soul is being prepared to enter into a deeper reliance upon God's guidance as it is being detached from its dependence upon the senses for its knowledge. In a word, they have to learn to trust God, and trust can only grow by trusting. This is done by choosing to *do* what they have come to *believe* is God's will for them as they learn to patiently endure the cross of self-doubt.

Conclusion

In his wisdom, St. John of the Cross shows us that at times we interpret experiences incorrectly—we sometimes interpret fair as foul, and foul as fair. In short, John helps us to interpret experience from a spiritual perspective and not merely psychologically. In this essay, we have explored three types of experiences that often indicate that God is calling a soul into deeper transformation but are commonly interpreted as indications of regression. Thus, chap. 14 of book 1 of *The Dark Night* helps us to correctly interpret indications of growth that we encounter on the spiritual path.

Notes

1 In this essay I use the word "soul" in the way that John uses it most frequently in his writings—to designate the whole of human nature. In general, John's use of the word soul (*alma*) is roughly equivalent to the word "person" in English.

2 C.S. Lewis, "After Ten Years," *The Dark Tower and Other Stories* (New York: Harcourt Brace Jovanovich, 1977), 137.

3 Carl Jung, "The Relations between the Ego and the Unconscious" in *Two Essays on Analytical Psychology* (New York: Princeton University Press, 1966), 169.

4 Josep Pieper, *The Four Cardinal Virtues* (New York: Harcourt, Brace & World, Inc., 1965), 145.

5 I am indebted to Ruth Burrows for the metaphor of the relationship between transformation and homoeopathic healing. See Ruth Burrows, *Ascent to Love: The Spiritual Teaching of St. John of the Cross* (Denville, NJ: Dimension Books, Inc., 1987), 50.

6 Catherine Mowry LaCugna, *God For Us: The Trinity and the Christian Life* (New York: HarperCollins Publishers, 1973), 407.

7 Edward C. Whitmont, *The Symbolic Quest* (Princeton, NJ: Princeton University Press, 1978), 19-23.

8 Marie-Louise von Franz, *Puer Aeternus* (Boston, MA: Sigo Press, 1981), 112-13.

9 Geneviève of the Holy Face (Céline Martin), *A Memoir of My Sister St. Thérèse,* trans. Carmelite Sisters of New York (New York: P.J. Kenedy & Sons, 1959), 67.

10 Paul Tillich, *The Dynamics of Faith* (New York: Harper & Bros., 1957), 22.

11 Mark Twain, *The Adventures of Huckleberry Finn* (New York: Bantam Books, Inc., 1982), 85.

12 Ibid., 89.

13 Joseph W. Ciarrocchi, *The Doubting Disease: Help for Scrupulosity and Religious Compulsions* (Mahwah, NJ: Paulist Press, 1995), 15.

14 David Fleming, S.J., *The Spiritual Exercises of St. Ignatius: A Literal Translation and a Contemporary Reading* (St. Louis: The Institute of Jesuit Sources, 1978), 229.

Constitutions of the Cerro, Or Treatise on Melancholy
Translation of a Work of Jerome Gratian: An Example of Teresian Humor

Michael Dodd
Madison, Wisconsin

Translator's Introduction

This brief work appeared in a modern Spanish edition by Fr. Ildefonso Moriones, OCD, in 1965. The original text, preserved in the Carmel of Brussels, was apparently written in 1582 after Fr. Jerome Gratian and St. Teresa had completed the last, difficult foundation they were to make together. All Carmelite men and women follow the ancient Rule of St. Albert, given in the early thirteenth century. Their particular constitutions specify the ways in which the different forms of life—enclosed nuns or active religious—are lived. One year before Gratian wrote this treatise, in 1581, the first official constitutions for the new province of Discalced friars and nuns were completed at a chapter meeting in Alcalá de Henares. These were the fruit of much thought, prayer, and effort by the Mother Foundress and her collaborator, as is evident from their surviving correspondence. Fr. Ildefonso Moriones suggests that while the two were waiting in Burgos for a resolution to the difficulties in making that foundation, they began to play with the idea of a parody of their seminal legislation, and the final result is the present work.

Although Gratian's writings were extensive, little has appeared in English translation. Some are historically significant for the family of St. Teresa's nuns and friars, providing through his autobiographical memoirs a firsthand account of the beginnings of the order. Other works are of a spiritual nature and somewhat heavy reading. This selection is not of such great historical moment nor is it difficult to read and enjoy. It illustrates the good humor which was part of the atmosphere of the early years of the Teresian movement. In highlighting human foibles, it speaks to us today. Not only religious, but members of almost any group or organization will recognize themselves and others in the following pages, despite the changes in customs and outlook in the past four centuries. The solid doctrine which appears at the end of the document is challenging and worth pondering on its own merits. On an historical note, it gives us insight into the mind of a man who was about to suffer greatly at the hands of the leaders of the community he had helped foster. One can only hope that he was able to follow his own advice and thus reach the holiness he desired.

I wish to acknowledge the assistance of Fr. Steven Payne, O.C.D., who first directed my attention to this work and who has encouraged me along the way. I also thank Fr. Stephen–Joseph Ross, O.C.D., for sharing his ideas on the meaning of the elusive term, *cerro,*[1] and its derivatives, upon which so much depends, and for assistance in deciphering the meaning of the mysterious *tabletas* mentioned in the chapter on obedience. Fr. Ildefonso Moriones, O.C.D. promptly and generously replied to a request for help with this same issue.

In many ways this version of the text might better be called an English paraphrase of the original. Part of Gratian's humor appears in the ponderous and repetitive style which mimics prolix legal documents. I have tried to retain enough of that to give the flavor, without overwhelming the reader with its tediousness. Also, some phrases and constructions were indecipherable to me and to expert linguists I consulted. In those cases, I have tried my best. In the spirit of the doctrine herein presented, I think it more important to enjoy the significance of this parody than to scruple about literal accuracy. In imitation of the Holy Parents, St. Teresa and St. John of the Cross, I bow to anyone who knows more about this than I do.

Jesus + Mary
Provincial Chapter of the Cerro
Which Deals with the Imperfections and Faults of Melancholics,
Which Arise from Sadness, Anger, Bitterness of Heart,
Disobedience, Despondency and a Wounded Spirit

Written in the Form of Constitutions,
Commanding Everything contrary to What Is Proper,
so as to Serve as Recreation for the Religious
as well as an Examination of Conscience

[Letter of Convocation]

We, Fray Melanco Cerruno, provincial of all the melancholics, the sad and bitter-hearted, the vexed, restless, scrupulous, ill-tempered, insufferable, and agitated, etc.:

Since the term of our office has now come to an end, we must have a chapter and elect a provincial. We order our subjects upon receipt of this patent and convocation letter, to gather in chapter and elect a delegate. Then, leaving behind a vicar for the convent, come as quickly as possible to our convent of La Culpa to deal with matters for the good governance of the order and to plot how, in the houses of the discalced friars and nuns, to break the rule and constitutions, introduce abuses, ruin the good spirit and perfection they seek, as well as the fruit they wish to give the Church by their example; and how to introduce at the beginning such imperfections and relaxations as may later cause notable harm, and many souls be condemned and—after laboring in this life—lose any reward and go to the dwelling of our great friend *Pero Botero*.[2]

Because we are so concerned about your health, we advise you always to travel at a bad time: in the summer from 8 a.m. until 6 p.m. so that you might enjoy the sun (this pertains to those coming by way of La Mancha and Andalusia); and in the winter, before dawn, in order to enjoy the cool. If there has been a lot of rain, you must go by way of the *Paso de los Pontones* and path of Gumiel, on the Burgos road.[3] Always and in every case, lose your way, even if it seems impossible to err. In every inn, forget and leave some of your baggage behind. Your pack animals should be very thin or seedy. Try to give bad example in everything while on the way, so that those who see you may despise religious. Because of you, the servants of God who stay in the monastery, keeping cloister and doing penance, may lose.

Meeting of the Priors and Delegates and
Examination of the Patent Letters

On the date designated for the chapter, the following religious met together with the Very Rev. Fr. Fray Melanco Cerruno:

From the convent of Disobedience, Prior Disobedient Backtalk and his companion, Fray Rigid Stiffneck;

from the convent of Sensuality, Fray Sensual Softy, prior, and Fray Relaxed Meddler, his companion, the enemy of chastity;

from the convent of La Avaricia, Fray Greedy Sharp, prior, and Fray Attached Toad, his companion, opponents of poverty;

from the convent of Inattention, Fray Inattentive Bozo, prior, and Fray Hernando Dozer, his companion, opponents of the Divine Office and spiritual things;

from the convent of La Gula, Fray Nabuzardan Glutton, prior, and Fray Sardanapal Discontent, socius, opposed to fast and abstinence;

from the house of Little Discipline and Bad Confession, Fray Pious Bamba, prior, and Fray Shameful Excuses, socius;

from the convent of Constant Chatter, Fray Goldfinch Talker, prior, and Fray Vociferous Self-seeking, socius, opponents of silence;

from the convent of Sloth, Fray Lazy Goof-off, prior, and Fray Purse Beggar, socius, opponents of manual labor;

from the convent of Dissension and Pride, Fray Nabucodonosor Proud, prior, and Master Moth of Corruption, socius, opponents of humility and peace;

from the convent of Carelessness and Neglect of Responsibilities, the Bachelor Fray Ignorant Simpleton, prior, and the Presentado Fray Careless Deviator as socius.

The said priors and companions presented their letters and patents and the other messages they brought for the said provincial chapter and Fray Melanco Cerruno received and feasted them very well.

The next morning, before proceeding to the election of the provincial and definitors, the Very Rev. Fr. Fray Melanco Cerruno, provincial, and the above mentioned chapter members assembled and ordered the reading of the rule and constitutions of the *Cerro* and everyone noted what needed to be deleted or added to them that they might be confirmed before the election of the provincial. Thus they read the chapters in the following order.

Constitutions of the Very Grave and Downcast
Fray Melanco Cerruno

We, Fray Melanco Cerruno, in our misfortune Provincial of all the *cerros*, the quarrelsome, and the difficult, wish poor health and misfortune to all the melancholics and the closed-minded and scrupulous who live in our convents.

Be it known that our Provincial Chapter petitioned that, since we live scattered among the discalced convents without a rule or constitutions and without a way of life, that We, as a good shepherd, ought to gather you together and impose constitutions and rules; which we do by means of the constitutions that follow below, which will serve for the quarrelsome and unpraiseworthy mode of life of our servants.

Chapter I: Concerning Obedience

1. First of all, let none of our subjects, in any case whatsoever, fail to object at least once or twice to that which obedience might demand of him or her. If they raise objections three or four or five times or even more, we will reward them when they appear before us. Use discretion, however, and maintain discipline. They must not only make their objection with disgust to what they are commanded, but so that the good and laudable custom of objecting not be lost, let them reply so rudely that all might see what obedience is.

2. We decree and ordain, therefore, that every time the superior reprimand or reproach them about something, they excuse themselves of the fault with good excuses. Some of our subjects might think that they fulfill the constitutions by excusing themselves with evasions and asking a blessing or pardon to begin the excuse, or by minimizing the extent of their guilt on the excuse of natural weakness or some other condition or lack of strength. In this way they are faithful to the constitutions; but in addition we desire that all excuse themselves bluntly for the sake of the scandal that it will give the little ones and the bad example shown those who think such things no real excuse.

3. We further decree and ordain that all our subjects must bear large *tabletas*[4] on their breasts so that they will never be able to prostrate themselves, even though the superior reproach them. And giving in to human weakness in case they do prostrate, let it be only when the

superior expressly demand it, and never do we desire them to do so politely. As for rising, they should not await the signal from the superior, but object, saying they thought it had already been given. And if they remain for some time prostrate, they should at least raise their heads and make excuses. And having not yet attained perfection, let them remain grouchy so as to burden the superior.

4. We further decree and ordain that they always judge the superior harshly, never looking on his or her actions with favor. At the very least, let them consider the superior to play favorites, loving some and unable to bear the sight of others. Let them hold the superior little experienced in matters of government. If the superior applies discipline, think it the result of personal rancor. If the superior is kind, consider it a sign that he thinks one imperfect and that he is kind because insensitive; so that the kindness will appear harsh. If the superior eat anything, consider it a relaxation. If he does not, it is hypocrisy. If he speaks sharp, serious words, put it down to pride and despise him. If he speaks lovingly and sweetly, put it down to lack of authority and hold him in contempt. And finally always go about annoyed with him and never speak to him about how things seem, but rather gossip about it in the corners with others, so as to tempt them and get them to join our confraternity.

5. They should be very anxious to give advice to the superiors and look out for the good of the community, suffering greatly if they see any imperfection in the house, exaggerating it in the scrutinies of the visitations, no matter how minor it be, saying that the one they have for superior is unfit.

On the other hand, if they reprimand you for giving advice to the superior, then stubbornly refuse to pay attention to anything on the grounds that it does no good. Nor ought you to say what you feel during the appropriate times [scrutinies] at visitations, but go from one extreme to the other.

6. Be most faithful in never giving any account of one's own inner state to the superior or to anyone else, nor share your thoughts, but let them fester inside your breast—first by saying it is nothing and you can resist the temptation, and later out of shame for having seen oneself fall. Such shame arises from presumption.

7. We ordain that, should the superior on some occasion mortify you or reprimand you, or say something harsh, you be disproportionately afflicted and become quite noticeably angry, gloomy, and arrogant, so that the superior should be depressed and the other brothers or sisters feel it and be scandalized. Then get headaches and other illnesses so you can always go about complaining. Superiors from that point on will not dare reprimand or correct you, and you can continue growing in your imperfections, vices, and bad habits.

Added by the Chapter

8. For the good of the congregation, the chapter fathers added the following stipulations, which are as binding as the others concerning obedience.

9. First, that in every instance, there should be two heads in each house so that the monastery and its perfection be destroyed. One should be the prior or prioress and the other, appointed by the demon, subprior or subprioress, or else one of the senior members of the community.

10. And this second head, in order to destroy obedience completely, should proceed in the following manner:

First, set yourself up to be very zealous in keeping the rule and constitutions in the house, and be self-deceived so as to think this zeal is a fruit of prayer.

Second, never speak to the superior privately and lovingly about what you feel.

Third, go about always examining everything that is going on and taking note of every minor thing, as though you were the zelator.[5]

Fourth, go around talking with the other members of the community about particular defects of the superior. If you are confessor, bring these up when others come to you in confession, so that the cancer might grow more secretly and do more damage.

Fifth, speak to the superior publicly and in front of the novices about these failings, showing great zeal for the order.

Sixth, bring up cases of conscience in which subjects are not bound to obey the superior in such and such a case, since he does not live as he ought, etc.

11. And when there is in the house this second head, the lawful superior should stubbornly insist that the other be ignored and that he or she be obeyed, exaggerating in his heart the value of obedience and doing nothing about other failings in the house.

12. From this manner of acting, great fruits will accrue to our *Cerro:*

First, since the superior deserves to be adhered to because of office, and the other to be adhered to because of zeal, they will proceed so foolishly that the wound will be incurable.

Second, those who have difficulties with the superior will rally to the support of the second head and so factions will form in the house.

Third, those who are servants of God, since they see this chaos about the ruling of the house, will be very upset and weaken in obedience and desire to be transferred to another house.

Fourth, the novices will be brought up with this spirit of disobedience and the order will be lost.

Fifth, all the members of the community will go about rash judging, upset, and scandalized. Afterwards, when they go to confession, they will not know how to present themselves. If the confessor is a [non-Carmelite] cleric who hears the nuns, he will lose his opinion of the order, for they will deal only with childish things and the confessor will be depressed because he cannot understand them. The second heads must make sure in every possible way to ingratiate themselves and be very concerned about the subjects; and especially in chapter to excuse them. Make every effort to become friendly with the provincials and other superiors, so that the prior and prioress may be constantly afflicted and upset.

13. Therefore the fathers added the qualities of a good superior of the *Cerro,* because when the superior is a good *cerruno,* obedience is lost in the entire house.

14. First, the good superior will seek to walk around with such a sad and unfriendly face as to become abhorrent to others.

15. When commanding or reprimanding something, it should be with such ill grace, rudeness, and harsh words, that it will appear he is moved more by hatred of the other than by desire for correct behavior. Thus others will not obey the superior, putting things down to rancor and not obedience.

16. Once the superior has begun to correct someone, never think about stopping. Don't forget to bring up past faults and corrections, but always throw them in their face, so as to be detested.

17. Have very little or no pity for those who are sick, and strive to get them back to full rigor so quickly that their health is destroyed. If they ask some dispensations, tell them it is a temptation and reproach them. Then the subjects will not ask for anything, but simply do it without permission or obtain permission from someone who has no right to give it.

18. Show great favoritism, fawning over and bestowing gifts on some and being very short and cold with others, so as to provide

growth for our *Cerro*. Because, if the devil makes them think the superior does not love them even when it is not true, what will they think when they see this kind of favoritism shown?

19. When they come to the superior for consolation, dismiss them harshly so that they lose heart about sharing their spirit with him and so seek new counselors.

20. Let such superiors pay no attention to the mandates of the provincials nor follow the prescriptions they have indicated, offering long-winded rationalizations, so that all the subjects might follow this example and themselves become disobedient.

21. Never consult with the members of the community about anything and never pay any attention to them, but follow your own opinions. Should some subject give you good advice, receive it rudely and reproachfully.

22. Do not allow your subjects to write to the provincial or to the Mother Foundress. Should someone say something in the visitation or write without permission, act so angry that you will be left as absolute ruler in the order.

23. Become very afflicted about the failings in the house, and so lose your prayerful spirit and never have a long-suffering and open heart.

24. The more prayer time is devoted to thinking about the running of the house (under the pretext that it is necessary), the faster they will lose their spirit.

25. If the prioresses should be very fond of penance or of frequent communion, they should agree with the sisters to overdo the one or praise the other to excess. When the superior corrects her, she can say she is only doing what the others do. In this way they can exhaust themselves in just a few days and be unable to do even what is obligatory.

26. When a nun goes to the prioress to be consoled about a problem with another religious, the prioress, our subject, should reproach

her and at the same time speak ill of the other party, so as to increase her hatred for her sister.

27. Finally, let our priors speak disrespectfully to their subjects, shouting at them, and so on, so that they lose their love and respect for obedience.

28. These and many other qualities are needed by the superiors of the *Cerro.* And the capitular fathers noted and added one little word more, concerning the prioresses: that what the religious tell them secretly in giving an account of their spiritual life, they should tell publicly in chapter, so that giving an account of their prayer to the superior should become odious to the religious—for this is a very important thing.

29. The above-mentioned fathers also commanded that they always be talking about elections in the houses and that they go among one another discussing whether so-and-so voted for such-and-such or if he did not vote for him; and if someone did not get all the votes, was it because of so-and-so? Let them be very fond of these discussions.

30. Let there be some who, when hearing confessions, advise the religious for whom to vote, but under the secrecy of the seal. If the provincial should try to find out who is doing this, they should be told they are not obliged to reveal the secret; and so the cancer of suborna-tion will not be cured.

31. When at the time of the provincial visitation, something be corrected or spoken about in the chapter, let there be lengthy discus-sions about who told the provincial, so that by this means, instead of profiting by the visitation, it should cause more rancor and bitterness. Then people will be afraid to say what they feel, and so will violate the provincial's command that they tell all they know—a command which is binding under mortal sin in serious matters. Afterwards they will be unable to confess it and will be left perpetually scrupulous.

32. Let subjects not give in regarding penances, but let them think it more perfect to be severe, even though this be contrary to obedience.

33. Let there be some in every monastery who become so put out with the superior that they say they must be transferred or else lose their minds or despair. This will introduce the spirit of unrest and dislike in every house of the nuns.

34. The above-mentioned Melanco and said fathers noted important points of doctrine for the monasteries of nuns, so as to destroy all perfection:

First, to destroy absolutely the custom now prevailing whereby the nuns give an account of their spiritual life to the superior, and to have this removed from the constitutions, so as to destroy everything.

35. So that this be well understood, five reasons are given:

First, say that the confessors are scandalized and that it is said that the discalced nuns go to confession to the prioress who has usurped that office. Even report it to the Inquisition.

Second, let the nuns say that they don't want to give this account to the prioress because she doesn't understand them, since, after all, the prioresses are only women and don't know as much as men, and they are not educated.

Third, say that what is told in secret is proclaimed in public and thrown in their faces.

Finally, let it be pointed out that the constitutions do not oblige them to give such an account, but only say that the one who wishes should, and that they only want to give such an account to a theologian or to a sister other than the prioress.

36. The fathers said that much profit would derive from this because this sister, giving no account of her spirit, would allow temptations to fester and would become a great *cerruna;* or else she would

fall into attachments to scholars or others outside the house or within with great harm to obedience and danger to her soul.

37. The second important doctrine is that in every house of nuns there be a novice mistress to whom the novices give an account of their spirit and communicate their thoughts without going to the prioress. In this manner, said novices, when they are professed, will be so attached to the mistress and so uninterested in obedience that they will be great subjects for us. Such would not happen if said novices, while having a mistress to teach them the ceremonies, were to give account of their spirit to the superior.

38. The third and most important doctrine is that the confessor and the prioress always take different approaches, so that what the prioress would do by way of governing, the confessor will always undo by way of the conscience, so that they be in this way great subjects of ours. Since they are obliged to obey the prioress by their vow of obedience and the confessor by the sacrament of penance, with these two such great obligations, they will be so hemmed in between two terrible *cerros* and thus go crazy climbing to the highest *Cerro*. They will be full of scruples without knowing how to escape, because the confessor will undo obligations imposed by the prioress and the prioress those created by the confessor.

39. This split between the prioress and confessor arises from many things.

First, from the ignorance of confessors who, not belonging to a religious order, wish to guide a soul in conformity with their understanding, not realizing the importance of obedience in religious life. So if they see anyone inclined to penance, they give full rein to that and even impose it as penance for confession so that the prioress cannot alter it. If the prioress tries to take it in hand, he feels it very much and says that she is meddling in the tribunal of conscience.

40. It also often happens when some sisters on bad terms with the prioress are so attached to the confessors and so clever that, with the devil's help, they confuse things until the confessor takes their part and they team up against the prioress.

41. The fathers thought that this teaching should be inscribed in letters of gold and that the nun who created this factionalism and dissension merited a great crown next to *Pero Botero's* cauldron.

Chapter II: Concerning Chastity and the Cloister

1. Let all our subjects be so chaste in everything that if by chance they see someone raise her eyes slightly or show some necessary courtesy to a secular, they think all is already lost. Let them always assume that things will come to a bad end, and say this, growling and murmuring. Let them never speak or mention this without exaggeration and malice, rash judging everything.

2. Also, should any of our nuns go to confession to a confessor from whose instructions one of our subjects receives profit, and they come to have the least particular affection for him, however harmless, she should think herself obliged to deal with him no more under pain of mortal sin. She should look for another until she finds one who will destroy her spiritual life by fostering her melancholy. The demon will take care that she find someone and continue tempting her so that she never feels secure about confessors.

3. Also since our subjects will never lack battles against sensuality, if by chance without fault they do not control their bodily reactions, let them afflict themselves about this in such a manner that they lose heart and prayer.

4. If they happen to hear something said about another's fall, let them become very frightened, with extreme prudishness and much presumptuous boasting about themselves.

5. The capitular fathers added, that a great *cerro* in every way guards against impure thoughts, always assumes they are consented to, judges them a sin, and afflicts himself to excess. Since the soul cannot keep these thoughts from happening, the religious will lose prayer and courage. Virtue will collapse so that what was no sin before, without the struggle, afterwards becomes sin.

6. Likewise with regard to bodily reactions, when these occur let them assume they are already in hell and that these things come because of their hidden sins, and afflict themselves to excess, and think that they are obliged to get rid of them and work industriously to do so. Since they are natural and frequently unsought and by the way they try to get rid of them they increase, the soul will lose all patience when they happen, especially if they occur during time for prayer and interior gifts. Thus they may cease praying, become lukewarm, and lose all virtue.

Chapter III: Concerning Poverty

1. We decree and ordain for the perfect keeping of poverty that, though in the main they have put aside possessions, they should under the same claim to poverty become so attached to a patched habit or some broken sandals that they become notably annoyed and upset should the superior take them away. If on the other hand the superior take away a new habit and give an old one, let them become sad and upset and try to cover the holes by never taking off the mantle and hiding when seculars visit or things like this.

2. Also let their hearts be tied to childish things, like a particular chaplet or a little cross or a holy picture or discipline or such things and if these be taken away, they should be notably upset. We command them, should they be corrected for this, to declare that it is no imperfection to love an image, or a blessed rosary or letters of pardon

because it moves their spirit. Out of love for our adversary mortification, they should carry them hidden where the superior will not see.

3. And for greater perfection, we add this point of perfection: when they are attached to such a thing, they go to the superior and beg that she command them to keep it under obedience, so that when they are reproached inwardly or outwardly about the said attachment, they can reply that they are doing it out of obedience. As they know very well that it arose from self-will, they will always go about afflicted.

4. The fathers added that, in order to keep poverty perfectly, their subjects should always bring up all the adversities that might occur, never forgetting them. Those that might happen in the future, they should keep in mind so that it seems like the sky is falling down on top of them and their whole spirit will revolve around solicitude for *quid manducabimus et bibemus et quomodo induemur?* (what will we eat and drink and how will we be clothed?) (Mt 6:25)

5. And should some religious, whether healthy or ill, ever lack any of life's necessities, then let him become sad and think that he must die, even repent of having professed the rule and become indignant toward the superior. Let him complain, exaggerating what is lacking, however minor it may be, saying there is no charity and that if it were someone else, they would not be left without. Forget religious poverty and the pleasure a religious soul should have when lacking some necessity.

Chapter IV: Concerning Divine Office and Spiritual Exercises

1. We decree and expressly order that every time our subjects go to mental prayer, their motive be to attain delight and gifts, and also that the brothers consider them spiritual.

Upon beginning prayer, they should strive to force themselves to produce tears, closing their eyes and clenching their teeth. Let them have no patience in considering the matter for meditation if they find it dry. If when they arrive God does not give them delight, which is what moved them to go to prayer, let them become restless and despondent, begin to become sad and turn their thoughts to earthly things. And then let them yawn and wriggle around a lot longing for prayer to be over. Let them think and even say that they were not made for mental prayer, and let them recall things that they need to do instead, so that they can leave, taking much care over what obedience has demanded of them.

2. Let them also be very attracted to visions and revelations. As for lightheadedness that often causes the imagination to act up, let them think these are visions and so tell others.

3. Let them neither know how to nor desire to give an account of their spiritual life to anyone except those who have great imaginations so they will be misunderstood. And if at times something extraordinary, no matter how minor, should occur, let them think that God is showing them great favors; at other times, as a result of any aridity or interior struggle, let them judge themselves already condemned and lost.

4. Let them never be satisfied with a simple presence of God, accompanied by a desire to do his will, to be humble, and to give obedience to the superiors. Let them believe this is not great prayer when there is nothing sensible about it, for that is where they place all the perfection of spirit.

5. And let what they take from prayer always be to do indiscreet penances and to go to communion without permission. And also desires for much solitude and abstinence, so that they get restless and despondent when the superior will not grant permission. If they have some good thought or desire, then they should forget it and remain as wretched as before, even more so.

6. We decree that when our subjects are very ill and have headaches, they must give themselves to prayer even more, until the prioress makes them stop so that they can then be angry and upset about that.

7. Let them desire to make progress so quickly and impetuously that if in four days they do not find the virtue they seek, with great despondency and distrust of gaining it, let them despair and cease the acts that they were making.

8. We decree that every imperfection they commit should bring them such despondency, affliction, and sadness that they lose the spirit of interior peace, mistaking this despondency for true contrition.

9. Let them wish to see others made perfect in four days and tolerate no imperfection. Instead of correcting them with patience and encouraging them by teaching virtue, discourage and afflict them, so that they may join our fraternity through the good teaching of the superiors and confessors under our obedience.

10. We decree and ordain that none of our subjects stick to one purpose. With desire for greater perfection, let them jump from one spiritual act to another so that they find rest and profit in none nor attain even one virtue.

11. Insofar as peace flees from our subjects, we desire them to keep following after it, always upset and longing for peace though never gaining it. And so we decree that under pretext of laying hold of it they desire to move from one house to another, from one superior to another, from one cell to another, finding things to unsettle them in what obedience lays on them, so that in this way their will may never learn to be quiet in one thing and will remain unsettled.

12. We decree for the guarding of the interior life that all our subjects keep recalling painful thoughts, such as whether they are predestined or damned to hell, whether God hates them, whether they

have some unknown faults for which they will be condemned, whether their past confessions were valid, whether they are resisting the divine will and other such thoughts; from such always comes that bitterness of heart we so desire and love.

13. Touching the Divine Office and the canonical hours, the fathers added that if on occasion for whatever reason one of our subject's attention wanders in the choir, however briefly, then it should seem to them that they have not prayed it satisfactorily. They should go back and recite the entire office, so that they are always short of time and full of scruples.

14. Let them be great friends of some old rubrics so that they think they do not meet their obligations by doing what is ordinarily recited unless the recitation is very burdensome. When chanting let them hold the final notes for a long time with great devotion, so that they slow things down and make choir hateful. And if they recite compline on a ferial day with the gradual psalms and a little office, let it seem that they did not fulfill the obligation because it was still daylight.[6]

15. And if anyone is sick, and the superior and doctor say they are not obliged to recite the prayers, let them not be persuaded but desire to recite so that they get headaches and a fever. Insist on this because it is important for our *Cerro* to disobey and to endanger one's health.

Chapter V: Concerning the Fast, Meals, and Penance

1. Our subjects should try very hard to fast too much and to perform indiscreet penances, in such a fashion and manner that will do them ill. Let them wear hair shirts to draw a lot of blood. Use the discipline and fast on bread and water until faint. Insist on wearing chains and iron collars. When sick at the stomach, do not eat right. Deprive oneself of the major portion of the necessary sleep. Study and preach too much, in order to do harm. Finally always try to ruin your health,

so that you can complain, saying that you cannot bear the penances and austerity of the order, and wind up lax and imperfect.

2. They should always have great scruples about collations. In those of the order, do not give them bread so that they ruin their heads and stomachs. In those of the Church, although the prior or prioress, seeing their weakness, says to take a bit more to eat, let them think they are not obliged to obey and refuse. Let them always disobey in this matter.

3. Let the food always be bad for the health: in the summer poorly cooked cabbage and in the winter salads of stale olives; and they must drink a lot of water so as to be always bloated. Let them take a lot of vinegar when it will do them harm. Finally, the dish should always arrive bland, without salt or spices, so that they hate the food. When they have to eat meat or take some treat on a Sunday, let them take too much so that they become gorged. Thus they must do either too much or too little until their health is gone.

4. Above all let them give up sleep, which is important for creating sloth and lightheadedness. If the constitutions command that they go to bed at eleven, they should babble on that it doesn't say they can't make prayer in bed, and they will do so and not sleep. Then they cannot get up in the morning and everything will be turned upside down.

5. Let the cooks cook poorly and leave everything dirty to destroy the appetite. Let them be great friends of doing penance, recalling the dishes and meals of our ancient fathers. If they take vetch to make broth, let them not change it for a month, until they are reproached for it.

6. The dispensers and the provisors[7] should be great *cerros*—mean—spirited, rigid, and disagreeable-and not let them have spices for the meals and give them transparent slices of cheese. They must always go around looking starved and crying about the poverty of the

house, so that those who find religious life hard will be further tempted and lose all joy and sweetness of spirit.

Chapter VI: Concerning Chapter, Visitation, Confession, & Communion

1. First, we ordain that in every convent one of the most advanced of our subjects shall be the gall of the convent; the which, under color of zeal for that house, will be scandalized by what he sees, no matter how small, and will complain and exaggerate it at visitation, to the confusion of the visitator or the superior in chapter.

2. Never tell things as they are but say that one particular instance is the way it always is. We declare that this exaggeration of things in chapter will make it so odious that they will end up taking nothing seriously nor profit from any advice but only take harm. Seeing that their administration is doing damage, they will be brought to confusion not knowing what to do and become excessively depressed and disconsolate.

3. If the superior does not believe them, let them insist strongly that they remedy that which they have imagined, even if it only be talking to seculars so as to defame religious life. If they are believed, they will make visitations and chapters so odious that instead of their being fruitful for amendment, they will create grave sins of hatred and discontent and other things.

4. We note that, although they do this under the title of zeal for the protection and good of the order, the motive from beginning to end will be their ill will toward those whose faults they declare.

5. If the prioress reprimand them for being malicious gossips, let them think and even say that the prioress is partial to the other party. They should try to make sure this feeling is only natural, because they will be unable to get rid of it and the harm that will follow will be irremediable.

6. Those who accuse others in chapter should do it so boldly that it seem born of rancor toward those accused. Though the fault be childish, what results will be a growing mortal hatred within.

7. Our subjects, male and female, should have a lively and sharp ingenuity for seeing the faults and imperfections of others, letting nothing escape them. They should, however, never come to understand or notice their own, though they be like the beam of a winepress. Whenever anyone challenges them, they must think it is only to quarrel and due to the other's ill will.

8. They should always let it show on their faces when they are corrected for faults in chapter, and talk about it at recreation, to nurture hatred and bad feelings important for our *Cerro.*

9. The one who presides at chapter should exaggerate each one's faults, however small or light they be, and go to extremes and be so vociferous that very serious things will be considered as nothing and the whole thing will turn out badly.

10. Let our prioresses at chapter throw in the face of their subjects things told in secret when giving account of their spirit. Or say things that seem to arise out of what was said in secret so that talking about one's spiritual life with the prioress will become hateful. This is most important for our *Cerro.*

11. Grave issues, secret or not, should be brought to the chapter, not to do away with sins but to defame the guiltless and so increase the gravity of the problem.

12. After the visitation there should be much talk about who told this, who told that, and the prior or prioress should show themselves so angry toward whoever told that no one will dare say what is the case. Since the command of the visitor obliges under mortal sin, they will remain in sin or at least with big scruples.

About Confession [and Communion]

13. First, let there be a lot of talk and gossiping about whether so-and-so takes longer or such-and-such takes less time so that the penitent become irritated and the confessor become furious.

14. Under title of good zeal, let them tell part of everything that goes on in the house and in the order to the confessor, thinking that, since he is the confessor, it is no sin to defame other religious.

15. By means of confession try to remedy some abuses and failings in the house, so that things that one said about another in confession go from tongue to tongue and, since the other will have confessed to the same priest, she will think he revealed the confession, and so this sacrament will become detestable.

16. Let the superiors rigorously insist that the subjects, all or some, not confess to others but only to the superior, so that said subjects will become desperate and stop confessing entirely either from fear or shame.

17. Use the confessional to tamper with elections; and under title of dealing with conscience and scruples, go to every priest in the house and accuse oneself of having determined to vote for so-and-so, having these reasons, so that this may draw the confessor to vote for him. Confessors should ask in confession for whom they have determined to vote, and if they say for so-and-so, advise them that he has some fault. Thus he will undermine him by means of confessions and escape punishment for it.

18. Let there be confessors who introduce discord by means of confession. This can be against the superiors, saying they are not obliged to obey in such and such a case, so that what obedience builds up the bad confessor may destroy. The damage that follows will be irremediable.

19. Never let them think they have declared fully the rash judgments they make against the superior unless they go into such detail

that they reveal the superior's faults. Perhaps they can persuade the confessor to believe it and fall into other rash judgments.

Since they never tell their own faults, they will never seem satisfied in confessing the judgments and problems they have had about the prior or prioress, unless they go into detail about the occasions when they had those temptations. Then, if the prioress does not go to that same confessor, the confessor will think she has great faults, is running away from him and looking for another confessor. If she does go to confession to him, since he will see that she doesn't mention these grave things in confession, he will think she lies. This will stir up a whirlwind from hell between the prioress and the confessor, to the destruction of that house, all brought on by our very dear *cerrunas.*

20. Whenever one of our subjects finds himself tempted by thoughts against the faith or a spirit of blasphemy, even though it pains them, let them think that they sin in this, and every moment want to confess it. Never let them be persuaded that it is nothing, although the confessor tell them that this is the case, nor let them want to believe this until, for the greater perfection of the *Cerro,* they think it necessary to confess to an inquisitor and try with all their might to obtain this.

21. Let our subjects become so attached to the confessor, it seeming to them that he understands them and no one else does, as if they did not all have the same power from Christ, that if they take him away, she make such a fuss that it gives occasion to assume there were other affections and everyone will get disturbed.

22. Since a spirit of blasphemy and temptations against the faith arise in some souls, so too can extremes happen regarding confessions and communion when they think that they always sin in going to them because they fail to do what they should. Such as these, under guise of avoiding sin, flee from confession and communion so much that they have to be forced against their will. Since they abandon the sacra-

ments, they lose these principal walls of the soul and they will be overcome by their enemies in many other things—for which the demons for their part are battling—until their spirit languishes and they fall into despair like people without hope.

23. In confession let them never be satisfied with the confessor. He should always appear to them not to know how to hear their confession. They should repeat and confess the same sins over and over and should not be at peace with what the confessor tells them. They should consider everything, no matter how small, to be a mortal sin. They should be wordy in confessing and often want to make general confessions. Never let them think the confessor understands them but consider him a man with little spirituality and less learning, so that they are not content with confession and want to change to another confessor. She must assume that the confessor and prioress join in persecuting her, and in this way we will close off the door to obedience, our main enemy.

24. Above all let them be given to scruples, judging every little thing, however small, as mortal sin so that they can never find peace or satisfaction.

25. They should have a very great desire for communion and be despondent if these are refused. At other times they should abstain from communion under pretext of humility and say they find themselves unsettled. Finally, let the desire for communion arise out of the pleasure they take in it and not for the honor and glory of God.

26. For any little scruple about mistakes in choir, knowing full well it is no mortal sin, we command them to stop going to communion for good, with no disposition to go to confession. In this way our contrariness will break their constitutions and they will lose the spirit that Holy Communion might give.

Chapter VII: Concerning Manual Labor and External Affairs

1. First, we ordain that they always be exceedingly busy, without giving their spirit a chance to breathe, and with a greediness and determination about the same work that they get overtired, so that they can in no way make prayer nor any spiritual exercise, no matter how easy it be.

2. We decree and ordain that they go around slack-mouthed and scowling, frowning and upset, especially when the prior or prioress has corrected them, so that they get notably despondent and depress the others. Should someone laugh, let it be without any composure, going from one extreme to the other. But they should guard themselves rigorously not to laugh or have fun at recreation, when the others are enjoying themselves, but then be very devout. Save laughter for the time of silence or in front of seculars when it is not appropriate.

Chapter VIII: Concerning Silence and Recreation

1. We decree, and ordain first of all, and if it be necessary, expressly command, that all our subjects be great enemies of recreation. If the superiors give permission to speak with the brothers to console them, refuse to do it, thinking these would be idle words; or, if they talk, let it be all worldly things. Much care should be taken in this.

2. They should be very anxious to know the news and oddities and things of the world, and about the health and events concerning their relatives, friends, and acquaintances, under pretext of piety, weeping over whatever happens outside. On the other hand, if they are corrected for this, let them go to the other extreme of refusing to commend their parents and relatives to God. At every recreation think that the others, because they laugh, are not devout but imperfect and that they alone are recollected and deeply spiritual.

3. At recreation there should be a lot of quarreling with one another so that they become irritated and have to go to confession.

4. Should anyone be angry with another, bring it up in recreation and let others know about the problem so that they be scandalized and the whole house upset.

5. Let our subjects be so extreme in keeping silence that, under the pretext of not wanting to break it, they refuse to share anything of their spiritual life nor let anyone know if they have any affliction. If they are asked for something necessary for the house or for the health of someone sick, they should refuse to answer out of zeal for silence, so that the one who asks gets irritated and loud and silence is even more broken.

Chapter IX: Concerning Humility and Peace

1. First of all, let our subjects be so humble that they run from anything that is said to them, keeping this point of honor so strongly in their heads that if someone says something as a joke, they think it is an insult.

2. In all things at all times they should follow their own opinion. If some subject should ever ask advice, they should be severely punished immediately the first time they do it. If another should offer advice about something that concerns them, let them refuse to accept it and not take it seriously, but criticize and complain, so that no one dare aggravate them by giving advice.

3. We command by virtue of the Holy Spirit and holy obedience that our subjects, male and female, each one in particular, be singular in all things, great and small, and never follow the community nor think what others are doing is right. In choir they should have their scapulars and mantles twisted, making faces to show how much they are pleased by the recitation. In the refectory, let them not eat what is

given to the community so that the superior will be burdened with finding them new foods. At bedtime, let them be vigilant to disturb those who sleep, and then fall asleep at Matins and fail to get up for prayer in the morning. At recreation time, they should always be filled with a spirit of prayer. Finally, let them strive to go a different way in every matter under this precept.

4. Let them meddle in the tasks of others, thinking that if they don't take it in hand, nothing will be done right. As for what pertains to themselves, they need take no bother, keeping peace of body. So they will want to turn their energy to what is not their concern and what is theirs, they will not do.

5. When our subjects are superiors, they must so want to make those they govern perfect that, if after four hours they see them still imperfect, they will become depressed and oppress and discourage them. They should reprimand them impatiently, thinking that since they are their subjects, they must be perfect. Let them not desire to humble themselves nor obey the infirmarian or anyone who looks out for their health, but go on [in poor health] and have the whole house upset and uneasy.

6. If in a house there are two of three of our subjects, they must love one another so much and get along so well that they get together to gossip, to judge, to complain, and to form factions, alliances, and parties against the rest. If the superior punish one of them, the others should make excuses and defend him, having great compassion for him and criticizing the superior. Finally, let our members be like a secret corruption that causes unrest and divisions in the whole house where they are, without the superior being able to understand clearly. This will be remedied only with great difficulty.

7. Let our subjects have so much charity and communion that when there is some difficulty, they will come up with gossip about

how the superior doesn't really love them, and that they heard the superior say such and such a thing, or that so-and-so is persecuting him. When they are zelators, they must find many faults, so that the office of zelator becomes hateful.

8. They should strive never to accommodate themselves to the circumstances of the other brothers, and be angry with everyone and cause them grief, and let their own moods be such that the superior will not be able to understand them nor the brothers tolerate it.

9. We advise that for the high perfection of the *Cerro,* they never be sincere with one another, nor with superiors, but always say one thing while keeping another in the heart. This moth will destroy the brotherhood, give birth to suspicion and rash judgments, remove equality from the house, cause factions, filling not only the souls we have, but the whole house with perpetual scruples and weariness of heart.

10. Let our subjects strive above all to be so zealous for perfection that they go around watching what others are doing and reprimanding them, never believing it is natural weakness or illness or that they can do no more. Never take pity on anyone nor believe anyone else is perfect, but hold all the rest imperfect. Thus they will make themselves hateful and abhorrent, and although afterwards they take note of things more wisely than the Gospel, they will not benefit anyone but just unsettle the house even more.

11. In everything let our subjects be impatient, and whatever little thing that is said to them, even as a joke, let them feel it, and grumble and frown and swell up, and answer back and become irritated and enraged so much that they lose their own peace. The whole house will get put out with them, watching every little word so as not to upset them; and although they only spoke plainly with them, they will have to confess that they spoke harsh words to a sister, or at least that they gave occasion for rudeness.

12. They should always be talking about who so-and-so is, what is her social class, what her lineage, if she served or was served. Then if they throw it in her face or talk about it in front of her, she will become annoyed or depressed; and if they murmur about it behind her back, others of our subjects should tell her so that rancor and factions will result.

13. In a convent where there are professed sisters from another convent, they should always be comparing other houses, saying that this was done in that house but not here, always praising the prioress and sisters of such houses, and sighing for it. Thus they make themselves abhorrent in the convent where they reside and introduce divisions among the various houses.

14. Our subjects will always use abusive language with frowns, passion, and ill grace.

15. The prioress should ordinarily be upset with the subprioress, so that the prioress try to subjugate her and mortify her excessively and treat her harshly, and the subprioress try to meddle in what is not her office and fight against the prioress about the choir.[8]

The novice mistress must be upset with the prioress or subprioress should they correct the novices or say anything to them; and they ought to be upset with her, believing that she is forming novices with no sense of obedience, but very attached to herself.

The cooks and the prioress should always be upset with one another, they because she does not give them spices to cook with, and she correcting them for poor cooking.

The provisor and turn sister[9] should fight like cats and dogs, the provisor because the turn sister doesn't turn things in, and the turn sister because she thinks the provisor is pestering her.

The sacristan and the keepers of the keys should be backbiting all the time, since the sacristan says they will not pay for some little thing that is necessary for divine worship, and they that she spends too much.

The infirmarian should fight with the whole house, thinking they have no charity; they should all want to get rid of her, saying she doesn't care for them well. The refectorian should say that the infirmarian goes into the refectory and messes everything up, taking silverware and napkins; the cooks that she takes their plates; the prioress that she is always whining; the sacristan that she turns things upside down looking for something for someone who is sick; the turn sisters that she is very discontent; the subprioress that she does not come to choir; the seamstress that she won't use inexpensive sheets; the prioress and treasurers that she spends too much on the sick.

Finally let all the lay sisters be put out with the choir sisters, the choir sisters thinking that the lay sisters are blabbermouths messing in what is not their concern, and the lay sisters that the choir nuns are very proud and hold them in no esteem.

Thus the *cerrunal* perfection of the whole house will go forward harmoniously as one.

16. And so that this perfection endure and be perpetual, we order that these divisions not be made public but stay hidden in the heart and every day they should bother the confessors about them, without seeing any change of heart. These will think things are very serious and will go around making rash judgments about the house, thinking it damned. In the end it will all be just foolishness, but very important for taking away the spirit they strive for, which the demon desires to destroy, and to introduce abominable sins when it is gone since that is the way he proceeds.

Chapter X: What Each of Our Subjects Is Obliged to Do in Office

The Office of Prior or Prioress

1. The office of the prior is: to afflict his subjects and say haughty and hurtful things; never to turn a good face on them; to show more love to some than to others; always to be afflicted and disturbed and show this to the subjects; to have no compassion for them when sick or weak; never to submit to the will of the provincial, but when the visitation is over remain in absolute control; never to take counsel with anyone nor let the community know what he is doing; to carry everyone around like a yoke; to be very rude and heavy-handed in speech; to have no patience with hearing or consoling anyone spiritually; never to be moved to pity the weak, the infirm or the burdened.

If he be a little ill, let him complain and never be content with what his subjects do for him nor appreciate the love they have for him.

He should be afflicted and weakened by despair if they are short of flour or anything else and always go around bemoaning the present necessities of the house and fearing those to come.

The Office of Subprior or Subprioress

2. Always try to team up with the outside superior of the house, lovingly consoling those whom one sees are tired or angry at the prioress and thus win them over to oneself.

Meddle in what is not your office and, under pretext that they are not going to choir, reprimand everything that is being done.

Always go about puffed up by your office, showing superiority to the others in the house so that they come to hate you.

Rebuke the prioress to her face and argue with her strongly whenever she offers any counsel about your office.

If someone makes a mistake in choir, correct her with so much agitation that it disrupts the choir and makes it reprehensible.

Should you ever be left in charge due to the absence of the prioress, strive to change everything that she has ordained.

Always go about unhappy and complaining that the Divine Office is not done correctly.

Complain about the prioress if she fails to come to the office. And finally, be the heaviest cross of the whole house for the prioress.

Of the Mistress of Novices

3. Be so heavy-handed that the novices are tempted to leave.

Train them to be disobedient to the prioress and be very attached to them.

So that the order may grow, let the novices you receive be *beatas*, cross-eyed with big noses, pasty-faced, with big teeth covered with tartar. If asked about their health they say that they have some stomach problems and heart pains. At the time they come to ask to receive the habit, let them sigh deeply and speak with a lisp, casting their eyes upwards in affectation.

Let the novice mistresses who care for them try to make them dislike the prioress, grant them many penances and do everything according to their own will so that when they come to profession, they may be great *cerrunas*.

Of the Offices of Keyholders, Dispensors, Cook, Infirmarian and the Rest

4. Let these meddle very much in the offices of one another.

Be upset if the superior asks them to do anything about their office except what they want. Let them go about always preoccupied, depressed, and proud when they hold office; put out with one another; judging that the others like to eat good food and so the cooks cook poorly.

And not only will they not do what the religious ask, they will not even give them a kind word in reply.

Important Doctrine

When they got to this point in the constitutions, Rev. Fr. Fray Melanco asked for attention in order to treat of a very grave doctrine, which he had discussed with Rev. Fr. Fray Moth of Corruption, prior of the convent of Dissension,[10] and he spoke in this manner:

"You already know, Reverend Fathers and my dear friends, how much I desire to destroy the convents of the discalced friars and nuns, to please my friend Satan, and for this reason I have given you constitutions and teaching as ingenious as I can; but it seems to me that in all these I have been beating about the bush and have not arrived at the root or the essence, which is what I want to say now, pointing out the steps by which one descends to hell by way of discord, anger and harshness, and hatred.

"You know that a religious is obliged under pain of mortal sin to follow the way to perfection, although not obliged to be perfect. And that perfection is no other thing than perfect love of God and neighbor, as Jesus Christ, their Doctor and Teacher declared. Responding to the question of what is the greatest commandment of the law, that is, the highest perfection, Christ said, 'You shall love God with all your heart and all your soul and all your strength; and the second like it is this: you shall love your neighbor as yourself.' In St. Matthew, chap. 5, when he speaks of love of enemies, he declares this to be the sum of perfection, because, having said 'Love your enemies, do good to those who hate you, pray for those who persecute and speak evil against you, so that thus you may be children of your heavenly Father who is in heaven,' he continues saying, 'Be perfect,' as if to say, 'Perfection consists in this.'

"What we must do with great diligence is get them to forget this high perfection and make it appear that everything consists in doing many penances, or going about outwardly composed, or having much delight and consolation in prayer and other things that they imagine, all the while going around with a heart full of hatred, rancor, and animosity, sinking little by little toward hell, until they arrive there by the steps that follow."

The Steps by Which One Descends to Hell

1. The first step is differences among people. It often happens that there are two people of contrary temperament and complexion and natural qualities, which is natural, being human. This can lead to liking nothing the other person says or does, but this is all normal and the soul does not sin by it.

2. The second is rash judging which is born of the first: because, since so-and-so does not share my perspective and her actions annoy me, this pushes my self-love to consider all my deeds as good and opposed to her, so that I wind up thinking hers are evil. If she goes about sad, I consider her neurotic; if happy, frivolous; if talking, gossipy; if silent, hostile, etc. And if she does commit any fault, no matter how slight, to me it appears very great and dangerous.

3. The third step is complaining about this same thing that I have judged about this other person, so that it seems to me that I will explode if I don't talk about it with one or another who is on my side. Then they go about complaining and judging the other person, too.

4. The fourth is the anger and rancor that is conceived in my heart so that I do not desire good for the other, but wish him ill and enjoy hearing bad things about him and when they punish or correct him, etc.

5. The fifth is letting the person know that I don't love him so that he may always go about at odds with me with open enmity between us.

6. The sixth is daring to say offensive things that will pain him and so create anger and rancor.

7. The seventh is to lay hands on him or wish him dead and other acts and thoughts that are mortal sins.

Annotations

It is worth noting about these steps that many souls do not arrive at the sixth or seventh and remain on one of the first five. Since in confession they do not mention injurious words or bad actions against the neighbor, everything else seems like foolishness to the confessors; they will not pay attention to them nor will they correct them, leaving them often upset—what they will call tried—and they lose heart and soon lose perfection so that these rancors fester and become wounds difficult to cure.

The second thing to note is that other souls fearful of God are on the first step, which is natural and beyond their control, and they think they are condemned, without hope and full of fear. Thus they afflict themselves and don't want to go to communion and arrive at a state of desperation.

The third thing to note is that the friends of one, those with the same points of view, join that one and the friends of the other gang up with him; and thus through only two who were tempted, the entire house separates into factions.

The fourth, on the point that one is annoyed with the other, regardless of what may be said in chapter to one's friends, it is not only unprofitable but increases anger and enmity so that chapter becomes hateful and faults irremediable.

The fifth thing to note is that, if the person I am angry with is the superior, other damage will follow which is very profitable for hell, such as disobedience and rebellion, with incurable blindness so that what they command by obedience will seem rancorous and so I am not obliged to obey.

Having finished this speech, Fray Melanco said, "This, my comrades, is the plan by which all well-ordered communities and convents destroy themselves and in the same way we can destroy the discalced friars and nuns without any doubt. So take courage and be diligent, for they will not take perfection from us."

And having said this he began to weep bitterly and to say, "Woe is me! Woe is me! My soul escapes me when I think of a way to teach their superiors to undo this *Cerro*, which is the universal weapon before which everything falls and it is this:

Brief, Clear, and Certain Plan for
Attaining the Height of Perfection

"Devote yourself to being very humble and love God tenderly. And put that person who has hurt you the most, whether inside or outside the convent, in your heart and together with the Heart of Christ love that one greatly. Let this be the first person you pray for. Ask nothing good for yourself that you do not first ask for the other. Make many acts and promises to God that if for the glory and honor of God, it were necessary for you to lose honor, health, and life, and even your own glory for the honor, health, and life, and even glory of that person, then you are determined to give all that good.

"By making these promises and desires often and continually kissing their feet interiorly and even the ground on which they walk, and orienting all your acts and resolutions in prayer, you will by this single road rise to the highest grade of perfection and attain heroic virtue and pull up the *Cerro* by the roots."

The priors, when they saw Fray Melanco weeping so, consoled him saying that no one could understand such teaching.[11] Then they called Srs. Ignorance, Passion, and Malice and charged them to hide this secret thoroughly so that the *Cerro* might reach its greatest height.

***

These are the Constitutions of the *Cerro*, which we command be kept in all evil and disobedience so that, little by little, true religion be destroyed and intolerable abuses introduced.

Let all know that no one can be excused from these, our constitutions, if he expects to become a happy *cerruno* or on the other hand be extremely unhappy seeing those who keep them taking such pride in their *Cerro*.

The things which were confirmed and expanded in our provincial chapter and signed with our names and accepted by all the priors of our province.

Fray Melanco Cerruno

Notes

1 The word *cerro* as used in this humorous work cannot be translated easily and consistently. The usual meaning is *hill,* but it also can mean *the neck of an animal* and is used in idiomatic phrases to mean *to go astray, to be irrelevant or foreign to the purpose* as well as *proud* with an implication of vanity. It also suggests *something closed off* (from the verb, *cerrar,* to close.) It sounds suspiciously like the Spanish word for zero, *cero,* and in another form, *cerril,* means *rude and unmannerly.* As Jerome Gratian uses it here, it implies closed-mindedness, self-absorption, being off the track, uncultured, stiff-necked, and obstinate. Even its more usual meaning of hill is in contrast to the mountain of Carmel. Fr. Stephen-Joseph Ross, O.C.D., has suggested that Gratian and Teresa used *cerro* as a sort of shorthand to refer to Gratian's painful experiences as a novice under the unbalanced Angel of San Gabriel at the monastery at Pastrana, located on *el cerro de San Pedro,* St. Peter's

Hill. Any of the foolishness suggested herein would smack of that *cerro,* indeed. All of this must be borne in mind to get the full flavor of *cerro* and *cerruno/a,* an inhabitant of or traveler on this dead-end way.

At the time Gratian wrote, the term *melancholy* covered a greater range of emotional disorders than gloominess. It could almost be translated *neurotic,* and the melancholy would include people who were hypochondriacs or even delusional. We note that the proper name of the fictional provincial, Melanco Cerruno, evokes all of the notions we have been discussing. Whether Gratian intended a further shade of meaning by the resemblance to the name of Luther's great disciple, Melancthon, we do not know. But it is a nuance that occurred to the translator.

2 *Pero Botero* was slang for the devil.

3 See F. 31.16-17.

4 *Tabletas* literally means small pieces of wood or tablets. Perhaps one might visualize these as a sort of breastplate which would prevent the wearer from being able to bow or bend over to prostrate when receiving a correction. Such a bow or full prostration was prescribed by the customs of Gratian's time.

5 The zelator was the religious assigned to keep watch over the community, to observe and report failings. The superior called upon the zelator regularly to note lapses in the observance. The purpose was to keep the religious conscious of how they were doing, although it is easy to see how something which was intended to build up the community could be turned to other purposes.

6 The custom at the time called for recitation of compline around 5 or 6 p.m., so that it was often still daylight though the office is for night. The gradual psalms are Psalms 120-134. The "little office" was a devotional exercise of oral recitation of psalms and prayers other than the official Liturgy of the Hours.

7 The provisor was the religious responsible for obtaining and distributing whatever was needed for the daily running of the monastery.

8 The subprior or subprioress traditionally was in charge of the celebration of the Divine Office in choir. Thus it was an easy arena for power struggles between superior and assistant.

9 The turn is a cylindrical cabinet, open on one side and placed in the wall between the enclosure and the public area of a monastery. It turns on an axis so that items can be placed in it on one side of the wall, the cylinder turned, and the item can be removed on the other side. This was the way that donations of food and other goods were given to the religious without anyone coming into or going out of the enclosure. The sister responsible for receiving these things was called the turn sister. She was to give everything to the provisor or the superior who would decide how to use it.

10 In the original list of priors and delegates, he figures as socius.

11 Despite the assertion that no one would understand such teaching, it is noteworthy that a similar piece of advice appears in *Alcoholics Anonymous.* In a personal account in the fourth edition (2001), a member writes of her struggle to deal with the problem of resentment.

> I looked through [some magazines]. A banner across one featured an article by a prominent clergyman in which I caught the word *resentment.* He said, in effect: "If you have a resentment you want to be free of, if you will pray for the person or the thing that you resent, you will be free. If you will ask in prayer for everything you want for yourself to be given to them, you will be free. Ask for their health, their prosperity, their happiness, and you will be free. Even when you don't really want it for them and your prayers are only words and you don't mean it, go ahead and do it anyway. Do it every day for two weeks, and you will find you have come to mean it and to want it for them, and you will realize that where you used to feel bitterness and resentment and hatred, you now feel compassionate understanding and love." *Alcoholics Anonymous* Fourth Edition (New York City: Alcoholics Anonymous World Services, Inc., 2001), 552.

The Holy Spirit, Mary, and Thérèse of Lisieux

Emmanuel J. Sullivan, O.C.D.
Carmel of the Espousals of Mary and Joseph
Brighton, Massachusetts

Our intention in this essay is to show that the teaching of the Church's newest and youngest doctor—St. Thérèse of the Child Jesus of the Holy Face—gives us a renewed and deeper understanding both of the Holy Spirit and of Mary of Nazareth. Thérèse does not present us with an in-depth study either of the Spirit or of Mary, but her words and, above all, her life evidence the constant presence and activity of the Holy Spirit. Like Mary of Nazareth, Thérèse speaks to us of the Holy Spirit more by the way she lives than by what she says.

Thérèse refers to the Spirit more implicitly than explicitly. When these references are made explicit, they clearly reveal that she anticipated Vatican II's teaching on both "The Universal Call to Holiness in the Church" and "The Blessed Virgin Mary, Mother of God, in the Mystery of Christ and the Church" in *Lumen Gentium*. Thérèse fully agrees with the Council when it affirms that all are called to holiness. The witness of her own life clearly shows that holiness consists in loving God and one another in all those everyday events that make up our lives. Thérèse also shows us that holiness of life, while it requires our complete and constant effort, is a reality that is more received than it is achieved.

When Thérèse speaks about Mary of Nazareth, she draws our attention, not to Mary's extraordinary graces and singular privileges, but to the human Mary we find in the Gospels. For Thérèse, as for Vatican II, Mary of Nazareth is one of us. When Thérèse relates Mary's life as presented in the Gospels, she sees herself in those

Gospel scenes. Only then does she tell us what must have been Mary's attitudes and concerns in those events. In Thérèse's writings, as in Vatican II's Marian teaching, we come to know a human but God-centered Mary, a woman who is imitable as well as admirable.

Thérèse's gift to the Church—her renewed understanding of the Holy Spirit and of Mary—reminds us that in our relationship to God the initiative is always with God, an initiative that God extends to all persons without exception. Thérèse helps us to grasp that most basic truth: our response to God is more God's work in us than it is our own accomplishment.

Thérèse and the Holy Spirit

Recent studies have shown Thérèse's intense and constant relationship to the Holy Spirit.[1] Like John of the Cross, she speaks of the Spirit with impersonal images, such as fire, wind, and living waters. Yet, clearly, the symbol for the Holy Spirit she prized most is the symbol of love, the most personal of all symbols. Thérèse's entire life and teaching speak to us of love: God's love for us and our love for God. Only in the light of her understanding of who the Holy Spirit is and what the Spirit's role is in our life can we hope to fully appreciate and make our own her understanding of God's love for us and our response to that love.

Unlike the present time in which we experience the beginnings of a renewed consciousness of the presence and the activity of the Holy Spirit in the lives of Christians and in the life of the Church, Thérèse lived in an age when little was said about the Spirit. In fact, in her time, the third person of the Blessed Trinity, if referred to at all, was most often called the Great Unknown member of the Trinity. As a child of her day, Thérèse does not say much explicitly about the Holy Spirit. As we shall see, however, the little she does say reveals that from her earliest years Thérèse associated the Spirit with our ability both to be loved by God and to love God in return.

Thérèse's autobiography, her *Story of a Soul,* was begun in 1895 and completed in 1897. It consists of three separate manuscripts: Manuscript A, which Thérèse wrote in 1895 at the request of her older blood sister Pauline, Mother Agnes, then prioress of the Lisieux Carmel, describing her early life up to her religious profession (S, 9-182); Manuscript B, a brief letter which Thérèse wrote in 1896 to her oldest blood sister, Marie of the Sacred Heart, also a member of the Lisieux Carmel, explaining her vocation to love (S, 183-200); and Manuscript C, which Thérèse wrote in 1897 at the request of Mother Marie de Gonzague, Pauline's successor as prioress, about her life in Carmel. (S, 201-59) In Manuscript A, when Thérèse recalls her preparation for and reception of the sacrament of confirmation, she tells how she prepared with great love for the visit of the Holy Spirit. She also states that she could not understand how anyone could fail to adequately prepare for "this sacrament of Love." (S, 80)[2]

In this first explicit textual reference to the Holy Spirit, she clearly equates the receiving of the Holy Spirit with the receiving of Love. Thérèse recalls several other incidents in Manuscript A that indicate that she came to see at a later date, if not when these incidents actually happened, that these events were not mere coincidences, but were the effect of the presence and the activity of the Holy Spirit in her life. These incidents include: her Christmas conversion, her obtaining her father's permission to enter Carmel, and her actual entrance into Carmel.

Thérèse's poetry also explicitly and revealingly refers to the activity of the Holy Spirit in her life during the same period recalled in Manuscript A. These poems, although written for the other members of her community, manifest her own deep convictions about the

Holy Spirit. Examples of references to the Holy Spirit may be found in the poem entitled "Living on Love" (P, 89–92). Thérèse composed this poem during her hours of adoration before the Blessed Sacrament on the 24th, 25th, and 26th of February 1895, although she committed the fifteen stanzas to writing only after the conclusion of the Forty Hours devotion. Her aim in the poem is to express her great love for Jesus and to tell how her main occupation is to love Jesus. By always using capital letters to begin words referring to the Spirit, Thérèse clearly indicates that she is referring not to something but to Someone. For example:

In stanza 2, she states, "Ah! Divine Jesus, you know I love you. / The Spirit of Love sets me aflame with his fire."

In stanza 6, she writes, "Divine Flame, O very sweet Blaze! / I make my home in your hearth. / In your fire I gladly sing: / 'I live on Love! . . .'"

In stanza 15, her words are, "I want to be set on fire with his Love."

Reading this poem leads one to conclude that the fire of love which sets Thérèse aflame with love for Jesus is in reality the fire that is the Holy Spirit.

At the end of Manuscript A, Thérèse describes an event that is the key to understanding her entire message. That event was the offering of herself to the Merciful Love of God, an oblation she made on 9 June 1895. (S, 180–81, 276–77) Thérèse's oblation does not explicitly mention the Holy Spirit; however, to fully appreciate the significance of the oblation for Thérèse, we must view it in the light of her understanding of the Holy Spirit, for the love that receives Thérèse's oblation is, in fact, the Holy Spirit. An examination of the act of oblation in the light of Thérèse's references to the Holy Spirit in the *Story of a Soul* and in her poetry has much to tell us about her life of prayer being in complete conformity with her life of faith. It is obvious that Thérèse's faith centers totally on Jesus. Yet, what is not always noted is that Jesus is never separated from the Holy Spirit. Jesus is Thérèse's only love and she realizes that Jesus' love for her and for all of us is truly the Holy Spirit.

When Thérèse speaks of the Holy Spirit, she is referring to the third person of the Blessed Trinity precisely in what theologians today call the temporal mission of the Spirit. For Thérèse, the Holy Spirit is Divine Love in Person who ever dwells in the Incarnate Son. On the day of Pentecost, the risen Jesus gave the Holy Spirit to all of his followers to be the heart or the principle of life in his Church. The Holy Spirit is not only Jesus' love for her; the Holy Spirit is also Thérèse's love for Jesus. By her total offering of herself to Merciful Love, Thérèse sought to make of her entire life a constant and continual act of perfect love for Jesus. At each moment, she would put into each of her actions all the love that had been given to her by the Spirit of Love. In fact, the Spirit of Love is the very love by which she would love Jesus and all others. Thérèse had no illusions about the difficulty and the effort required to make of one's life a perfect act of love. She also knew that the Spirit, who inspired this desire within her, would enable her to reach the fulfillment of that desire. Her life tells us that, for Thérèse and for all who follow her teaching, the Spirit of Love would be the very love by which she and they would love God and love all the children of God.

Manuscript B of the *Story of a Soul* was written by Thérèse in September of 1896 (S, 183–200) at the request of her oldest sister and godmother, Sister Marie of the Sacred Heart. On several previous occasions, Marie had apparently verbally asked Thérèse to put into writing an account of her little doctrine. Now, as Thérèse is about to begin what both sisters realize may well be Thérèse's final retreat, Marie repeats her request in writing. Thérèse hastens to reply to her sister. She tells Marie that Jesus has also confided those same secrets to her. In fact, Thérèse goes on to say that it was Marie herself who taught Thérèse "how to gather the divine instructions." (S, 187) Thérèse promptly expresses her willingness to comply with her sister's request.

According to John Clarke, O.C.D., her American translator, Thérèse's reply to Marie is "the jewel of all Thérèse's writings" (S, xiii). In these three sheets of folded paper, Thérèse reveals the secrets of her own heart. She gives us in these brief pages a clear and beautiful account of her "little way." In doing so, she quotes those texts from the Old Testament that led her to her little way of loving God. (S, 188)

In part of Manuscript B, Thérèse addresses Jesus directly. She tells him how much she desired to love him and how she was attracted to all vocations. She saw in each and every vocation a way to express her love and gratitude to Jesus. Finally, she comes to the realization that what makes all and each of these vocations pleasing to God is not so much what is done but the love with which it is accomplished. Thérèse then recognizes that the Church itself has a heart that is burning with love. She states: *"I understood it was Love alone* that made the Church's members act, . . . that LOVE COMPRISED ALL VOCATIONS, THAT LOVE WAS EVERYTHING, THAT IT EMBRACED ALL TIMES AND PLACES. . . . IN A WORD, THAT IT WAS ETERNAL!" (S, 194) She goes on to say that, in the excess of her delirious joy, "I cried out: O Jesus, my Love. . . . my *vocation,* at last I have found it. . . . MY VOCATION IS LOVE! Yes, I have found my place in the Church and it is you, O my God, who have given me this place; in the heart of the Church, my Mother, I shall be *Love*. Thus I shall be everything, and thus my dream will be realized." (S, 194)

The explicit references to the Holy Spirit in Manuscript B refer only to the Holy Spirit's inspiration of those Old Testament texts that helped Thérèse in her coming to understand what she calls her "little doctrine." Yet, in Manuscript B, the explicit mention of the Love is ever present. For Thérèse, love burning in the heart of Jesus has, since Pentecost, become love burning in the heart of the Church. Telling us that her vocation is to be Love in the heart of the Church means that to love Jesus as he desires to be loved demands loving him with the very same love with which he has loved us. That love burning in the heart of Jesus is the Holy Spirit.

Thérèse concludes Manuscript B with the request that, at the end of her life, Jesus plunge her into the Abyss of Love to which she has already offered herself as a victim. (S, 200) These words recall Thérèse's offering to Merciful Love. In asking to be totally united with that love by which she is loved, is she not asking to be inundated by the Holy Spirit? She who desired to make her life a constant and continual act of perfect love has, at last, discovered how to attain the goal of her desires. By her union with the Holy Spirit, Thérèse becomes, both in time and in eternity, an act of perfect love.

In the fall of 1896, not long after completing Manuscript B, Thérèse wrote "How I Want to Love" (P, 173), a beautiful poem telling how she would make her life a constant act of perfect love. In three revealing stanzas, she tells Jesus that she wants to please him and that she is ready to accept the trials of this exile. She asks Jesus to change all her works into love. The second stanza is the most revealing and the most beautiful:

> It's your love, Jesus, that I crave.
> It's your love that has to transform me.
> Put in my heart your consuming flame,
> And I'll be able to bless you and love you.
> Yes, I'll be able to love you and bless you

As they do in Heaven.
I'll love you with that very love
With which you have loved me, Jesus Eternal Word. (P, 173)

Thérèse wrote Manuscript C, the third and final manuscript for the *Story of a Soul*, in June and July of 1897 at the request of Mother Marie de Gonzague, then prioress of Lisieux Carmel. (S, 203-59) In that manuscript, Thérèse explains that in the most recent year of her life she received the grace to grasp the true meaning of charity, namely, that love must be expressed not just in words but also in deeds. (S, 219) Thérèse affirms, too, her deep appreciation for the new commandment that Jesus gave his disciples at the Last Supper. It is not enough that we love others as we love ourselves, for Jesus explicitly stated, *"A new commandment I give you that you love one another: THAT AS I HAVE LOVED YOU, YOU ALSO LOVE ONE ANOTHER."* (S, 219) Thérèse finally realizes that it is precisely as Jesus has loved us that we must love one another. Thérèse comments insightfully on the new commandment. She tells Jesus himself that never would she be able to love others as he did "unless you, O my Jesus, *loved them in me."* (S, 221) She states that it was because Jesus wanted to love others in us that he gave us this new commandment. She says: "Oh! how I love this new commandment since it gives me the assurance that your Will is *to love in me* all those you command me to love!" (S, 221)

After giving an extended account of how love for one another is practiced in our daily lives, Thérèse again speaks directly to Jesus. She tells him that she desires only to love him and make him loved. She also tells him that, in order to love him as he loves her and to love others as Jesus loves them, "I would have to borrow your own Love, and then only would I be at rest." (S, 256) Thérèse marvels at the love Jesus has bestowed on her; she even dares to say that it seems it could not be greater. She thus unhesitatingly asks Jesus *"to love those whom you have given me with the love with which you loved me."* (S, 256) In the next sentence, Thérèse admits that in heaven she may find that others have loved Jesus more than she and thus were more deserving of God's love. But here on earth she cannot conceive a greater immensity of love than the one bestowed on her without any merit on her part.

When Thérèse writes of loving both Jesus and one another with the very love with which Jesus has loved us, is she not referring to the Holy Spirit? Surely it is in and by the Spirit that Jesus loves us. Thérèse apparently realized that it is in and by the Holy Spirit that we are to love Jesus and one another.

Thérèse and Mary

More than one authority on Thérèse has noted that Thérèse herself has drawn our attention to the similarity of what she experienced on the day of her First Communion and what she experienced at the shrine of Our Lady of Victories in Paris before entering Carmel. In the first instance, Thérèse tells about her union with Jesus, one that she would not call a union, but a fusion with Jesus, a oneness with Jesus. In the second instance, Thérèse speaks of her union with Mary. (S, 123) Thérèse does not use any special term to describe this union. Yet, this later union has so impressed Theresian scholars that they have no hesitation in referring to Thérèse as a miniature of Mary, or as an icon of Mary. Some even speak of Thérèse's welcoming smile as a reflection of the welcoming smile that Mary and her son have for each one of us.[3] At Paris, Thérèse experienced a union with Mary that would never be interrupted. Later, in the darkest moments of her trial of faith, Thérèse would affirm that Mary was never absent from her life. (LC, 81)

In May 1897, just months before her death, Thérèse wrote her last poem and dedicated it to Mary. Entitled "Why I Love You, O

Mary!" (P, 211–20), the poem's twenty-five stanzas are an uninterrupted defense of the human Mary. Here Thérèse says everything she would like to say about Mary if she could preach but one sermon on her. Throughout the poem, from beginning to end, Thérèse describes only the joyful and sorrowful events in the lives of Jesus and Mary. Never does she mention the glorious events, nor does she depict Mary except in relationship to Jesus. Thérèse focuses her attention on the human and the suffering Mary. Above all, she presents to us the simple, ordinary, and truly human Mary. As we read the poem, we also see a clear portrait of Thérèse herself as simple, ordinary, and very human. Because she imitated Mary so well and so closely, Thérèse, in portraying her model, portrays her own self.

Thérèse wrote this poem when she had been experiencing her great trial of faith for well over a year. The stanzas reveal that Mary is always present to Thérèse at this most difficult time. Like manuscript B, this poem was written at the request of Thérèse's eldest sister, Sr. Marie of the Sacred Heart. However, before being asked to write the poem, Thérèse had said, "There is still one thing I have to do before I die. I have always dreamed of saying in a song to the Blessed Virgin everything I think about her." (P, 211) The poem has been aptly described as "a journey through the pages of the Gospel, where Thérèse discovered Mary's love for God and for others, her poverty, her contemplative silence, her simplicity, her faith, her hope, her receptivity and obedience in accepting the will of God. . . . The Gospel tells us who Mary was and Thérèse's heart revealed to her in her experience of daily life in communion with the Virgin, Mary's true personality."[4]

Thérèse always sees Mary as someone who seeks to love God and others precisely as she is loved by God. We have few, if any, of Mary's spoken words in the incidents recalled in the poem, but Thérèse's presentation of those incidents helps us to see that Mary's actions speak to us of how one who truly loves God responds to both joy and sorrow. In recalling these various Gospel scenes, Thérèse vividly portrays Mary as truly one of us, yet as one who also has been gifted by God to lead us to God. A few quotations from the long poem show us Mary as Thérèse saw her.

Thérèse has no hesitation in approaching Mary, nor in believing that she is Mary's child, "For I see you human and suffering like me." (st. 2) Of Mary's humility she tells us, "This hidden virtue makes you all powerful" and "attracts the Holy Trinity into your heart." (st. 4) "You made visible the narrow road to Heaven." (st. 6) Speaking of Mary's silence in time of trial, Thérèse declares that "your eloquent silence . . . . speaks to me of the greatness and power / Of a soul which looks only to heaven for help." (st. 8) Seeing Mary's search for Jesus, her lost child, Thérèse states, "Mother, your sweet Child wants you to be the example / Of the soul searching for him in the night of faith." (st. 15) Thérèse, who in her own life saw suffering as inseparable from loving, asks: "Mary, is it thus a blessing to suffer on earth?" And Thérèse herself answers: "Yes, *to suffer while loving is the purest happiness!"* (st. 16) For Thérèse, Mary was a person who shared and enjoyed simple pleasures: "Instead of scorning pure and simple joys, / You want to share in them, you deign to bless them." (st. 18) The many other verses that could be cited to show how the human Mary strove to love as she had been loved are perhaps best captured in one final quote from stanza 22: "You love us, Mary, as Jesus loves us, / And for us you accept being separated from him. / *To love is to give everything. It's to give oneself."* (st. 22)

Our examination of Thérèse's autobiography and some of her poems clearly reveals that she anticipated Vatican II's teachings on the universal call to holiness and Mary of Nazareth's humanness. The new awareness of the universal call to holiness and our consciousness of the truly human Mary, in turn, deepen our understanding of the Holy Spirit's role both in bringing us to and in sustaining us in sanctity of life. In the account of her life, Thérèse tells us that Jesus teaches her without the sound of words, that he guides her and inspires her as to what she is to say and to do. (S, 179) Jesus accomplishes these same activities in our present world through the power and the presence of the Holy Spirit.

The Holy Spirit did for Thérèse what the Spirit had already done even more abundantly for Mary of Nazareth. More than any other human person, Mary was indwelt by the power and the presence of the Holy Spirit. The Gospel passages which tell us how Mary pondered the events surrounding Jesus' birth and infancy indicate that Mary looked to the Spirit who had overshadowed her at the Incarnation to guide, to inspire, and to teach her what to say and do. In discovering her own vocation to be love "in the heart of the Church," (S, 194) Thérèse also discovered Mary's vocation. Thérèse asserts that she will do in heaven what she desired most to do here on earth, namely, to love Jesus and to make him loved. Thérèse's most quoted statement is perhaps "I want to spend my heaven in doing good on earth." (LC, 102) These words also aptly describe the heavenly occupation of Mary of Nazareth. For both Mary and Thérèse, to love Jesus and to make him loved is their sole occupation both in time and in eternity.

Thérèse believes that to love Jesus as he desires to be loved, we must borrow the very love by which he loves us. That love is the Holy Spirit. Only the Spirit of love who overshadowed Mary at the Incarnation enables and empowers Thérèse to love as she is loved by Jesus; indeed, the same Spirit of love must also enable and empower all who respond to the universal call to holiness. In her offering to merciful love, like Mary in her Magnificat, Thérèse expresses her awareness of being totally and gratuitously loved by God. Her one desire is to love God and to make God loved. As did Mary of Nazareth, Thérèse would make of her life a constant and continual act of perfect love. Neither Mary nor Thérèse had to wait until eternity to hear the words from the lips of Jesus, "I have loved you with the very love by which the Father has loved me." By their very lives, both Mary and Thérèse witness to their awareness of and response to the presence and the activity of the Holy Spirit within them. The Spirit of love brought Jesus to Mary and Thérèse; and that same Spirit brought Mary and Thérèse to Jesus, the Spirit who is the very love of the Father and of the Son.

Conclusion

We are all called to holiness of life. To attain that goal, we must possess an awareness of being loved by God and of being capable of loving God precisely as God desires to be loved. The Spirit of love, who makes us aware that we are loved by God, also enables and empowers us to love God as God desires to be loved by us. While holiness of life requires our earnest, constant, and generous effort, it remains true that sanctity is more received than it is achieved. For us, as for Mary and Thérèse, holiness of life is more God's work in us than it is our own accomplishment.

Notes

1 Michel De Goedt, " L'Amour de Thérèse de l'Enfant-Jésus pour Marie, Mère du Sauveur," *Teresianum* 48 (1997): 115–37; François–Marie Lethel, *L'Amour de Jésus: La Christologie de Sainte Thérèse de l'Enfant-Jésus* (Paris: Desclée, 1997); Francois–Marie Lethel, "L'Amour de Jésus," in *Thérèse de l'Enfant-Jésus: Docteur de l'Amour* (Venasque: Editions du Carmel, 1990), 113-55; Ivan Marcil, "Thérèse de Lisieux et l'Esprit Saint," *Teresianum* 51 (2000): 385-413.

2 English quotations from the writings of St. Thérèse are taken from the translations of her works by the Institute of Carmelite Studies. Her writings cited in this essay are *Story of a Soul: The Autobiography of St. Thérèse of Lisieux,* trans. John Clarke (Washington, DC: ICS Publications, 1975); *Her Last Conversations,* trans. John Clarke, OCD (Washington, DC: ICS Publications, 1977); *The Poetry of Saint Thérèse of Lisieux*, trans. Donald Kinney (Washington, DC: ICS Publications, 1996). Citations are noted in the text following each quotation, giving the book and page number. In these citation, S = *Story of a Soul*, LC = *Last Conversations,* and P = *Poetry.*

3 In addition to those Theresian scholars listed in note no.1 above, see also: Emile Neubert, *Sainte Thérèse de l'Enfant-Jésus et la Sainte Vièrge* (Paris: Alsatia, 1962); Jean la France, "Le Rôle du Saint-Esprit dans L'acte D'Offrande à L'Amour," *Vie Thérèsienne* 33 (1969): 7-16; Marie Dominique Philippe, *L'acte d'Offrande: Retraite avec La Petite Thérèse* (Versailles: Editions-Saint Paul, 1997).

4 Joseph Chalmers, O.Carm, and Camilo Maccise, OCD, *Back to the Gospel: The Message of Thérèse of Lisieux* (Rome: Casa Generalizia Carmelitani Scalzi, 1996), 27

Blind Hope in Divine Mercy

Charles Niqueux, Priest of Notre–Dame de Vie
Translated by Salvatore Sciurba, O.C.D.
Carmel of the Espousals of Mary and Joseph
Brighton, Massachusetts

When St. Thérèse of Lisieux discovered her place in the Church, she identified with the love that is its heart: "In the heart of the Church . . . I will be love." (S, 194) Such a desire for personal identification with Love indicates the great love that motivated Thérèse, but also her very great understanding of God-Love.[1] This desire especially manifested what was Thérèse's grace. In discovering Love as the heart of the Church, Thérèse only recognized and expressed the quality of the grace that dwelt in her, the quality of the love that took hold of her. This grace let her know what she was, "the child of the Church" (S, 197), prescribed her mission to her—to love and make Love loved—and indicated to her its universal scope, for it is identical to the Love that extends to "all times and places."

Grace is the free gift of participation in the life of God. Grace bears in it, as its principle, all the potentialities that God has placed in it in view of the place that each must occupy in the Church and the function that each must fulfill in it. "To occupy this place, to accomplish this mission," wrote Fr. Marie-Eugène in *I Want to See God,* "are inseparable aspects of our perfection, or rather constitute and specify it."[2]

How did Thérèse attain sanctity? At each stage of her life, we see Thérèse unconditionally give herself to Jesus, abandon herself to his Love (L, 794-97), and progressively accomplish, led by this Love, everything that God gave her by way of light and life for the Church.

How was she able to present such docility and such availability to the purifying, transforming action of the Spirit of Love? By offering herself to this Love and by placing no limits, "no restrictions" (L, 541-43), on its action in her. For if Thérèse offered herself to merciful Love, it was because she saw herself—and always wanted to be ever more so—under the impulse of the Holy Spirit who allowed her to accomplish all her hopes, all her desires to love in him, discovering her place in this Church and her mission for eternity.

Thérèse put all her spiritual, interior energy in the practice of the theological virtues of faith, hope, and love;[3] she also turned to God in prayer and was nourished by the Eucharist. Moreover, she completed this theological activity by offering God the humble collaboration of her good will in every opportunity for renunciation and service that the events, circumstances, and people amply provided in her life as in everyone's.

The theological virtue of hope holds a significant place in the development of the Christian's spiritual life. Unfortunately, this virtue is little known and taught, while its practice is considered indispensable for fidelity and progression in the love that unites us to Christ. Thérèse responded to this lack: she brings us the luminous example of her life and teaching. The doctrine of the "little way" reveals to us Thérèse's perfect hope. It shows us the power of hope on the heart of God. To reach sanctity, the doctrine of the "little way" teaches us how to abandon ourselves in poverty, confidence, and humility of heart to the transforming action of love.

1. The Movement of Hope

Hope, the Virtue of Activity

The theological virtue of hope is completely directed toward its end: the possession of God and the salvation promised in his Son. St. Paul speaks of hope in the Letter to the Romans: "We have been saved, but in hope. For to see what one hopes for is no longer to hope; how can one hope for what one sees? But to hope for what we do not see is to wait patiently." (Rom 8:24-5)

St. John of the Cross, whose doctrine Thérèse profoundly absorbed, speaks of hope as a power of going beyond, of detachment from all that is not God, to direct oneself to God alone. He tells us: "By hope, the soul detaches its heart from all things, it hopes for nothing of what this world gives or can give; it lives on in expectation of eternal goods." (N.2.21.6) Once again: "It is so stripped of every possession and every support that it cares only for God, it raises its eyes to God alone." (N.2.21.9) St. John of the Cross especially shows how perfect hope, because it is completely poor, conquers God and "obtains all it hopes for." He adds: "Without this green livery of hope in God alone, vainly would the soul set out after the conquest of love. It would have obtained nothing, because hope alone triumphs over all trials." (N.2.21.8)

Of the three theological virtues, only hope accomplishes this movement to God, this movement of the will to possess him:[4] "Hope implies a movement toward what one does not possess."[5] Thus hope enables progression toward the goal: "Faith discovers; charity possesses in the embrace; hope is entirely given over to the object it knows by faith and which it does not possess in the entire measure of love's desires," wrote Fr. Marie-Eugène.[6] Hope is truly "the virtue of movement in the spiritual life; it is the motor that moves it and the wings that lift it up."[7]

"A Giant's Race"

This movement of hope, completely directed toward the possession of love, dominated Thérèse's life; it was its total dynamism. Nonetheless, Thérèse did not attain the full possession of God's love, which she manifested at the end of her life, without encountering countless obstacles along the way. She knew all kinds of difficulties and failures;[8] suffering marked each stage of her life.

Thérèse's childhood was marked by the death of her mother when she was only four years old; by the departure of her sister Pauline, her second mother, for Carmel; next came that strange illness which resulted in emotional wounds from which Thérèse was cured by the Virgin's smile on 13 May 1883. Thérèse experienced many setbacks that marked each step toward the fulfillment of her Carmelite vocation. Even when she received permission to enter, she would have to wait three months more. In Carmel, her reception of the habit and her profession would be postponed; she would never be a chapter member.[9]

Above all, Thérèse experienced suffering. Suffering for those she loved, especially with the onset of her father's illness: "Ah! On that day I did not say I could suffer more." (S, 157) She also experienced dryness in prayer,[10] the voluntary privation of affective bonds with her sisters and, even more intense, the trial of faith that afflicted her beginning on Easter 1896. Finally, there were the "great physical and moral sufferings"[11] she endured throughout her final illness.[12]

We always see her react with an abundance of confidence in God, with hope in his all-powerful action: "God has always come to my aid; he helped me and led me by the hand from my childhood. I count on him. I am assured that he will continue to help me until the end." (LC, 50) She said again during her last illness: "What difference does it make? Suffering can reach extreme limits, but I am sure that God will never abandon me." (LC, 73)

Thérèse, however, did not arrive all at once at this acceptance of suffering.[13] She recognized that she had shed many tears when suffering took her by surprise.[14] Though Thérèse found "happiness and joy on earth," it was nonetheless in the midst of suffering that it was given to her.[15] Still, she always lived this suffering in love, in communion with the sufferings of Jesus, in order to share in the fullness of the redemption. She always lived it in the great desire of saving souls.

How can we understand this capacity of going beyond, of disengaging, of acceptance that Thérèse manifested throughout her life and which is not a question of will, but founded on the certitude that God would never abandon her?

To understand this, we must return to the Christmas grace of 1886. Thérèse said that she then received the grace of a "complete conversion," which brought her out of her "swaddling clothes." Thérèse was, in fact, paralyzed by her extreme sensitivity, which she had not yet mastered. Here, by this great effort, she found again the basic balance that would permit her to progress in every respect and to begin what she herself would call "a giant's race": ". . . and on that luminous night that illumines the delights of the Holy Trinity, Jesus, the gentle little child of one hour, changed the night of my soul into torrents of light. . . . On that night when he became weak and vulnerable for my love, he made me strong and courageous. He clothed me with his weapons and since that blessed night, I have been overcome in no battle, but on the contrary, I go from victory to victory and thus began a giant's race!" (S, 97)

What dominates in Thérèse, throughout the account she gives of the Christmas grace, is the certitude that this conversion, though accomplished by an act of courage on her part, is before all else a gift of God, a gift of his infinite mercy.[16] "In an instant Jesus did the work I was never able to do in ten years, satisfied with my good will which was never lacking." (S, 98) This action of God is bestowed on Thérèse instantaneously. In this transformation that God accomplished in her, Thérèse discovered the relationship between human time, that of her efforts, and God's time which is given at every moment; for her, the only thing that counted was the instant in which God acted to transform her and when she herself was able to give herself.[17]

Henceforth, for Thérèse, the all-powerful, merciful action of God would be associated with her experience of an extreme poverty. This union, experienced in its weakness through which the strength of God was manifested, was the entire dynamism of Thérèse's life. This was not an acquired conviction but a certitude founded on her experience which marked out the depths of her grace and her life. Thus Thérèse, who was always the little one in the Martin family, who knew emotional weakness, interior suffering and powerlessness, would use her powerlessness to attract God's action. Such was the most profound fruit of the Christmas grace of 1886 in Thérèse's heart. Her doctrine of the little way would develop on this foundation. The conversion of Pranzini, the criminal, obtained through her prayer, was the first accomplishment, the first verification of this absolute confidence in the merciful, infinite power of Jesus.[18]

From this time on, Thérèse was filled with this absolute confidence in the infinite mercy of God, in the omnipotence of his love which was able to fulfill the most secret desires of her soul: "More than ever, I understand that the littlest events of our lives are directed by God; he is the one who causes us to desire and who fulfills our desires." (L, 1015) Thérèse had the certitude that God guided each step of her life and that this love is foreseeing: it is the love of a father for his child. God-Love only wants the welfare of his child. Thérèse responded to this love with absolute confidence and absolute abandonment to merciful love.

How can we understand, not only the dynamism that Thérèse maintained throughout her life to deal with all her difficulties, and the strength she manifested in her sufferings, but also such an expression of her aspirations and such certitude in her mission, as evidenced by the many sayings reported in the *Last Conversations?* Thérèse herself gives us the answer. She greatly hoped and desired, greatly expected from God—and God surpassed her expectations and fulfilled all her hopes. (S, 208)

2. Hope at the Service of Love

The Desire for Heaven and the Desire to Love

Heaven had always been for Thérèse the object of a profound hope. From her early childhood, she learned how to turn to heaven to find God there, and throughout her life, she would have an exalted idea of heaven. (LC, 43) Before all else, heaven was for her the place of perfect communion among all; it was the place where all the dear beings who had already left this land of exile were to be found. Everyone was to aim for it.

Even more, for Thérèse heaven was the time of every accomplishment. Thérèse, sensitive and penetrating, painfully experienced the imperfection that affects human relationships even in the most generous of intentions. In heaven all the misunderstandings of this life, all the failures to comprehend, will come to an end. It will be the time when everything appears in its full truth and in its real light.

Heaven also represented for Thérèse the hope of the fulfillment of her most intense personal desires. Since she never did her own will on earth, God would have to grant her everything in heaven. (LC, 91) Thus, this would be the time of her "revenge" for all the love that she was not able to give here below and which she would dispose of without measure.[19] After having been "in chains," not being able to act as freely as she would have liked, heaven would also be the time for her conquests. (LC, 144) We would be greatly mistaken in judging this representation of heaven as purely ideal. It was brought about by a growing experience of love that was completely interiorized. On the day of her First Communion, Thérèse received Jesus for the first time; it was a fusion in love and unity between Thérèse and Jesus who came to her and to whom she gave herself without reservation: "For a long time, Jesus and little Thérèse had looked at each other and understood each other. On that day, it was no longer a look but a fusion; they were no longer two, for Thérèse had disappeared like the drop of water that is lost in the depths of the ocean." (S, 77)

Thérèse spoke about this day as a "day of heaven." It was within herself, however, that she would henceforth discover all the riches of heaven. After the Christmas grace of 1886, this interiorization would become stronger. Thérèse noted, as an essential effect of this grace, that she grew "in the love of God." More than heaven, the very reality of love itself drew her: ". . . it was not that heaven did not stir up my desire, but then my heaven was no other than the Love I felt—like St. Paul—that nothing could separate me from the divine object that delighted me!" (S, 112; cf. Rom 8:39)

Thérèse's hope then tended both to heaven, whose riches and beauty she sensed, and to the love that dwelt in her and took hold of her. These two realities were of different orders. The first one belonged to the knowledge she had of future realities in the light of faith but also to her great sensitivity and affection. The second, divine love or the love of Jesus, was the outpouring of love in her that united her to God himself. Thérèse's representation of heaven would be swept away by the very vision of God in glory. The love communicated to her would remain forever, for that is what united her to God; it would not pass away. Thérèse recognized the distinction between the idea she had of heaven, exalted as it was, and the reality she perceived more deeply in love, and for which she hoped. She expressed it in a paradoxical manner: "I have so exalted an idea of heaven, that, sometimes, I wonder how, at my death, God could surprise me. My hope is so great, it is such an object of joy for me, not by sentiment, but by faith, that something above all my thoughts would be needed to fully satisfy me. Rather than be disappointed, I prefer to keep an eternal hope." (LC, 43)

Thérèse would express just as paradoxically her anxiety of not being able to love in heaven as much as she desired on earth: "Nonetheless, I sense it, O Jesus, after aspiring to the highest regions of Love, if I cannot attain them one day, I would have tasted more sweetness in my martyrdom, in my folly, than I will taste in the joys of the homeland, unless by some miracle you take from me the remembrance of my earthly hopes." (S, 197)

Thérèse's hope is expressed then in this twofold expectation: that of heaven and that of love. The two realities overlap. The first is acquired at the end of life as the reward for good works, whereas love is already present and is at the root of good works. The love lived here below will be the same as that which will continue its work in heaven, whereas faith will give way to the vision of God and hope will cease when love is possessed.

On 9 June 1895, Thérèse pronounced her Act of Offering to Merciful Love. In this prayer, she gave herself completely to divine love, manifested in Jesus. In order to express the perfection of the gift in love, this Act borrowed the language of hope. By reading it attentively, we discover all the theological hope of Thérèse who, moved by love, tends toward the source from which it proceeds: Jesus in the Trinity.

In the very first place, Thérèse expressed the great desire that moved her in this Offering: "O my God! Blessed Trinity, I want to love you and make you loved." In the next to last paragraph, Thérèse returns again to this sole desire to love which she henceforth wants to live with each beat of her heart: "In order to live in an act of perfect love, I offer myself as a victim holocaust to your merciful Love."[20]

The hope of heaven is also present in the Act of Offering. Thérèse is not unaware of this essential element of the Christian faith, namely that "God is the rewarder of those who seek him." (Heb 11:6) Heaven, as participation in God's happiness, is fully the object of her hope: "I hope to go and find my joy in you in the homeland." (S, 277)

Thérèse especially hoped to receive the glorification to come as resemblance to Jesus. When she pronounced her Act of Offering, she had already suffered greatly and, through her love of the Holy Face, she participated in the passion and the cross: "In heaven I hope to resemble you and see the holy wounds of your passion shine in my glorified body." (S, 277) Therefore Thérèse does not expect the glorification of what she is, or of her good works; she desires to be associated with the glory of Jesus himself for the sole love of whom she gives herself and wants to act: "I want no other throne, nor other crown than you, O my Beloved." (S, 277)

Thus, the Act of Offering reveals to us an essential aspect of the hope that moves Thérèse to give herself to this merciful Love: before all else, she hopes to be consumed here below in love. This desire does not first of all aim at her personal sanctification, even if Thérèse always did want to be a saint. (cf. S, 13-14) This desire has as its goal the overflowing in her of "the waves of infinite tenderness" that are in God and which find few souls to inundate.[21] As for the hope that tends toward heaven, Thérèse completely abandons herself to love itself. This love alone explains the impatience of her love: "May this martyrdom, after preparing me to appear before you, make me die of love, and may my soul go forth without delay in the eternal embrace of your merciful love!" (S, 277)

Manuscript B: "The Love that Hopes for Everything"

Manuscript B is an essential text for the understanding of Thérèse's hope as it is linked to the desire to love.[22] In the second section of this text, Thérèse addresses Jesus himself: "Forgive me Jesus if I become irrational in wanting to repeat my desires, my hopes that reach the infinite." (S, 192) In the continuation of the text, Thérèse will express the object of her hopes and the desire for their accomplishment: "Forgive me and heal my soul by giving it what it hopes for!"[23]

First of all, Thérèse will express her desires to embrace every vocation to manifest to Jesus her desire to love. It is only by raising the stakes in her desires that Thérèse finds the proper disproportion to express the intensity of her love. The disproportion of her desires is however entirely motivated by the sole desire to act for Jesus alone. The "for you" is essential. It shows Thérèse's purity of intention in her desire to love.[24] Thérèse is not unaware of her weakness, her complete powerlessness which she will express in as impressive a manner as she expresses her desires to love in the parable of the little bird. But she wants no other measure for her love than the very love of Jesus. She knows, along with St. John of the Cross, that "love is only repaid by love"[25] and that to love Jesus we must borrow the very love by which Jesus loves.[26] This purity of love is the basis for the perfection of hope in Thérèse and makes her experience her poverty.

Thérèse, therefore, finds the answer to her immense desires in love itself. The organic structure of the Church, where members discover themselves in the complementarity at the heart of the whole body, does not suffice for her and leaves her unsatisfied. "The answer was clear but did not fulfill my desires; it did not give me peace," Thérèse wrote. Only love, which St. Paul says is the "excellent way that surely leads to God," responded to her hope and gave her the key to her vocation: "Yes, I have found my place in the Church and this place, O my God, you have given me. . . . In the heart of the Church, my Mother, I shall be love . . . thus I shall be everything . . . thus my dream will be fulfilled!" (S, 194; cf. 1 Cor 12:31)

Thérèse found in love the reality of what motivated her and inspired her desire to be everything. She is not yet in full possession of the goal of her hope, since here below love can always grow and deepen. Nonetheless, a new certitude dawns on her, which brings her peace: "Why speak of a delirious joy? No, this expression is not right, it is rather the calm, serene peace of the navigator who sees the beacon that is to lead him to port." The peace that accompanied hope expressed the certitude of being close to hope's goal. Thérèse continues: "O luminous Beacon of love, I know how to reach you, I have found the secret of making your flame my own." (S, 195)

This last sentence is the key to Theresian hope and reveals its perfection: love alone must guide her to the complete fulfillment of her desires.[27] Thérèse knows by experience that she possesses this love in a stable manner: "Ah! Since that happy day [of her Offering to Merciful Love] it seems to me that *Love* penetrates and surrounds me, it seems to me that at each instant this *Merciful Love* renews me, purifies my soul and eradicates every trace of sin from it." (S, 181)

Thus this love which acts because it is love, is also that which "hopes for everything" (1 Cor 13:7), according to St. Paul's expression. For a long time already, the hope by which Thérèse lived was not a hope that brought her to God for his gifts,[28] nor even for the promised glory,[29] it was a perfect hope that sprung from her love for God and associated her with his life.[30] Thérèse discovered that the love of

God which is infinite put no limitations on her hopes, placed no boundaries on her desires to love. Thus Thérèse's desires, "greater than the universe" (S, 193) and which "extended to infinity" (P, 210), were neither dreams nor folly; they were the desires of love. They revealed her mission to her and led her to give herself to it in an even more complete self-gift.

In the last part of this chapter, we will see how Thérèse, immersed in the trial of faith, would be associated with the mystery of redemption. In that night, her love and hope would bring her to sinners. In order to grasp this enlargement of her personal hope at the service of love, we must first see how the trial of faith is also a trial of hope. This was a trial that led Thérèse to live an even greater personal poverty; that led her to affirm in an even more explicit way the primacy of her desire to love over the desire for heaven, thus enabling her to completely accomplish her mission to love and make Love loved.

"The Thought of Heaven Was So Sweet to Me"

The trial of faith Thérèse experienced, shortly after the feast of Easter 1896, represents a very painful interior trial that would last until her death. Before entering into this trial, as early as 1891, Thérèse had experienced doubts regarding the existence of heaven: "I then had great trials of all kinds (even to the point of wondering if there was a heaven)." (S, 173) Thérèse would confide these doubts and trials to Fr. Alexis Prou who had come to Carmel to preach the annual retreat. His response was to ask her to abandon herself to the love of God. Thérèse wrote: "He launched me full sail on the waves of confidence and love which attracted me so strongly, but on which I dared not advance."(S, 174) Thérèse progressed in love and confidence through the experience of these trials and doubts about the existence of heaven that so profoundly strengthened her hope.

In the trial of faith, the existence of heaven became the object of her suffering and of her night. "I then enjoyed so lively, so clear a faith that the thought of heaven constituted all my happiness. I could not believe that there were evil people who had no faith. I thought that they were speaking against their beliefs by denying the existence of heaven, of the beautiful heaven where God himself wanted to be their Eternal Reward." Thérèse then continues, clearly specifying the object of this trial: "During those very joyful days of Easter time, Jesus made me feel that there truly were souls who had no faith, who by the abuse of grace lost this precious treasure, the source of the only true and pure joys. He permitted my soul to be enveloped by the thickest darkness, and the thought of heaven, so sweet to me, was from then on a subject of struggle and torment." (S, 211)

In the following lines, Thérèse recalls several times the suffering that the thought of heaven would henceforth provoke in her. It became impossible for her to "find again the very sweet image of the homeland"; her torment increased when she sought "to rest her tired heart from the darkness that surrounded her by the remembrance of the luminous country" (S, 213) which was the object of her desires.

This trial bears on Thérèse's faith where the very reality, the very existence of heaven was concerned. The veil of faith that expressed the obscurity inherent in this virtue became "a wall that was raised to the heavens and covered the starry firmament." (S, 214) For heaven is "eternal salvation, it is the work of the Lord, it is the consummation of Jesus' love."[31] This was not merely the representation Thérèse made of heaven but the reality itself, the hope for the possession of God: "When I sing of the happiness of heaven, the eternal possession of God, I feel no joy, for I simply sing of what I want to believe."[32] Elsewhere and during the course of her illness, Thérèse would say that it was indeed on the existence of heaven, and not on the existence of God, that her trial hinged.[33] This trial of faith was then also, and perhaps even more radically, a trial of hope.[34]

The depth of this trial was manifested in the words Thérèse felt rise up in her as the expression of the voice of sinners: "You dream of light, a country scented with delightful perfumes, you dream of the *eternal* possession of the Creator of all these wonders, you believe you will one day emerge from the fog that surrounds you! Go ahead, go ahead, rejoice in the death that will give you, not what you hope for, but an even more profound night, the night of nothingness." (S, 213)

Thérèse's hope is put to the test both in terms of its object (the eternal possession of the Creator of all these wonders) and in terms of its act (the movement: go ahead!). These words are like a parody on hope and on its movement toward God to receive from him the fulfillment of his promise. In this trial, Thérèse was asked to continue to advance with the certitude of being deceived on the goal she pursued.[35]

Thérèse reacted valiantly in this trial. She does not confront her enemy head on but turns to Jesus by faith: "knowing that it is cowardice to fight a duel, I turn my back to my adversary without deigning to look him in the face; but I run to my Jesus and I tell him I am ready to shed my blood to the last drop for him to confess that there is a heaven." (S, 213-4)[36] By thus turning to Jesus in the moment of trial, Thérèse does not only accomplish this act of anagogic faith recommended by St. John of the Cross in times of temptation. In this movement to Jesus is also expressed the perfect love of the one who has no other support than Jesus himself to proclaim her faith and to profess the existence of heaven.[37]

The trial was long and intense. Thérèse recognized that, earlier, she would have been "overcome by discouragement," her hope would have been shattered.[38] During these last months of her life, Thérèse actually lets us see to what extent the thought of heaven lost its reality for her and became painful.[39] She also recognized the spiritual fruits of this trial: "Now it removes all that could have been naturally satisfying in the desire that I had for heaven." (S, 214) Shortly before this trial began, she questioned herself about the way she was following. This way, composed of confidence and abandonment to God, but also of humble acceptance of the ordinary life of Carmel, seemed to have necessarily maintained her in rest. Thérèse stated: "Truly I have no great exterior trials and to have interior ones, God would have to change my life. I don't think he will; nonetheless, I cannot always live in peace. What way will Jesus find to test me?" The trial of faith would be the response to the desire of love that Thérèse expressed by this lack of satisfaction: "The answer was not long in coming and showed me that the One I love does not lack the means; without changing my life, he sent me the test that was to mix a salutary bitterness with all my joys." (S, 250)[40]

"My Heaven on Earth"

But more profoundly than this personal aspect of purification, Thérèse lets us understand how, in this trial, her hope was definitively enlarged to the dimension of the love that possessed her. On 13 July 1897, she said: "I cannot think of the happiness that awaits me in heaven; one sole expectation makes my heart beat: it is the love I will receive and that which I will be able to give."[41] The next day she wrote to Fr. Roulland: "the thought of eternal beatitude scarcely moves my heart; for a long time suffering has become my heaven here below . . . what attracts me toward the homeland of heaven is the Lord's call, it is the hope of finally loving him as I have so desired and the thought that I will make him loved by a multitude of souls who will bless him eternally. (L, 1142)

Stripped of everything that heaven represented as expectation and personal joy, Thérèse's hope took on the measure of her love, revealing its scope in all its grandeur and immensity. It was motivated entirely by the mystery of redemption and the salvation of souls:

> I sense that I am about to enter into rest. But I especially sense that my mission is about to begin, my mission to make God loved as I love him, to give my little way to souls. If God grants my desires, my heaven will be spent on earth until the end of the world. Yes, I want to spend my heaven doing good on earth. This is not impossible, since in the heart of the beatific vision, the angels watch over us.
>
> I cannot pursue my own happiness, I cannot rest as long as there are souls to be saved. . . . But when the angel says "time is no more!" then I will rest; I will be able to rejoice, because the number of the elect will be complete and everyone will have entered into joy and rest. My heart trembles at this thought. (LC, 102)

This development of hope in love which Thérèse then lived reaches its universality in this night of faith that accompanied her until her death. In this night, which united her so profoundly to Jesus' passion, Thérèse mystically accomplished her vocation to love and make love loved before she accomplished it in glory after her death. In the last part of this study, we will return to this mystical dimension of Thérèse's hope which embraces the whole Church. Before that, we must consider Thérèse's hope in itself in order to understand how this hope reached its perfection by giving itself to all the aspirations of love.

3. "You, Yourself, O My God, Be My Sanctity"

Thérèse very appropriately expressed the nature of theological hope when she wrote in her Act of Offering: "I want to clothe myself with your own justice and receive from your love the eternal possession of you. I want no other throne or crown but you, O my Beloved!" (S, 277) Hope is a theological virtue because it makes us desire God alone whom we do not yet fully possess in this life. Hope makes us desire God both as the end to which we proceed ("the full possession of you") and as the motive on which we must rely to arrive at this end ("to receive your love"). The rapport between the twofold object of hope goes from divine help to the possession of God: one hopes for God's help in this life to obtain eternal happiness from God.[42] One can truly desire to possess God who is infinite only by relying on God's help, which is also virtue, power, and infinity. Thus St. John of the Cross says the soul that has attained perfect love hopes only in God.[43]

This is why "the more the soul hopes from God, the more it obtains, and it hopes more to the extent that it empties itself more," says St. John of the Cross. Only the hope that hopes solely in God, in God's love, with no other support, will obtain from God the full possession of God. Hope becomes more perfect and soars more profoundly to God as one's motivation is purified in the soul. St. John of the Cross shows us again that the perfection of hope is in its purity and not in the intensity of its desire. Hope will be purer to the extent that it relies on God alone.[44] Thérèse absorbed this teaching of St. John of the Cross; she made it her own and lived it perfectly in order to present it in an adapted form that bears the characteristics of her grace and genius.

The "Arms of Jesus"

What most characterizes the life of St. Thérèse of the Child Jesus is this primacy accorded to the action of God, a primacy that is found explicitly in her doctrine of the little way. She experienced God's action through love and consequently by the Gifts of the Holy Spirit; this did not begin only at the time of her religious life in Carmel but went back to her childhood.[45] How does Thérèse express her experience of the primacy of this divine help? A major text of the Third Manuscript gives her whole doctrine on the question of divine help in its relationship to hope. (S, 207-8) It was the novelty of the elevator that inspired this very simple comparison to her.

The logic of her experience is both consistent and absolutely rigorous. Thérèse begins with the certitude of the hope that is in her, the great desire for sanctity she always had: "Mother, you know that I always wanted to be a great saint." She confronts this certitude in her weakness and natural imperfection to acknowledge that she absolutely cannot rely on her own strength: "God would not inspire desires that are impossible to attain; then despite my littleness, I can aspire to sanctity; for me to grow is impossible, I must bear with myself as I am with all my imperfections."

She searches for a means that would be in proportion to the aspirations she bears within her. The image of the elevator permits her to express the help that comes from someone other than herself: "I would also like to find an elevator to lift me up to Jesus, for I am too little to climb the steep stairway of perfection. . . . The elevator that must lift me up to heaven is your arms, O Jesus!" The image of Jesus' arms expresses the divine character of this help and indicates its omnipotence. To correspond to this action of God, Thérèse knows that not only must she not seek to grow but also that she is obliged to remain little.

Her littleness is not an obstacle to sanctity; nor is it a means that appeals to divine help only to support her efforts: Thérèse does not simply ask Jesus to help her climb the stairway of perfection, enabling her to progressively climb each of the steps. Thérèse goes much further in the perception of the primacy of God's action. She expects God to lead her to the summit of perfection according to a properly and almost exclusively divine action. In such a perspective, God's action no longer has as its goal to qualify the virtuous action of the soul; rather it substitutes itself for this action as the principle of the accomplishment of this activity.

The powerlessness is no longer an obstacle but, on the contrary, a necessary condition, an essential disposition of her soul, so God's action might be more complete and the work of transformation more perfect. Even though Thérèse must supply a certain activity, make certain efforts, they are simply a collaboration with God's activity. Actions that are ordinarily powerless manifest good will, safeguard humility, and lead to the more ardent desire of God's help.

Thérèse found a completely theological response to her aspirations which were completely ordered to the possession of love: to attain sanctity, she would place all her hope, all her confidence in the omnipotence of God's action within her and in an always more peaceful acceptance of her poverty.

"The Action of God"

Hope is only Christian and theological when it relies on God alone and when it leaves the primacy to God in the work of transformation and union by love, which is what the image of Jesus' arms—just seen—expresses. In the *Last Conversations,* when commenting on a verse from the Book of Job, Thérèse would say: "This saying of Job: 'If God killed me, I would still hope in him,' delighted me in my childhood. But it was a long time before I established myself in this degree of abandonment. Now I am in it; God put me in it, he took me in his arms and placed me there." (LC, 77)

This text is quoted not so much for the verse from Job, but to emphasize the passivity of Thérèse who was taken by God's action, which explains the last sentence: "God put me in it, he took me in his arms and placed me there." Such passivity belongs to love itself. Love in the natural order makes us capable of loving and being loved, of grasping and being grasped. The love God gives us permits us to love God truly and makes us loveable in God's eyes.

St. John of the Cross says in his *Spiritual Canticle* that the more God "honors and exalts" a soul by his grace the more "he is taken with love for it" and renews the gift of his grace to it. "When God truly loves more, he grants more graces." The holy doctor adds: "Who can say how much God exalts a soul that pleases him? It is impossible to conceive of this. One can only say that here he acts as God and for the sake of showing his magnificence."[46] Thérèse of the Child Jesus marvelously understood this law of supernatural love and abundantly made use of it. Her entire little way is based on this passivity of love to continually attract God's love and action. Her hope, perfect because it was completely poor, would leave to God complete freedom to bestow on her his love and life.

The perfection of the hope Thérèse expresses in terms of abandonment is the fruit of the divine action she recognizes in herself. Only this action of God orders the movement of the soul, giving it a measure that is, not more human, but divine. It purifies theological hope by depriving it of all supports other than God. The soul's movement which is qualified by the virtue of hope will be "ordered," according to St. Thomas's expression, by God's action. The divine action is accomplished by the Gifts of the Holy Spirit—as St. John of the Cross teaches, especially in regard to the virtue of hope. This is why hope must be purified of every support other than God; it must sustain itself in absolute poverty, so that it can be put in motion by this supernatural action of the Holy Spirit: "If the soul wanted to act by its own strength, far from deriving some profit from the work it was forcing itself to do, it would only hinder, by its awkward natural operation, the supernatural work God accomplishes in it by his gifts."[47]

Relying on Romans 8:26, Thérèse states this law of divine action in her own way: "'We do not know how to ask as we should, but the Spirit asks in us with sighs that cannot be expressed.'(St. Paul) We have only to give over our soul, to abandon it to our great God. What does it matter if we have no gifts that shine externally since the King of kings in all his glory shines within!" (L, 863) It is necessary to enter into this passivity where God's action dominates, since God alone can lead the soul to the goal God has set for it; God alone fully knows the place and mission he has determined for everyone in his love.

Thérèse has rediscovered, beginning with her experience and living knowledge of the supernatural realities within her, the great theology of hope—that which gives God absolute primacy in the movement toward the Good that God is. Only God can dispose us to the complete possession of God. No action, no human work, however holy it might be, can dispose us to it—not even great desires for heaven, not even acquired merits. "These are the spiritual merits that make us unjust when we complacently rest in them and when we think they are something of importance," wrote Thérèse in the letter of 17 September 1896 to Marie of the Sacred Heart. (L, 999) She likewise wrote to Céline: "Do not be afraid, the poorer you are, the more Jesus will love you. He will go far, to great lengths to seek you" (L, 1038). To a novice who was saddened by her weaknesses Thérèse also taught: "We are happy to feel weak and miserable, because the more we humbly recognize this, expecting everything freely from God with no merit on our part, the more God lowers himself to magnificently fill us with his gifts."[48]

Poverty, the absence of desire, and weakness, recognized and acknowledged before God, almost irresistibly attract God's Love. For the property of love is to give itself, to extend itself, and it does so to the extent it finds poverty and weakness which permit it to manifest what it is by nature: the free gift of itself. We must now develop this last point to understand how Thérèse teaches the perfection of hope.

The Role of Poverty: "To Receive from Your Love the Eternal Possession of You"

It is actually poverty that perfects hope, or more accurately, that creates the necessary dispositions for the perfection of hope. For only an action of God can perfect the theological life in what is essential. God alone can perfect this theological activity in proportion to its object. Let us recall that hope is a theological virtue having God as object and motive. We hope to obtain the eternal life that will be the vision of God and the source of our happiness. We also hope that God will give us his grace to move toward this goal. We expect this help from God alone, that is, it becomes the object of our hope.

Hope will be more perfect to the extent that we only hope in God, counting only on God to attain sanctity. For, as we know by experience, our hope is far from having this purity. If it is true that we indeed hope for eternal life, we also expect that our Christian life will strengthen us, that it will give us a certain assurance, some certainties, a certain stability in our personal, social, and familial life—a balance. All these gifts are surely desirable, and we must not refuse them when they come our way or when we succeed in acquiring them. What weakens our Christian hope is the attachment to these gifts. This attachment is as harmful as the gifts are spiritual: gifts of the intellect, gifts of the will, gifts of the heart, and even supernatural gifts that are gifts of grace.

The result of this attachment is that we no longer hope in God for himself but for his gifts. There is a potentially more serious consequence: we may rely on these gifts to claim sanctity, to have rights over God. In this case God must, in fact, in all justice, reward us in proportion to our actions. Only poverty of heart will enable hope to attain its perfection, its purity.

Here again, Thérèse has profoundly grasped the teaching of St. John of the Cross. She has truly made her own his doctrine on the absolute poverty that alone can obtain everything from God. God always gives himself freely, but he gives himself to the extent that he finds the heart free from all attachment. In the *Ascent of Mount Carmel* St. John of the Cross writes: "The soul must then let go of all that is not God to be united with God. . . . Every possession is in fact opposed to hope; this virtue has as its object, St. Paul says, 'what it does not possess.' Thus the more the soul (the memory) empties itself, the more hope it acquires; consequently, the more hope it possesses, the more it is united with God. For the more a soul hopes in God, the more it obtains from him. For, I repeat, its hope increases in proportion to its renunciation; it is when it is perfectly stripped of everything that it perfectly enjoys the possession of God and is united with God."[49]

This teaching does not differ from that of Jesus to the rich young man in the Gospel: "If you want to be perfect, go, give all you have to the poor, then come follow me." (Mt 19:21) Jesus thereby teaches what he is and what he himself lives: "The Son of Man has no place to rest his head." (Lk 9:58) St. Paul will take up this great antinomy of the spiritual life: "You know, in fact, the generosity of our Lord Jesus

Christ, who for your sakes became poor, rich though he was, so you can become rich by his poverty." (2 Cor 8:9)

How Thérèse Lived Poverty

This was the poverty Thérèse desired, since it gave God to her more surely than if she saw him. This poverty would be the result of her activity but also the result of God's activity. The theological virtues are the means God has given us to attain him, to know him, and to love him. We must live from their strength and exercise them so they can fortify and purify us. But even given our good will and fidelity, without a special intervention of God, these virtues would always remain very imperfect in their activity.

In order to remain poor and little, Thérèse would renounce everything that could make her grow up in her own eyes or in the eyes of others. She only wanted to act to please Jesus. In the material realm, she would live poverty with much seriousness and sensitivity, preferring the ugliest and least convenient objects. In that, she would fully live out the demands of the Carmelite Rule, adding to it a note of sensitivity and discretion. It is especially in the moral realm that her intense need for poverty is revealed. She knew that what pleased God were not her great desires to work for his glory or even her great desires for martyrdom: "Ah! I really feel that this is not at all what pleases God in my soul. What pleases him is to see me love my littleness and my poverty; it is the blind hope I have in his mercy. . . . This is my treasure." (L, 999)

In order that the love of this littleness, of this poverty grow, Thérèse would practice an asceticism entirely directed toward humility of heart. She would eliminate every search for the extraordinary in this realm. "For Thérèse everything that stood out or required the expenditure of strength was extraordinary, anything not in the line of ordinary duty."[50] At the same time, Thérèse would show a very great generosity in the accomplishment of her tasks, seeking to please her sisters in everything and doing little favors for them. Manuscript C is filled with facts and details that show how Thérèse's love was poured out in the least details.

Thérèse developed this attitude at every opportunity. What especially pleased her was to find herself weak and imperfect despite all her efforts. "When I committed a fault that saddened me, I knew well that this sadness was the result of my infidelity. But do you think I remained there? O no, not at all! I immediately said to God: 'My God, I know that I deserve this feeling of sadness, but let me offer it to you nonetheless as a trial sent by you in love. I am sorry for my sin, but I am content to have this suffering to offer you.'" (LC, 71)

For Thérèse, discouragement in the face of apparently useless efforts indicates that one does not yet have enough confidence in God's mercy. For even in the activity that is within the reach of all, Thérèse affirms the primacy of God's action. We must tirelessly begin again the same efforts, knowing well that we will not succeed in even climbing the first step of the stairway of perfection leading to sanctity. Yet, and here we are at the heart of Thérèse's teaching, "God only asks good will from you! From the top of the stairway, he looks at you lovingly. Soon, overcome by your useless efforts, he will come down himself and, taking you in his arms, will bring you to his kingdom where you will remain forever."[51]

The Passive Purification of Hope

Thérèse's hope would not have been so powerful and so pure if God had not intervened by a direct action to make it perfect. Along with the theological virtues—perfect in themselves to attain God, though we use them imperfectly—God gives us grace, the means to permit God to act in order to perfect this theological activity. In the Christian tradition, these means are called the Gifts of the Holy Spirit. This passive aspect of grace allows us to be moved by God in order to perfect our lives as children of God. Thérèse, with an extreme intuition into supernatural realities, knew how to find the essential dispositions to attract this act of God to her, which was infinitely more efficacious than all our virtuous, meritorious activity. She would not want to acquire merit for herself; it would always be for others.

How was this action of God expressed by her from the perspective of hope? By an experience of the void, of the nothingness she discovered within her. Thérèse noticed within her this poverty which was not the fruit of these efforts: "I can rely on nothing to have confidence, on none of my works." (LC, 137)

This profound awareness that she had of her weakness is completely contemplative. It was the fruit of the encounter of her poverty with the transcendence of God who developed this filial fear in her; Thérèse knew herself to be a child of complete dependence on God. Above all, she feared relying on her own strength, for this would be an infidelity that could cause her to lose union with God.

> I never stop saying to God: "O my God, I beg you, preserve me from the unhappiness of being unfaithful."
>
> Of what infidelity are you speaking?
>
> Of a thought of pride voluntarily entertained. If I said to myself, for example, I acquired such a virtue, I am sure I can practice it. Then that would be relying on your own strength, and when you do that, you may fall into the abyss. But I would have the right, without offending God, of making little mistakes until my death,

> if I am humble, if I remain little. See the children; they never stop breaking things, tearing things, falling, all the while loving their parents very, very much. When I fall, that makes me see my nothingness even more, and I say to myself: what would I do, what would become of me, if I relied on my own strength?

Thérèse illustrates these reflections with the example of St. Peter who denied Christ because "he relied on himself instead of relying solely on the power of God." (LC, 140)

Thérèse recognized that everything good she did came to her from God at the very moment; she recognized "that God placed the treasure in his little child's hand, so he can make use of it when he needs it." She added: "But it's always God's treasure." (LC, 139) It was poverty that created the constant need of God.[52] The filial fear of separating oneself from God, the source of all good, proceeded from love. Hope, purified by poverty, strengthened by the action of God, became the abandonment of the little child in her Father's arms.

4. The Role of Hope in the Little Way

Let us specify the role occupied by the virtue of hope in Thérèse's understanding. The role of the theological virtue of hope in the little way emerges from its theological, or more accurately, Christological foundation.[53]

"He Humbled Himself Even More"—the Condescension of the Son of God

To save us from sin, from the consequences of sin, and to unite us to himself, the Word of God, the Son of God, lowered himself by becoming man and taking on our human condition of weakness and suffering. Even more, as the Letter to the Philippians says: "He humbled himself, becoming obedient even to death, death on a cross. Therefore God exalted him. . . ." (Phil 2:8) It was by this movement of extreme humiliation, the sign of God's excessive love for us, that Christ merited his resurrection and glorification. We are associated with the fruits of his passion and resurrection by a communion of grace and love.

Thus Thérèse understood that the more love lowers itself to give itself, the more it manifests its profound nature. "It is the characteristic of love to lower itself," she wrote in the first pages of her Manuscript A. In the following pages she shows that God did not create only great souls, the holy doctors, the martyrs, but God also created littler, simpler souls. Such is the child who knows nothing or—this is her own expression—" the poor savage who has nothing to guide him but the natural law, and it was to their hearts that he deigned to lower himself; these are the wild flowers whose simplicity delights him. By thus descending, God shows his infinite grandeur." (S, 14)

In the allegory of the little bird at the end of Manuscript B, Thérèse expresses how all her hope rests in this capacity that love has to tend toward the one who is weak and confident: "Therefore, for as long as you desire, O my Beloved, your little bird—[namely Thérèse]—will remain without strength and without wings, its eyes always fixed on you. It wants to be fascinated by your divine gaze, it wants to become the prey of your love. . . ." These first lines indicate Thérèse's faith and fidelity to remain in expectation of God's action, and what dispositions of littleness she maintained in this expectation. Then comes the movement of hope itself: "One day, I hope, adored Eagle, you will come to seek your little bird, and returning to the fire of your love, you will immerse it for all eternity in the burning abyss of this love to which it offered itself as victim." (S, 200) This movement is truly a law of the presence of God's love here below and of his transforming action in hearts. This is why all Thérèse's experience rests in "the habitual movement of the Incarnate Word."[54]

Thérèse's Communion with This Condescension

Thérèse goes even further. She experienced that the greater the condescension, the more God's love is manifested for what it is: "Yes, for love to be fully satisfied, it must lower itself, it must lower itself to nothingness and it must transform this nothingness into fire." (S, 195) Thérèse would thus participate in this condescension by her own littleness, by lowering herself as well.

In a letter to her sister Céline dated 25 April 1893, she expressed this communion with the condescension of Jesus by comparing it to a wild flower that collects a drop of dew. Thérèse is addressing Céline, but she herself is the dewdrop that, hidden in the wildflower, must refresh it by its simple presence.

> During the night of life she will have to remain hidden from every human glance, but when the shadows begin to fade, when the wildflower becomes the Sun of Justice, when he comes to carry out his giant's race, will he forget his little dewdrop? Oh no! As soon as he appears in glory, the companion of his exile will appear there too. The Divine Sun will cast over her one of his rays of love, and immediately will present to the angels and saints the little dewdrop who will shine like a precious diamond, and who, reflecting the Sun of Justice, will become like him. But that is not all. The Divine Star, by looking at his dewdrop, will draw her to himself; she will ascend like a light vapor and take her place for all eternity in the heart of the burning fire of uncreated love and will be united with him forever. Just as on earth she was the faithful com-

> panion of his exile, of his scorn, in heaven she will reign eternally. (L, 785)

To share in this intimate communion with the mysteries of Jesus, Thérèse knew that she had to remain very little, like a dewdrop. She knew as well that this littleness, when it is lived in love, powerfully attracts God's transforming action. For Thérèse, to be little "was to recognize her nothingness, to expect everything from God, like a child expects everything from his father; it is not to be anxious about anything, not to seek to earn any fortune." (LC, 138) Littleness and poverty are closely linked in her thought. They are the essential dispositions of heart which form humility and which attract God's gift.

Thérèse knew that sanctification is not measured by human standards; that everything good she could do would always be insufficient to merit the sanctity she desired, that all human works are tainted with imperfection.[55] She would rely neither on her strength nor on her good works to earn heaven, but only on the love of God who gives to the extent that poverty provides greater receptivity. In a letter addressed to Sister Marie of the Sacred Heart, Thérèse expressed this very intense connection between transforming love and poverty of heart:

> O my dear sister, I beg you, understand your little daughter, understand that to love Jesus, to be his victim of love, the more weak one is, without desires, without virtues, the more one is suitable for the operations of this consuming, transforming love. . . . The sole desire to be a victim is enough, but you must consent to always remain poor and weak, and that is the difficult thing for "true poverty of spirit is hard to acquire. It must be sought after far off," said the psalmist. . . . He did not say that it must be sought after among great souls, but "far off," that is, in lowliness, in noth-

> ingness. . . . Ah! Let us keep from all that shines, let us love our littleness, let us love not feeling anything, then we will be poor in spirit and Jesus will come to seek us, far off as we may be, he will transform us into flames of love. . . . (L, 999)

Thus is the theological hope that reveals to us Thérèse's holiness. Moved by love, hope becomes confidence. Lived ordinarily in poverty, it turns to God as toward its father and creates the filial attitude of abandonment. As Fr. Marie-Eugène wrote: "confidence is theological hope inspired by love; abandonment is the hope that is no longer expressed only by distinct acts but which creates an attitude of soul."[56]

The little way indicates how we are to dispose ourselves to such a transformation by placing ourselves under God's action. It especially tells us how to keep alive this hope and this confidence through the trials and fatigue of daily tasks, even in the midst of suffering itself. Even more, Thérèse shows us how to offer our poverty to God so that he may come to us. She teaches us to appear before God "with empty hands" in order "to receive from your *Love* the eternal possession of *yourself.*" (S, 277)

5. Thérèse's Maternal Hope

We might criticize Christian hope for being too individualistic. The aspiration to happiness, the "possession of heaven," according to Thérèse's expression, seems in fact to emphasize the very personal character of such an aspiration. However, Christian hope is completely open to the other, to the very measure of Christ's love to which it directs the aspirations and desires of the heart. By hope, the Christian is led to participate in love according to the "mind of Christ" (Phil 2:5), as St. Paul says, adding that "Christ died for us while we were still sinners." (Rom 5:8) If such a love includes all men and women in the same plan of salvation, how can one hope to receive this salvation for oneself without expecting it with the same hope for all?

Thérèse, who lived the demands of love to the extent of complete self-giving, gives us the enlightening answer of her example. The hope that moved her developed from merciful love. This love grasped her, protected her from her childhood, and manifested itself as an "unfathomable abyss." (S, 256) Love, without which all would be in vain, was the root of her hope and made her participate in the activity of Christ's life in the Church. At the heart of the Church, Thérèse desired to be identified with love. This love thirsted to expand, to give itself.

"My First Child"

The Christmas grace of 1886 was Thérèse's fundamental experience of God's merciful love for her. She received this love in the light of Christmas. God's love only takes possession of a soul to associate it with his richness: "More merciful to me than he was to his disciples, Jesus himself took the net, cast it, and withdrew it full of fish. He made me a fisher of souls; I felt a great desire to work for the conversion of sinners." (S, 99)

Thérèse took care to specify that this desire, though not new in her, nonetheless acquired a new intensity. In Manuscript A, Thérèse placed the account of Pranzini's conversion a few lines after that of the Christmas grace. Between these two relatively detailed accounts, she briefly relates how her great desire to work for the conversion of sinners was more explicitly attached to the mystery of the passion and cross of Jesus. "One Sunday, when looking at a picture of our Lord on the cross, I was struck by the blood that fell from one of his divine hands and I was distressed to think that this blood was falling to the ground without anyone rushing to collect it; I resolved to keep myself in spirit at the foot of the cross to receive this divine dew flowing from it, understanding that I then had to pour it over souls." (S, 99)

In these first lines, Thérèse looks at the mystery of the cross and understands what her attitude before it must be. To share in this mystery and absorb its fruitfulness, she will keep herself in spirit at the foot of the cross. Thérèse also tells us what her association with fruitfulness was: she understood that she had to pour this "divine dew" over souls. By her love, she penetrated the meaning of Christ's offering: all the love of Jesus is offered her so she can offer it in turn. By gathering this scorned love in solitude,[57] Thérèse wanted to extend it to those who do not stand at the foot of the cross. Her love is already maternal: it receives only to give, it bears within it the hope of richness.

With this first explanation of the love that dwelt within her and the love that the image of Jesus on the cross obtained for her, Thérèse also includes Jesus' cry from the cross: "I thirst." "These words inflamed within me a very vivid and unknown ardor. I wanted to give my Beloved to drink, and I felt myself devoured by a thirst for souls. It was not yet the souls of priests that attracted me but those of great sinners, and I was burning with the desire to snatch them from the eternal flames." (S, 99)

Pranzini's conversion was to confirm her in the depths and nature of her desire. A few minutes before his execution, Pranzini kissed three times the crucifix offered to him. For Thérèse, this sign was a confirmation of her powerful desire to save souls "I had obtained the 'sign' I asked for, and this sign was the faithful reproduction of the graces Jesus had given me to attract me to pray for sinners. Was it not before the *wounds of Jesus,* seeing his divine *blood* flow, that the thirst for souls entered into my heart? I wanted to give them this *immaculate blood* to drink which would purify them from their stains—and the lips of *'my first child'* were pressed to the sacred wounds! What an unspeakably sweet answer!" (S, 100)

By designating Pranzini as her "first child," Thérèse reveals to us the maternal character of the love that motivated her. Love is essentially maternal because it is foreseeing. Was this not the way Thérèse designated the love that God manifested for her?[58] Thérèse knew this love of God that manifests its tenderness when united with suffering, thus creating resemblance.[59]

The Table of Sinners

In her trial of faith, the hope by which Thérèse hoped for Pranzini's conversion was to be extended to sinners. In this trial, Thérèse shared the experience of the darkness of those who do not believe in heaven, in salvation: "During those joyful days of Easter time, Jesus made me feel that there really were souls who had no faith, who by the abuse of grace lost this precious treasure, source of the only pure and true joys." (S, 211) By being deprived of the joy received from the approaching hope of heaven, Thérèse too shared their condition. She accepted this trial as a gift of Jesus by which he associated her with the redemption and the hope of its fullness.

Thérèse expressed the redemptive value of this trial very clearly. She understood the light of redemption: to save us from our sins, Jesus did not remain outside the world, but he came among us and, for our sakes, he who was without sin became sin. (2 Cor 5:21) Thérèse understood that she had to be willing to enter into this movement of the redemption in order to intercede for sinners and ask forgiveness in their name.

Therefore, this trial took on the figure and obedience of Christ who, for our salvation, "became obedient unto death, even death on a cross." (Phil 2:8) Thérèse was "willing to eat the bread of suffering"; she "did not want to get up from this table filled with bitterness . . .

before the day" fixed by God; she was indeed "willing to eat alone the bread of the trial until it pleased God to bring her into the light of his kingdom." In this trial, she implored as the only grace never to offend God. This is why she could use this trial to ask for the justification of all those for whom she shared the darkness: "But can she not also say in her name, in the name of her brothers: *'Have mercy on us, Lord, for we are poor sinners!'* Oh! Lord, send us away justified. May all those who are not yet enlightened by the luminous torch of faith see it shine at last." (S, 212)

At the heart of the trial, Thérèse professed her faith in heaven and her hope; she hoped thereby to merit for sinners the possession of heaven: "I tell him (Jesus) that I am happy not to enjoy this beautiful heaven on earth so that he might open it for eternity to poor unbelievers." (S, 214) In her hope for heaven, Thérèse brings with her sinners, "her brothers," to whom she is bound by love.

"Draw Me and We Shall Run"

This hope for the salvation of all has its foundation in love. The hope that makes us desire a good we do not yet possess only concerns the one who hopes. Theological hope, considered in itself, makes us desire the eternal possession of God for ourselves. This aspect of "for self" is essential to Christian hope and to its universalism. Actually this is what permits the progressive invasion of the whole being by love and brings about union with God. The hope for others is developed from the love we have for them. It is by loving them that we hope, for them, what we hope for ourselves. Since the love of God could not be true without the love of others, hope for self is also at the same time hope for others.

In the second part of her last manuscript, Manuscript C, Thérèse speaks in particular about love of neighbor. With astonishing clarity she establishes this connection between hope for others and love. First of all, Thérèse explains how God himself enabled her to better understand what love of neighbor was: "This year, my dear Mother, God gave me the grace of understanding what love is." (S, 219) Thérèse clarified this development of the second commandment, "like the first," by referring to Jesus' discourse at the Last Supper. For Thérèse, whose heart burned more with love than those of his disciples on Holy Thursday, the commandment to love our neighbor was truly the new commandment: "Oh! How I love it since it gives me the assurance that your will is to love in me all those you command me to love!"[60] For Thérèse, all the newness of the commandment resides in the assurance that it is Jesus himself who loves in her when, despite her weakness and imperfection, she loves those whom God has entrusted to her.[61]

In the continuation of Manuscript C, Thérèse again takes up this perspective of hope linked with love. A verse of the Song of Songs enables her to understand how she would accomplish her mission:[62] "Jesus gave me a simple way to accomplish my mission. He made me understand this saying from the Song of Songs: *'Draw me, we will run after the fragrance of your perfumes. . . .'* Lord, I understand, when a soul lets itself be captivated *by the intoxicating fragrance of your perfumes,* she cannot run alone, all the souls she loves are drawn after her; this happens without constraint, without effort, it is a natural consequence of her attraction to you." (S, 254) Thérèse completes this interpretation of the Song of Songs with two images: the torrent that carries off everything in its wake and the iron that, inflamed by the fire, becomes incandescent like it.

The Prayer of Jesus

However, in an even more profound manner than in these comparisons, Thérèse will find the measure of her hope in the priestly prayer of Jesus. To express her hope, she will take up Jesus' priestly prayer and make it her own.[63] She will appropriate all its words and, with them, the very hope of Jesus, a hope that effects the accomplishment of the mystery of the Church. Thérèse realized that God alone knows the glory he has reserved to each one. Thus can she not ask, like Jesus, that those whom God has entrusted to her share his glory? However, this is not the perspective she first assumes when she takes up Jesus' request, but rather the perspective of the unity that is the first mark of the Church.[64] "I simply want to ask that one day we all may be reunited in your beautiful heaven." (S, 256)

The foundation of this hope and that of the prayer that expresses it is the love that God manifested to Thérèse, the depth of which she cannot measure. In a few lines, Thérèse brings together all the dimensions of her life from the perspective of love: "You know, O my God, my only desire has been to love you; I seek no other glory. Your love protected me from my childhood, it grew with me, and now it is an abyss whose depth I cannot sound. Love attracts love, therefore, my Jesus, mine soars to you. I would like to fill the abyss that draws it, but alas! it is not even a dewdrop lost in the ocean! To love you as you love me, I must borrow your own love, only then will I find rest. O my Jesus, perhaps it is an illusion, but it seems to me that you could not fill a soul with more love than you have filled mine; that is why I dare ask you *'to love those you have given me as you have loved me'* (Jn 17:23)." (S, 256) Thérèse's hope was sustained by the love God manifested to her and which she wanted to return to him. It is so universal, so broad because Thérèse allowed herself to be fully drawn by this love of Jesus. In him she discovered the nature and scope of her mission.

"All My Hopes Have Been Fulfilled"

Thérèse lived her desire to love in the hope and expectation of its complete fulfillment. Thérèse attributed the sufferings of the last months of her life to this great desire "to save souls." [65] In it she saw the fulfillment of all her hopes: "It is unbelievable how God has fulfilled all my hopes. When I read St. John of the Cross, I begged God to effect in me what he says, namely, the same thing as if I lived to be very old; finally to consume me rapidly in Love, and I was answered." (LC, 177)

To die of love would be the heart of Thérèse's hope and its most intense source. She desired the death of love which, for her, was the death of Jesus on the cross—a death that was obscure, hidden in suffering and anguish.[66] Death lived out in the love of Jesus accomplishes the paschal mystery. All Christian hope is centered in him since under the apparent triumph of death is hidden the triumph of love. Thérèse expresses this pull toward the paschal mystery in the last stanza of the poem "To Live by Love":

> To die of love is my only hope
> When I shall see my bonds broken.
> God himself will be my reward.
> I want no other goods,
> I want to be inflamed by his love.
> I want to see him, to be united with him forever,
> That is my heaven, my destiny:
> To live by love! (P, 92)

Notes

This essay originally appeared as a chapter in *Thérèse de l'Enfant-Jésus. Docteur de l'Amour* (Venasque [France]: Éditions du Carmel, 1990), 237-

70. Quotations from St. Thérèse's writings in this chapter have been translated directly from the French of Fr. Niqueux's essay. For the benefit of English readers, references to these quotations in the text and the Notes are to the ICS (Institute of Carmelite Studies) English translations of Thérèse's writings. The citations note the volume and page numbers in the ICS translations. The abbreviations for these translations are: S = *Story of a Soul* (3rd ed., 1996), LC = *Last Conversations*, L = *Letters*, and P = *Poetry*.

1 From a theological point of view, the comprehension of the mystery of God signifies his full possession at the end of earthly life. That is why the comprehension of the mystery of God is the object of the theological virtue of hope, but it is also what brings it to an end just as the face-to-face vision of God brings an end to faith. While vision is radically opposed to faith, hope, which in this life tends to the full possession of God in and by love, already permits a certain comprehension of it (cf. St. Thomas Aquinas, *Summa Theologica,* I, q. 12, a.7, ad 1). Thérèse does not generally use the verb "see" in a theological context except to affirm, as she would do during her last illness, that she never desired to see the saints or to have visions (cf. LC, 4 June, p. 55; 4 Aug., 4, p. 132; 11 Aug., 5, p. 146; 11 Sept., 7, p. 188). In the first Manuscript, she only uses the word "vision" to speak of the prophetic vision of her father's illness. (S, 45-47) It actually occurred between 1879 or 1880.) On the other hand, Thérèse, gifted with a great theological sense, willingly uses the word "understand" each time she wants to express how a new, important penetration into the things of God is realized for her. The use that she makes of it exceeds the simple notional comprehension and includes a connotation of the reality itself in the area of charity (for example, S, 13-14, 27, 194ff., 211-12, 219, etc.).

2 P. Marie-Eugène de l'Enfant-Jésus, *Je veux voir Dieu* (Venasque [France]: Éditions du Carmel, 1988), 662.

3 Before entering Carmel, Thérèse was delighted to have been able to teach children, to open them to the riches of the grace of baptism: ". . . it was a great pleasure for me to see with what candor they believed everything I told them. Baptism must place in souls a very deep seed of the theological virtues since from childhood they are already evident and the hope of future benefits is enough to allow for the acceptance of sacrifices." (S, 112)

4 *Summa Theologica*, I-II, q. 62, a. 3, ad 3.

5 Ibid., q. 67, a 4.

6 *Je veux voir Dieu,* 825.

7 Ibid., 835.

8 Thérèse encountered many difficulties of a relational nature with those around her. She also suffered from her own make-up. She would speak of

the trial of timidity that she experienced: "It cost me a great deal to ask to do penances in the refectory because I was shy. I would blush but I was still faithful to the practice twice a month." (LC, 180, 2 Sept., 3; cf. LC, 69, 30 June, 2: "My timidity came from an extreme embarrassment that I felt when anyone had anything to do with me.") She also expressed the uneasiness that her body caused her, being little: "My body always was an embarrassment; I was not comfortable in it, though little, I was ashamed." (LC, 118, 30 July,1)

9 In the *Last Conversations*, Thérèse recalls all the delays she experienced and that they were painful to her. "I think that for my death, the same patience that was needed for the other great events of my life will be called for. Look: I entered Carmel young and nevertheless, after all had been decided, I had to wait three months; for the reception of the habit, the same thing; for my profession, the same thing again. Well, for my death it will be the same, it will come soon but I will still have to wait." (LC, 6 July, 2, pp. 74-75)

10 Cf. S, 149: "God gave me the grace of having NO illusions upon entering Carmel. I found religious life to be as I imagined it; no sacrifice surprised me and yet, you know, dear Mother, my first steps met with more thorns than roses! Yes, suffering opened its arms to me and I threw myself into them with love."

11 On 3 August 1897, Thérèse qualified the sufferings of her illness: "I have suffered a long time, but little sufferings. Since 28 July, they have been great sufferings." (LC, 3 Aug., 8. p. 131)

12 Thérèse, even though she manifested and experienced a great capacity for suffering, never voluntarily sought suffering, nor greater sufferings. When suffering presented itself to her, she desired to welcome it as a sign of God's love and the means to be united with Jesus for the salvation of souls. "I never wanted to ask God for greater sufferings. If he increased them, I bore them gladly and joyfully since they came from him. But I was too little to have the strength myself. If I asked for sufferings, they would be my sufferings and I would have to bear them alone, and I could never do anything by myself." (LC, 11 Aug., 3, p. 145)

13 "Yes, that's right. Actually, I am no longer, as in my childhood, open to every pain. I am resurrected; I am no longer at the place one may think. . . . Oh, don't feel sorry for me. I have come to no longer be able to suffer because all suffering is sweet to me." (LC, 29 May, p. 52)

14 "Since my First Communion, since I asked Jesus to change all earth's consolations into bitterness for me, I have the perpetual desire to suffer. However, I do not think of making my joy out of it. It was a grace granted to me later. Until then, it was like a spark hidden under ashes, and like the flowers of a tree that must become fruit in their time. But always seeing my

flowers fall, that is, letting myself go to tears when I was suffering, I said to myself with astonishment and sadness: 'But these will always only be desires!'" (LC, 31 July, 13, p. 123)

15 "I have found happiness and joy on earth, but only in suffering; for I have suffered a great deal here below; souls must be told this."(LC, 31 July, 13, p. 123)

16 Cf. LC, 8 Aug., 3, p. 142: "Today I thought about my past life, about the act of courage I formerly made at Christmas and the praise addressed to Judith came to mind: 'You acted with a virile courage and your heart is strengthened.' Many souls say: 'But I don't have the strength to accomplish such a sacrifice.' Let them do what I did: make a great effort. God does not refuse the first grace that provides the courage to act. After that, the heart is strengthened and one goes from victory to victory."

17 For Thérèse, love never manifests itself so well as when it transforms in an instant: "Céline, it seems to me that God does not need years to accomplish his work of love in a soul, a ray of his heart can in an instant make his flower blossom for eternity." (L, 714)

18 "I felt in the depth of my heart the certitude that our desires would be satisfied, but in order to give myself the courage to continue to pray for sinners, I said to God that I was indeed sure he would pardon the poor miserable Pranzini, that I believed it even if he did not confess and gave no sign of repentance, so confident was I in the infinite mercy of Jesus, but I asked for a 'sign' of repentance for my simple consolation. My prayer was answered to the letter." (S, 100)

19 Cf. S, 64: "Fortunately, I would have heaven to avenge myself. My spouse is very rich and I will draw from his treasures of love to return to you a hundredfold all you suffered on account of me."

20 For Thérèse's entire Act of Offering to Merciful Love, see S, 276-77. On 8 August 1897, Thérèse, when someone had taken her by surprise as she was looking at the heavens, remembered that, since her Act of Offering, everything she did, even the most insignificant things like looking at the heavens, was done by love. "Ah! She thought I was looking at the firmament while thinking about the true heaven! No! It was simply because I was admiring the material heavens; the other is more and more closed to me. Then I immediately said to myself with great sweetness: 'Oh yes, it is indeed by love that I look at the heavens; yes, it is by love for God since everything I do, movements, gazes, everything since my Offering is done by love.'" (LC, 8 Aug., 2, p. 141) From this simple reflection, we better perceive how Thérèse lived this Act of Offering and how it was inscribed especially in the area of the will by leaving sensitivity in an impression of poverty.

21 At the end of her first Manuscript, Thérèse offers a commentary on her Act of Offering which emphasizes the motive. (S, 180-81)

22 For the structure of this text and its detailed analysis, see F. M. Léthel, *Connaître l'amour du Christ qui surpasse toute connaissance. La Théologie des saints* (Venasque [France]; Éditions du Carmel, 1989), 528-53.

23 S, 192. This perspective is the one developed by John of the Cross in stanzas 9 to 11 of Spiritual Canticle B (the one Thérèse had at her disposal). "The soul in these stanzas again addresses her Beloved and brings before him her complaint. Impatient love such as that which torments her brings neither respite nor repose. She ceaselessly repeats her anguish, always hoping to find a remedy." (*The Spiritual Canticle* [B], 9.2)

24 In the continuation of the Manuscript, Thérèse will return to this anxiety concerning the purity of her love. "But is PURE LOVE in my heart? Are my immense desires not a dream, a folly? Ah, if it were so, Jesus, enlighten me. You know I seek the truth." (S, 197)

25 Cf. S, 195, which is inspired by St. John of the Cross in *Spiritual Canticle* B. 9: "For the payment of love is love, and the soul insofar as she has attained the perfection of love can only desire the increase of her love." (*The Spiritual Canticle* [B], 9.7)

26 Cf. S, 256: "To love you as you love me, I must borrow your own love, then alone will I find rest."

27 "In the spiritual marriage, the soul continues its journey to God. His love possesses her only in shadow. The living faith that illumines it becomes each day more desirous of light. Its hope, purified by love, becomes more ardent, though peaceful. Love itself remains the self-communicating good, the impulse of which nothing could thereafter hinder. It is more dynamic than ever. Living faith supplies it with certitude that enlightens in the shadows. Hope puts at its service swift wings to cross with sure and rapid flight the distances that separate it from its infinite object. Love becomes a living flame in making an ever more complete gift of itself." (*Je veux voir Dieu*, 982-83)

28 L, 809 Cf: "He does not want us to love him for his gift. *He himself* must be our *reward.*"

29 Cf. S, 196: "Riches and glory (even the glory of heaven) do not lay claim to the heart of the little child. . . . What it asks for is love."

30 St. Thomas Aquinas shows that perfect hope is attained when it is in total dependence on charity; in fact, since all charity has value for eternity, it alone is able to communicate its perfection to all things. Cf. *Summa Theologica,* I-II, q. 17, a. 8.

31 Léthel, *Connaître l'amour du Christ,* 523.

32 S, 214. In these pages, all Thérèse's words have great significance. Thus, this statement that faith and hope have to do with the will: "I sing what I want to

believe."

33 Cf. LC, 3 July, 3, p. 72: "Ah! But I believe in the Thief! It is on heaven that everything bears. How strange and inconsistent!"

34 Faith and hope are united in the love of their object which is God, known and desired. "To believe in the benefits to come is nothing other than hope," wrote St. Augustine, *Enchiridion,* II, 8. The trial that touched Thérèse in her belief in the existence of heaven also touched her in her hope. This trial especially moved her to manifest a greater love for God and men.

35 The deception about the end of hope had to do with the trial of faith since faith is founded on the word of God that cannot deceive nor be deceived.

36 Thérèse symbolically lived this confession of faith by carrying on her person the Creed written in her own blood.

37 Having arrived at the threshold of his passion, Jesus said: "No one takes my life, I give it freely." (Jn 10:18) In this night of faith, Thérèse fully offered the suffering of this new deprivation that took all enjoyment from her of her own salvation as she also entered into her own passion.

38 Cf. S, 214. The church teaches that discouragement and despair are faults against the virtue of hope.

39 Cf. LC, 5 Sept., 1, p. 184, To Mother Agnes who asked her if she was sad to leave her, Thérèse replied: "No! . . . If there were no eternal life, then yes! . . . but perhaps there is . . . indeed, it's certain!" Likewise, as quoted in LC, 15 Aug., 7, p. 150: "I wonder how God can hold back so long from taking me. . . . Thus, you would say that he wants to 'delude' me into believing that there is no heaven! . . . All the saints I so love, where are they nested? . . . I am not pretending, truly I see nothing at all. But I must indeed sing strongly in my heart. 'After death, there is life immortal,' otherwise, it would turn out badly." Mother Agnes understood the depths of this trial and when Thérèse entered into this agony, she went to pray before the statue of the Sacred Heart that she would not die in despair.

40 This last statement of Thérèse is brought to light by the teaching of St. John of the Cross on spiritual joy. The saint recalls that Christians must attribute all joy to God alone and desire only to please God in everything they do. "They should desire in secret that only God be pleased and joyful over their works. They should have no other interest or satisfaction than the honor and glory of God" (*Ascent of Mount Carmel*, 3.27.5).

41 LC, 13 July, 17, pp. 94-95. According to Thérèse, the thought of heaven always accompanied this hope of being able to love without limits. "Oh! How beautiful our religion is. Instead of shrinking hearts (as the world believes), it raises them and makes them capable of *loving, loving* with a love that is *almost infinite* since it must continue after this mortal life, which is given to us to acquire the homeland of heaven where we will find the dear

ones whom we have loved on earth." (L, 865-66)

42 Fr. S. Pinckaers explains thus the division of the object of hope: "Hope, like faith, is a virtue of imperfection, contrary to charity, which effectively unites to God. Faith and hope preside at the passage from the imperfect to the perfect. They must contain an element of perfection, of union with God: it is the adhesion of faith to first truth and the reliance of hope on divine help; thus an element of imperfection directed to perfection. This is the state of man, still imperfect, who seeks his completion in the order of truth—this will be the Beatific Vision—and in the order of appetite—this will be perfect beatitude. The principal element is adhesion to God who orders all the movement." (Servais Pinckaers, *Le renouveau de la morale,* Téqui, 1978, 230).

43 *Spiritual Canticle* [B], 28. 4: "The soul rejoices only in God, it hopes only in God, it fears only God, and it is afflicted only according to God."

44 *Ascent of Mount Carmel,* 3. 15. 1; *Je veux voir Dieu,* 827.

45 *Je veux voir Dieu,* 310-311.

46 *Spiritual Canticle* [B], 33. 8.

47 *Ascent of Mount Carmel,* 3. 13. 3.

48 Sister Marie of the Trinity, *Une novice de sainte Thérèse* (Paris: Les Éditions du Cerf, 1985), 110.

49 *Ascent of Mount Carmel,* 3. 7. 2.

50 *Je veux voir Dieu,* 852.

51 *Une novice de sainte Thérèse,* 111.

52 An example: when someone admired her patience in her trial, she replied: "I do not have a minute of patience. This is not my patience. You are always mistaken." (LC, 18 Aug., 4, p. 153; cf. LC, 20 Sept., 1, p. 193)

53 For a detailed study of the Little Way, see Conrad de Meester, *Dynamique de la Confiance, Genèse et structure de la "voie d'enfance spirituelle" chez Ste. Thérèse de Lisieux,* Paris, 1969, and especially p. 359 and following for the theological character of hope and confidence.

54 *Je veux voir Dieu,* 1031.

55 Cf. Act of Offering to Merciful Love, S, 277.

56 *Je veux voir Dieu,* 837.

57 Beginning with the texts of Isaiah on the Suffering Servant, and more particularly Is 63:3-5, Thérèse felt that the mystery of suffering and the cross is only discovered in solitude. (L, 862)

58 Cf. S, 174: "God is more tender than a mother."

59 Cf. L, 896-97: "He finds you worthy of suffering for his love and this is the greatest proof of tenderness he can give you, for suffering makes us like him."

60 S, 221: "Ah! Lord, I know you do not command anything impossible. You know better than I my weakness, my imperfection; you well know that I

could never love my Sisters as you love them, unless you yourself, O my Jesus, *love them in me.* It is because you wanted to grant me this grace that you have given a *new* commandment."

61 Here we find again Thérèse's concern to give to God's action and influence the first place in her own activity. This activity, imperfect in itself, finds a new perfection when Thérèse is united with Jesus. "When I am charitable, it is Jesus alone who acts in me; the more I am united with him, the more I love my Sisters." (S, 221) After emphasizing this primacy of God's action, Thérèse tells us how she brings her contribution to this action, how she tries to convince herself of the good intentions of those around her.

62 Thérèse speaks of the mission she must fulfill very concretely to the novices entrusted to her and to the two missionaries she supports by her prayers and letters. We can expand the sense of this mission on the spiritual plane since Thérèse wrote concerning the second missionary she was asked to take on: "I think as you do, Mother. *'The zeal of the Carmelite must embrace the world.'* I hope I can by the grace of God be useful to more than two missionaries."(S, 253)

63 Thérèse did not hesitate to transpose to the feminine the excerpts from chap. 17 of John's Gospel which she quoted at length, applying to herself the words of the prodigal son's father to his older son: "EVERYTHING *I have is yours.*" (Cf. S, 255-56)

64 Cf. Niceno-Constantinopolitan (commonly called Nicene) Creed.

65 Cf. LC, 30 Sept., p. 205: "Never would I have believed that it was possible to suffer so much. Never. I can only explain this by the ardent desires I have to save souls."

66 Cf. LC, 4 July, 2, p. 73: "Our Lord died on the cross in anguish and this was the most beautiful death of love. This is the only one that was seen. No one saw the death of the Blessed Virgin. To die of love is not to die in transports. I admit it frankly, it seems to me that this is what I am experiencing."

"Something Surprising": Reflections on the Proclamation of St. Thérèse of Lisieux as "Doctor of the Universal Church"

Steven Payne, O.C.D.
Carmelite House of Studies
Nairobi, Kenya

> MARTYR. . . . Ah! in spite of my littleness, I would like to enlighten souls as did the *Prophets* and the *Doctors.* I have the *vocation of the Apostle.* I would like to travel over the whole earth to preach your Name. . . . But *O my Beloved,* one mission alone would not be sufficient for me, I would want to preach the Gospel on all the five continents simultaneously and even to the remotest isles. I would be a missionary, not for a few years only but from the beginning of creation until the consummation of the ages. (S, 192-93 [B 2v-3r])[1]

At the beginning of October 1999, the National Shrine of the Immaculate Conception in Washington, DC, hosted two Masses honoring St. Thérèse in the presence of her relics, which had been brought "on pilgrimage" to the United States. The crowds were larger than anyone expected, standing-room-only, even though both liturgies were at noon on a weekday. In the evenings, when the relics went to Whitefriars Hall on Webster Street, or to our Discalced Carmelite monastery on Lincoln Road, the pilgrims just kept on coming.

The same story was repeated virtually everywhere the relics traveled in their four-month tour. The Detroit papers reported, for example, that upwards of 50,000 people came to view and pray before the relics while they were at the Little Flower Shrine in Royal Oak, Michigan, the church built by the famous radio-priest, Fr. Charles Coughlin.

I have to confess a curious feeling when I was looking out over the huge crowd in the National Shrine, because my mind went back to a similar occasion two years before, in October of 1997. Then also there had been a Mass in the upper church of the shrine, the high point of a weekend celebration honoring the centenary of the death of St. Thérèse and her upcoming doctorate. Then also Bishop Patrick Ahern delivered the homily. We had spent over six months organizing the festivities. We had notified all of the local newspapers, thinking there would be a keen interest among religion editors in the news of a young twenty-four-year-old nun being declared a "doctor of the universal church," only the third woman to be given this title. But the media barely responded, and the Shrine itself was only a little over half full—a respectable showing, but far fewer than I had expected.

A few weeks later, as it happens, I was in St. Peter's Square when Pope John Paul II officially declared Thérèse a doctor. The crowd was very large, but evidently not as large as for her beatification in 1923 and her canonization in 1925.[2] And interestingly, the most emotional moment for me (and for many, I suspect) came not with the actual declaration itself but immediately afterward, when members of various missionary groups threw flower petals over the *reliquary* that had been placed in front of the altar.

And so I wondered: What, if anything, do the differences in the turnouts mean? Admittedly, the visit of the relics has been better publicized than previous celebrations, as a truly national event. The secular media's interest is certainly piqued by the idea of the remains of a dead saint being carted around the United States in this day and age for the people's veneration.

But it goes beyond that. There is something immediate and concrete about Thérèse's relics that people related to in a very deep and personal way. Granted, you didn't really "see" anything; no one outside Lisieux knows precisely what the ornate wooden reliquary contains. Granted, too, there are plenty of Thérèse relics already distributed all over North America. Still, when you observed the people coming to visit the reliquary, or when you heard what they said when they were interviewed by local news reporters, it seems clear that they were relating not to the *bones* but to the *person* of Thérèse, that they somehow felt very close to her in that context. Far from treating the relics as magic talismans, many came not merely to ask favors but also out of a sense of gratitude for favors already received. Whatever one may think of the countless stories of "roses," it's quite clear that this simple woman who died virtually unknown over a century ago has touched more lives more deeply than we can ever imagine. It demonstrates that, whatever the changes in the Church since Vatican II, there is still this deep well of Catholic "popular religion" or "popular piety," which in recent years has seldom been tapped or expressed, and which in this case, fortunately, was not hijacked for ideological purposes by any particular faction. Young and old, women and men, liberals and conservatives (whatever those slippery terms mean today), laity and religious: all kinds of people came because Thérèse somehow speaks to them about how to find God in the midst of what seem to be the very hidden, undramatic, ordinary lives that most of us live.

A Saint with a "Doctrine"

Does all of this mean that the bestowing of the title "doctor of the universal church" on St. Thérèse is ultimately irrelevant to the average Catholic? Was Rome merely casting around for just any new honor to add to those she already has been given? (As one friar said to me jokingly, "Now all that's left is to have her declared mediatrix of all graces!") If so, we could simply pass over this unusual Vatican decision in silence and move on.

However, there is obviously more to it than that. Notice, for example, that Pope John Paul II, who was not shy about multiplying blesseds and saints, did not choose to name any other doctor during his long pontificate. Notice, too, that virtually all the local news stories, as the relics progressed around the country, considered it at least worth mentioning that Thérèse is the latest and youngest "doctor of the church." More than that, almost every pilgrim interviewed spoke not just of her example but also of her *teaching,* of her "little way" of confidence in God's merciful love, of her message that we can become saints by doing ordinary things with extraordinary love, or however they chose to express it.

Compare that with virtually any of the other thirty-two "doctors of the church," even those most popular, like St. Anthony of Padua. With all due apologies to the Franciscans, although Anthony has a very devoted following and is much loved, one would probably find few ordinary believers who have actually read any of his works or could identify him with any particular "doctrine." Or consider, at the other extreme, St. Thomas Aquinas; with all due apologies to the Dominicans, one could argue that people can significantly benefit from Thomas's doctrine without knowing many details about his life. With Thérèse, however, her life and her "doctrine" are one and inseparable. Certainly, ordinary believers regard her as a model and patron, but they also spontaneously look to her as a *teacher* with a specific message that they can understand and put into practice; in contrast to the sublime writings of so many other doctors which are gathering dust on the shelves, ordinary people actually read and reflect on *Story of a Soul!* In that sense, to adapt Keith J. Egan's felicitous phrase, Thérèse was already a doctor *in* the church long before she was declared a doctor *of* the church.[3] Once again, as with her beatification and canonization, it's as if the hierarchy were simply formalizing and catching up with what the sense of the faithful, the *sensus fidelium,* had already decided. If in one sense Pope John Paul II *created* a new "doctor of the universal church," in another sense he just officially *recognized* a role Thérèse is already playing among the people of God.

When the pope suddenly announced in late August of 1997 that he intended to name Thérèse a doctor within a few weeks, even the Carmelites were caught a bit off guard. To be sure, there had been rumors for years that this might be coming. We all knew, for example, that the diocese of Bayeux and Lisieux, as well as Bishop Patrick Ahern of New York, had written to all of the bishops' conferences around the world asking them to petition for Thérèse's doctorate, and many had done so. But the story also went round that when Pope John Paul had visited Lisieux back in June 1980, the Carmelite nuns there had reportedly asked him when he was going to make Thérèse a doctor, and he had supposedly replied "Be patient! You Carmelites already have two!" Some speculated that Thérèse's comments in her autobiography about feeling within herself the vocation of priest would work against her, given the Vatican's strong position on the women's ordination issue; others thought that being a woman might work in her favor.

At the beginning of 1997, the centennial of Thérèse's death, word had come down that the Discalced Carmelite generalate and appropriate curial congregations should prepare the necessary documentation and hold the necessary hearings. The results were later published in the official *Positio*,[4] which comes to more than 1100 printed pages and is described in more detail below. But it was a case of "hurry up and wait"; after a mad rush to get all of the paperwork completed, still nothing was certain.

As always, the pope selected his times and settings carefully. Breaking the news of Thérèse's upcoming doctorate at the Twelfth

World Youth Day in Paris on 24 August 1997 gave him the perfect opportunity to recommend her as an example to the French and especially to the young (as he did again at the 2002 World Youth Day in Toronto). He actually bestowed the title a few weeks later at a Mass in St. Peter's Square on 19 October, which also happened to be Mission Sunday and the opening of the academic year for the pontifical schools of Rome. In his homily and Angelus message for the occasion, therefore, the Holy Father naturally emphasized Thérèse's role as co-patroness of the missions, and encouraged the pontifical students and faculty to "treasure [her] teaching."

More than that, however, the pontiff frankly acknowledged that some might consider Thérèse an odd choice for the doctorate, especially since she "does not have true and proper doctrinal corpus."[5] As he stated in his homily: "Everyone thus realizes that today something surprising is happening. St. Thérèse of Lisieux was unable to attend a university or engage in systematic study. She died young: nevertheless, from this day forward she will be honored as a doctor of the church, an outstanding recognition which raises her in the esteem of the entire Christian community far beyond any academic title."[6]

He went on to say: "Indeed, when the Magisterium proclaims someone a doctor of the Church, it intends to point out to all the faithful, particularly to those who perform in the Church the fundamental service of preaching or who undertake the delicate task of theological teaching and research, that the doctrine professed and proclaimed by a certain person can be a reference point, not only because it conforms to revealed truth, but also because it sheds new light on the mysteries of the faith, a deeper understanding of Christ's mystery."[7]

In other words, according to the pope, in naming Thérèse a doctor the teaching authority of the Church is proposing her not only as a spiritual model but also, as he put it, a "reference point" for evangelization and for theological studies. This is a claim that I imagine more than one theologian might find surprising, even alarming. What exactly does it mean for Thérèse (or any other saint, for that matter) to be named a "doctor of the universal church" and thus a "reference point"? Why and how does this happen? What, if anything, does someone like Thérèse have to offer the discipline of theology? I don't pretend to have a clear and complete answer to these questions, but perhaps I can make a start by briefly touching upon four points: 1) the history of the title "doctor of the church"; 2) the process by which Thérèse came to receive this honor; 3) the arguments given for and against bestowing it upon her (especially by the official theological consultors); and 4) some of the theological and pastoral implications of Thérèse's "doctorate."

History of the Title

As one might expect, the expression "Doctor of the Universal Church" appears nowhere in the Bible. Nevertheless, in the Hebrew Scriptures and the New Testament, as elsewhere in the ancient world, we see a deep preoccupation with the discovery and faithful transmission of knowledge and truth. Long before the internet and distance learning programs, when written texts were a scarce commodity and most learning took place in the context of a direct mentoring relationship, it was only natural that people be concerned about identifying reliable teaching and trustworthy teachers.[8]

In the Hebrew Scriptures, the ultimate teacher is (of course) God, the source of all truth and wisdom. In the New Testament, Jesus, incarnate Wisdom, is *the* teacher *par excellence* because of his privileged relationship with the Father. In fact, "teacher" is one of the most common titles given to Jesus in the Gospels, along with "rabbi" ("which means teacher," according to John 1:38). Jesus himself says, in Matthew's Gospel: "But you are not to be called rabbi, for you have one teacher (διδασκαλοζ) , and you are all brethren." (Mt 23:8) This perhaps explains why the disciples after the resurrection did not immediately describe themselves as teachers, διδασκαλοι, even though they were constantly instructing others in the Christian faith. Indeed, in John's Gospel it is the *Holy Spirit* whom Jesus promises to send who teaches the disciples and guides them into all truth. (cf. Jn 14:26; 16:13)

Yet, in two famous Pauline passages on the variety of gifts bestowed on the body of Christ, we read that "God has appointed in the Church first apostles, second prophets, third teachers (διδασκαλουζ), then workers of miracles, then healers, helpers, administrators, speakers in various kinds of tongues" (1 Cor 12:28), and again that "his gifts were that some should be apostles, some prophets, some evangelists, some pastors and teachers (διδασκαλουζ), for the equipment of the saints, for the work of ministry, for building up the body of Christ, until we all attain to the unity of the faith and of the knowledge of the Son of God." (Eph 4:11-13) The precise duties and status of these "teachers" is not entirely clear, but they appear to hold an important place within the organization of the early Christian community, and it seems reasonable to assume, given the Jewish antecedents, that their responsibilities included instruction in the faith and the interpretation of Scripture. Significantly, the Vulgate would translate the Greek word for teachers in these passages with the Latin term "doctores," the cognate of our English word "doctors." Thus, in the Latin West, it was possible to argue from the Bible that among many other gifts, God had given "doctors" for the sake of the Church, and that their role was not merely to communicate abstract knowledge but to help believers to interpret and clarify God's revelation in Scripture.

In the post-apostolic era, bishops quickly emerged as the Christian community's leaders and guardians of the faith. "Ever since, at least in the older Christian denominations, bishops have been seen as holding the most authoritative official teaching position in the Church," notes Bernard McGinn in his book, *The Doctors of the Church.*[9] At the same time, though, the early church recognized that many others also played an important role in instructing the faithful.

During the period of the first four councils and the great Christological and Trinitarian controversies of the fourth and fifth centuries, a number of writers (such as Basil, Cyril of Alexandria, Ambrose, Augustine, and John Chrysostom) distinguished themselves as faithful expositors of Scripture and powerful champions of orthodox doctrine. Other writers began treating them as reliable authorities who could be invoked in the battle against heresy and referred to them variously as "fathers" or "doctors." The terminology was still somewhat fluid, and the list of those who merited this title was still evolving. Most were bishops, but not all. (According to one source, Augustine himself, one of those most often listed among the "doctors," was among the first to use the term of a non-bishop, St. Jerome.)

By the time of Bede the Venerable (d. 735), however, four figures had emerged as the Latin Church's preeminent "doctors," namely, Ambrose, Augustine, Gregory the Great, and Jerome. Why precisely four? That's not entirely clear, but the number offered rich possibilities of symbolic comparisons: four evangelists, four doctors, and so on. However, the first official papal approbation of the title "Doctor of the Church" came only much later, during the pontificate of Boniface VIII, with the decretal *Gloriosus Deus* in 1298. There Boniface characterizes Ambrose, Augustine, Gregory, and Jerome as "great doctors of the Church" who, with their exalted teaching, "revealed the mysteries of the Scriptures, untied knots [i.e., dissolved perplexities], clarified difficulties, and explained what was uncertain" *(scripturarum aenigmata reserat, solvit nodos, obscura delucidat, dubiaque declarat).* Boniface also decreed that their feasts would henceforth be celebrated as duplex feasts alongside those of the apostles and evangelists. As Umberto Betti points out, this was not so much a formal declaration of the doctorate as a pontifical decision to raise the liturgical rank of these four saints, already acknowledged for their singular doctrinal importance to the Church.[10] Thus "doctor of the church" comes to assume here a significance as much liturgical as doctrinal, in terms of how the Church remembers and celebrates its most prominent post-apostolic teachers. Incidentally, this liturgical connection also explains, in part, why so far there are no *martyrs* among the doctors, since—liturgically—martyrs rank higher than doctors. (If you've already got the gold medal, there is no point in having it bronzed!) Whether the practice may one day change, and whether the Church might one day grant the title of doctor to martyred saints such as Cyprian, Irenaeus, or Edith Stein, remains to be seen.

In any case, there matters stood until the pontificate of Pius V, who in 1568 incorporated the three great patristic doctors recognized in the Eastern church—Basil, Gregory Nazianzen, and John Chrysostom—into the "common of doctors" in the Tridentine reform of the Roman Breviary; he also added a fourth name, Athanasius, thereby establishing a symmetry between the four doctors from the East and four from the West.

An even more significant step, however, was the same pope's declaration of Thomas Aquinas as a "doctor of the church" in 1567,[11] and Sixtus V's bestowal of the same title on Bonaventure in 1588. Given the impact of their teaching upon the Church, Aquinas and Bonaventure were both obvious candidates. But their choice clearly demonstrated that "doctors of the church" had not died out with the patristic era and need not be limited to authors who followed one particular theological method. This was also perhaps the beginning of a less fortunate trend; Thomas (a Dominican) had been declared a doctor by a Dominican pope, Bonaventure (a Franciscan) by a Franciscan pope, and soon different orders and national groups were lobbying for "doctors of their own." In any event, from this point on the Congregation of Rites (again, a liturgical connection!) was entrusted with examining candidates for the doctorate, and it has continued to do so down to modern times.

By 1588, then, the West had its first ten official "doctors of the universal church." This number remained unchanged throughout the seventeenth century, but in the eighteenth, the pace picked up again: Anselm of Canterbury was declared a doctor in 1720, Isidore of Seville in 1722, Peter Chrysologus in 1729, and Leo the Great in 1754. In the nineteenth century, nine names were added to the list: Peter Damian, Bernard of Clairvaux, Hilary of Poitiers, Alphonsus Liguori, Francis de Sales, Cyril of Jerusalem and Cyril of Alexandria, John Damascene, and Bede the Venerable. In the last century, prior to the Second Vatican Council, the list was again expanded to include Ephraim the Syrian, Peter Canisius, John of the Cross, Robert Bellarmine, Albert the Great, Anthony of Padua, and finally Lawrence of Brindisi, declared a doctor by John XXIII in 1959: thirty preconciliar doctors in all, and all of them male.

When you consider this peculiar list of saints for a moment, you begin to realize that "doctor of the universal church" must be an analogous term at best, since those so designated differ enormously from each other in their background, their areas of contribution, and their impact. Peter Canisius (who has the unique distinction of being declared a doctor at his own canonization ceremony) is most famous for the catechisms he wrote, Peter Damian for his severe letters, Anthony of Padua for his sermons, and Ephraim for his hymns. Some (like John of Damascus) wrote much, others (like Cyril of Jerusalem) relatively little that has survived. Some (like Augustine, Bernard, Aquinas, Bonaventure) are still widely read and studied today, while the teachings of others (like Peter Chrysologus or Lawrence of Brindisi) are all but forgotten. Most of those chosen before the nineteenth century were known for their contributions to major questions of dogmatic and systematic theology, while more recent choices are primarily known for their spiritual teachings. Yet all of those before Vatican II were clerics: one deacon, nine priests, fifteen bishops, three cardinals, and two popes (and, as one commentator asks, does declaring a pope a "doctor" really add any magisterial weight that his teaching does not already have of itself?).[12]

Not surprisingly, then, there has been significant discussion over the centuries of what exactly it means to be a doctor of the church and what the qualifications are. The classic criteria were succinctly summarized in the eighteenth century by Cardinal Lambertini, the "defender of the faith" in the Congregation of Rites, who would later become Pope Benedict XIV. In his famous words, "To become a doctor of the church three things are necessary: namely, eminent doctrine; outstanding holiness of life. . . ; and a declaration passed by the supreme pontiff or a legitimately assembled General Council."[13] It sounds simple enough! The second and third criteria have never posed any special problem in the past, since so far the title "doctor" has only been bestowed by papal authority (not yet by a council) and only on officially recognized saints. It is the requirement of "eminent doctrine" which has proved most difficult to spell out, especially since "eminence" is, at least to some extent, a matter of opinion, and judgments can vary. When the Congregation of Rites was discussing the doctorate for St. Alphonsus Liguori, for example, they observed that there are greater and lesser doctors of the church, and that the "eminence of doctrine" required is not to be judged in any absolute sense but always "relative to some great effect achieved in their own way throughout the Church by [the candidate's] ingenuity, holiness, and doctrine." As a consequence, they said, "it is worthless to try to influence the Holy See to provide a formal declaration of Doctor of the Church unless there is some sort of previous judgment of the Church that signifies a true benefit"—a fruitless plea on their own part, perhaps, to be spared the pressures of lobbyists!

In fact, in the years before Vatican II there were growing misgivings about the apparent multiplication of doctors, and opinions were forwarded to the Council that "only the saints who have brought renown upon the Church with their really eminent doctrine should be awarded the title."[14] The Council never took up this question. In fact, a number of these saints officially honored in the past for their "eminent doctrine" were never even mentioned in the conciliar documents. Though the Congregation of Rites had always insisted that "doctors of the church" deserved a higher degree of liturgical celebration than lesser saints and that candidates should be chosen accordingly, in the reform of the liturgy after the council several doctors were demoted to optional memorials.

As for recent changes in the process, when the Congregation of Rites was divided in 1969 into two offices—the Congregation of Divine Worship and the Congregation for the Causes of the Saints—it was the latter which continued to oversee the causes of proposed doctors. John Paul II added a further refinement with the 1988 Apostolic Constitution *Pastor Bonus,* which required that the Congregation for the Causes of Saints obtain a vote on the "eminence of doctrine" of proposed candidates from the Congregation for the

Doctrine of the Faith. Thérèse was the first one to be considered under these new rules, as we shall see.

The most important innovation in modern times came in 1970 when Paul VI declared Teresa of Avila and Catherine of Siena to be "doctors of the universal church," thereby bestowing the title for the first time on nonclerics (one of them, Catherine, a member of the laity) and decisively rejecting the opinion that women were excluded from the rank of doctor because of their sex.[15] This opened the floodgates to all kinds of new petitions to bestow the doctorate, and in 1972 Paul VI suspended further declarations until the requirement of "eminent doctrine" could be studied more thoroughly.

Texts from some of the ongoing discussions of the matter within the Congregation for the Causes of Saints were published[16] in 1981; participants in the discussion suggested, for example, that among the various elements pointing toward eminence of doctrine were orthodoxy (at least by the standards of the candidate's own time), personal originality (not merely repeating what had already been said), extensive written documentation, worthy expression, continuous use by theologians and pastors, and a significant contribution to the study of Divine Revelation. Being a "man [or woman] of action, a sacred speaker, a promoter of a particular devotion, a pious writer, or a theologian" is not enough by itself.[17] Moreover, candidates should be chosen, they said, not merely on the basis of past intellectual accomplishments, however important in their day, but also in the light of the Church's ongoing and future requirements. To be acceptable, one contributor wrote, candidates should be "doctors" not just for their own time but for all times.[18]

It seemed that everyone involved was struggling to articulate some way to preserve the prestige of the title while leaving the door open to new kinds of doctors to meet the Church's emerging pastoral needs. These were the kinds of issues still not fully resolved as the Congregation for the Causes of Saints was being asked to consider the case of St. Thérèse. Suddenly all of the seemingly abstract questions arising out of the complex history of the title and the evolution in its requirements became very concrete.

How Thérèse Became a "Doctor of the Universal Church"

As one might imagine, Thérèse presented a very challenging case. Pope John Paul II himself has underscored her limited academic background. During her brief life of twenty-four years, the last nine spent in the Carmel of Lisieux, she never published any writings, never wrote a book as such. At the time of her death of tuberculosis in 1897 she was virtually unknown outside the convent and the family circle. What she left behind were the memories others had of her holy life (especially the recollections of her three older siblings in the same community: Marie, Pauline, and Céline), and a series of occasional texts written mainly for family, acquaintances, and other Carmelites. It was evidently her sister Pauline, known in the Carmel as Mother Agnès of Jesus (because she served for a time as prioress), who came up with the idea of using some of these texts in place of the usual obituary letter, notably the three manuscripts describing what Thérèse called "not . . . my life properly so called" but "my *thoughts* on the graces God deigned to grant me" (S, 15 [A 3r]), texts composed at different times at the request of Mother Agnès herself, her sister Marie, and Mother Marie de Gonzague (the prioress at the time of Thérèse's death). Pauline even discussed this idea with Thérèse, and the latter (who had earlier brushed aside the suggestion that these texts were publishable) gradually warmed to the idea. As her death approached, Thérèse had a growing sense of a posthumous mission, and a conviction (using one of her favorite arguments) that God would not inspire such desires without intending to fulfill them. It occurred to her, in other words, that these "autobiographical" writings might be precisely the instrument through which her mission would reach a multitude of little souls. As she observed, "there will be something in it for all tastes, except for those in extraordinary ways." (LC, 143) However, by that point Thérèse was too weak to edit and rewrite anything herself, and so she entrusted the task completely to Pauline (at least according to the later testimony of the Martin sisters).

Whatever Thérèse had in mind, Pauline certainly took her job to heart. "She divided the three manuscripts into eleven chapters and composed a twelfth, in which she related Thérèse's last months and death. The book concluded with some extracts from her letters, a good number of her poems, and the testimony of her novices."[19] Pauline (Mother Agnès) edited Thérèse's words freely, correcting her mistakes, polishing her style (as she thought), modifying or deleting passages that seemed too personal or that might embarrass those who were still living. Mother Marie de Gonzague approved the work but insisted that it be rewritten to appear as if the autobiographical sections had all been addressed to her. She in turn passed the text along to a good friend of the monastery, the Norbertine priest Godefroid Madelaine, who made further suggestions, obtained the bishop's imprimatur, wrote a preface, and proposed the title by which the work eventually became known: *Histoire d'une âme,* or *Story of a Soul.* Two thousand copies were printed a year after Thérèse's death, and the Lisieux nuns wondered how they would ever get rid of them.[20]

Of course, the rest is history. To everyone's surprise, the first printing sold out rapidly. Because of the increasing demand, *Histoire d'une âme* had to be reprinted every year, and it would eventually be translated into more than fifty languages. By the time of Thérèse's canonization in 1925, in the French language alone, over 400,000 copies of *Histoire d'une âme* had been sold, along with 800,000 copies of a brief summary of her life and doctrine entitled *Call to Little Souls,* 300,000 copies of an even shorter work called *Abridged Life,* and half a million copies of her *Pensées*. Between 500 and 1,000 letters were arriving at the Lisieux Carmel every day.[21]

This outpouring of enthusiasm for Thérèse was certainly due in part to the so-called "shower of roses," the extraordinary number of favors attributed to her intercession, which her devotees saw as fulfillment of her promise to "spend her heaven doing good on earth." (The "shower of roses" phenomenon in itself would make a wonderful dissertation topic in the sociology of religion.) Whatever one may think about some of these reports, they certainly manifested a widespread conviction that this young woman was still a powerful and living presence in people's lives.

But even apart from her role as intercessor, Thérèse was regarded from the beginning as someone with a particular *message*. In his preface to the first edition of *Story of a Soul* in 1898, Père Madelaine had already praised Thérèse's "theology that the most beautiful spiritual books only rarely attain to such a high degree."[22] Other authors, including popes, bishops, and theologians, quickly followed suit, nearly always mentioning what she had called her "little way," which her sisters dubbed "the little way of spiritual childhood." Thérèse was celebrated for having rediscovered for our times the Gospel precept to "become like little children," not relying on our own accomplishments or despairing over our failures but abandoning ourselves with complete trust into the arms of Jesus, surrendering totally to a God who is all-merciful love. For her, this recognition of God as merciful love became, we might say, a hermeneutical principal in the light of which all other doctrines were interpreted. I will say more about this in the final section.

The impact of her seemingly simple message was so immediate and profound that already by 1928, not long after her canonization, there were petitions from the United States, Poland, England, Argentina, Brazil and elsewhere that she be named a "doctor of the church." Credit for the first *official* request, however, goes to the noted Jesuit P. Gustave Desbuquois, who at the first Thérèsian Congress in 1932, held in the crypt of the new basilica in Lisieux, created a sensation by arguing in detail why she should be named a "doctor."[23] He mentioned, for example, her retrieval of the biblical themes of "spiritual childhood" and "Merciful Love," her emphasis on what we now describe as "the universal call to holiness," and the fact that Pius XI, in his many statements on Thérèse, had already characterized her as a great Christian teacher and a "word of God" for our times. Desbuquois's proposal was unanimously and enthusiastically endorsed by the congress participants, including some bishops and cardinals, and within a year 342 bishops signatures from all over the world had been collected, when the process suddenly ground to a halt. The future Pope Pius XII, Cardinal Pacelli (at that time secretary of state), writing to Mother Agnès on behalf of Pius XI, indicated that it was better not to speak anymore of the doctorate for Thérèse, "even if her doctrine did not for that reason cease to be a sure light for souls seeking to know the Gospel spirit."[24] We don't know Pius XI's reasons for certain, but it has often been suggested that this pope who so often praised Thérèse's teaching and called her "the star of my pontificate" was simply unprepared to bestow the doctorate on a woman. Already some years earlier, when the Discalced Carmelite provincial of Milan had proposed Teresa of Avila as a doctor, he had simply replied "obstat sexus," though he did not close the door on the future possibility.

However, as already mentioned, any reservations about declaring women "doctors of the universal church" were removed in 1970 when Paul VI bestowed the title on Teresa and Catherine of Siena. So Thérèse's cause was taken up again. During 1973, the centenary of her birth, Cardinal Garrone petitioned Rome for her doctorate, as did the postulator general of the Discalced Carmelites in 1974, who was told that all further concessions of the doctorate had been suspended until the whole matter could be studied further. Nevertheless, the petitions kept increasing, not only from the general chapter of the Discalced Carmelites but from bishops' conferences all over the world, and from many individual members of the hierarchy. Unfortunately, lack of space prevents us here from reviewing in detail this growing avalanche of requests.

What was going on during all this time in the Vatican congregations?[25] Already on 31 August 1992 the Congregation for the Causes of the Saints, in accordance with the required procedure, had requested from the Congregation for the Doctrine of the Faith (CDF) the necessary opinion on the eminence of Thérèse's doctrine. Four years later there was still no vote, but the CDF released its "norms and criteria" for evaluating doctrinal eminence. These "criteria" would prove crucial: 1) the existence of a charism of wisdom, a fruit of the Holy Spirit; 2) excellence of spiritual and theological doctrine; 3) a doctrine at the service of the faith and Christian life; 4) [quality of] the sources of their theological and spiritual doctrine; 5) large diffusion of their doctrine; and 6) a relevant message of lasting value.[26] Though these criteria need some teasing out and hadn't necessarily been designed with Thérèse specifically in mind, they made it somewhat easier to argue in her favor, as we shall see. For one could make a strong case that she had met all of these six requirements: that she had drawn upon the Scriptures and classic Christian sources, for example; that she clearly offered an excellent spiritual doctrine; that it had been widely diffused; that her message was relevant and of lasting value; and so on.

In December of 1996, presumably because the centenary year of Thérèse's death was about to begin, the Vatican Secretary of State asked for a progress report on Thérèse's doctorate from the Congregation for the Causes of the Saints. At the beginning of February 1997—remember, this is only about eight months before the actual declaration!—members of the two congregations met. The CDF promised a vote on her doctrinal eminence for April, while the Congregation for the Causes of the Saints asked the Discalced Carmelite postulator general, Fr. Simeon Fernandez, to start pulling together as soon as possible the necessary background material. So at the beginning of April, under a strict deadline, a committee of Discalced Carmelite experts on Thérèse somehow managed to compile the *Informatio,* which comprises some 800 pages of the *Positio,* in about a week. This *Informatio* section, presenting a case for the "eminence" of her doctrine, includes among other things a biography of Thérèse; a history of her causes of beatification, canonization, and the doctorate; an overview and analysis of her writings and doctrine; a huge bibliography; a long listing of all the petitions received, and of the many saints, blesseds, popes, cardinals, bishops, theologians, religious congregations, and others who have acknowledged her influence.

This *Informatio* was then forwarded to the congregations for their study. However, since the Congregation for the Doctrine of the Faith had not managed to hold their promised vote by April, a compromise procedure had to be devised with the pope's approval, which involved several joint meetings to consider the further input of various theological consultors and to vote on the question. It wasn't until the end of May that their work was done.

We can't go into all the details of the process here, but as far as the theological input was concerned, the Congregation for the Doctrine of the Faith passed the *Informatio* along to five theological experts, and the Congregation for the Causes of the Saints (CCS) to two theological experts, for their opinions on the question of whether to grant the title "doctor of the church" to Thérèse; of these, six were favorable and only one opposed. The one opposed did not so much object to the Thérèse doctorate per se as question its opportuneness. While, like many others, he underscored her lack of a doctrinal corpus, his remaining arguments, e.g., that this declaration would favor one religious order too much, or that it would be difficult to think of a twenty-four-year-old girl as a real "doctor," seemed fairly weak.

These seven theological opinions, together with the original *Informatio,* were then forwarded by the respective congregations to a host of theological consultors. In the case of the CDF, nineteen consultors voted in favor, two more were affirmative "iuxta modum" (that is, with certain reservations), and one was against. In the case of the CCS, seven consultors voted in favor, two more were affirmative "iuxta modum," and three were negative. When the consultors' votes are added together, then, there were twenty-six consultors in favor, four more in favor with some reservations, and only four out of thirty-four against. With this kind of majority, it was easy for the subsequent consistory on 17 June to unanimously approve the doctorate and pass their judgment along to the pope. And that, in a nutshell, was the process by which Thérèse was named a "doctor of the universal church."

The Opinions of the Consultors and Others

What, then, about the third point, namely, the reasons for and against Thérèse's doctorate, as stated by the theological experts and consultors and others? To begin with, no one questioned her great holiness or the tremendous influence she has had within the Church. Most of the concerns expressed, however, had to do with what several describe as her "lack of a doctrinal corpus." Certainly she was no systematic theologian after the model of Thomas Aquinas or Bonaventure, and left comparatively few writings. Most of her theological insights are scattered here and there throughout her autobiographical manuscripts, poems, letters, and so on, and they are often too sketchy to allow even the best commentators to construct a full-blown Thérèsian "system." Several consultors asked whether it was too soon for Thérèse, and whether including her among the doctors would both detract from her "littleness" and further debase the title, making the requirements so loose that practically any saint would qualify. If Thérèse can be a doctor, they wondered, then why not Ignatius of Loyola, Maximus the Confessor, Mechtilde of Magdeburg, Elizabeth of the Trinity?

Well, one might respond, why not indeed? As a matter of fact, the process for Bernardine of Siena's doctorate has already been completed for some time, and awaits only the papal proclamation, while the doctoral causes for Veronica Giuliani, John Bosco, and John of Avila are well underway. Any loosening of the requirements, one could argue, had already occurred long before Thérèse's case came up. After all, do Anthony of Padua or Catherine of Siena have a large body of theological writings or a "doctrinal corpus"? Has Lawrence of Brindisi influenced as many theologians, or has any message of Peter Chrysologus been cited as often by the magisterium? It may be true that the standards need tightening up rather than loosening. Yet as a number of the consultors favoring Thérèse's cause point out, the particular kind of insight into divine revelation that "doctors" provide for the people of God must evolve as the needs of the Church evolve. Without denying the perennial value of the great doctors of the past, the Church may also require new kinds of doctors today who still play a significant teaching role, but in a different way. One can reasonably argue that the requirement of "eminent doctrine," however much attenuated or reinterpreted in Thérèse's case, still remains intact, which is why we are unlikely ever to see the title bestowed on, say, Joan of Arc or Theophane Venard; though they were personal favorites of Thérèse, they are not identified with a particular message to the Universal Church, as she is.

Related to this, I had expected some of the consultors to raise the tricky question of whether there should be different standards for male and female doctors, given the historical fact that until recently women were not usually afforded the opportunity for higher academic studies, nor given the chance to systematically develop a "doctrinal corpus" comparable to that of Aquinas or Augustine. Interestingly, however, there were almost no reflections on the significance of Thérèse's gender, though one theologian asked slyly if this doctoral cause might be just a consolation prize to women from the Vatican for its recent decisions rejecting the possibility of women priests.

Actually, in reviewing the *Positio,* it becomes clear that a whole series of factors providentially converged to make it possible for the consultors to acknowledge "doctrinal eminence" in Thérèse's case. First, there were the important debates earlier in this century over the integrity of her writings. Mother Agnès's editorial modifications were probably necessary at the beginning to present to the world the as-yet-unknown Thérèse according to the literary and devotional conventions of the time, but when Thérèse's devotees learned years later that Mother Agnès had introduced over 7000 changes in the *Story of a Soul* alone, there was a great concern over whether Thérèse's message had somehow been adulterated or falsified and a growing demand for the original texts. As a consequence, a complete facsimile edition of the autobiographical manuscripts behind *Story of a Soul* was published in 1956, and some years later a committee of experts began working on a thoroughly annotated critical edition of all her works. The result was the "Nouvelle Édition du Centenaire," which has won all sorts of scholarly awards and would be the envy, I think, of any "doctor of the church." Thus the consultors had at their disposal a reliable edition of Thérèse's authentic texts, accompanied by the most up-to-date critical apparatus and theologically informed interpretive notes that one could ever want. Then, too, they were aware that Thérèse's doctrinal mission had been endorsed by such great theologians of our times as Yves Congar and Hans Urs von Balthasar; the latter had even worked for the CDF and written a major study on our saint.

More than that, as the consultors duly noted, an entire series of popes had cited Thérèse frequently in statements which, without explicitly speaking of her "eminent doctrine," clearly implied it. Though her name doesn't appear in any of the final decrees of Vatican II, she was mentioned fifteen times in the published acts, more than eleven others who had already been declared "doctors." Again, although her doctorate wasn't official at the time the *Catechism of the Catholic Church* was published, only nine "doctors" were quoted more often in its pages. Moreover, of her six quotations, only one is found in the fourth part, on Christian prayer; the rest occur in sections on the canon of Scripture, on merit, on the holiness of the Church, and on the meaning of Christian death and the communion of the saints. The fact that she is cited so often by the *Catechism* in an explicitly doctrinal context, that so many popes had recommended her message, and that so many bishops, entrusted with the responsibility for authentic teaching, had called for her doctorate, is mentioned again and again by the theological consultors as supporting the "eminence" of Thérèse's doctrine. When a saint's *doctrine* has been so consistently invoked by the magisterium, how could he or she *not* be properly called a "doctor"?

Notice also that while the Congregation for the Doctrine of the Faith sometimes seemed to be deliberately dragging its feet, the way they formulated the criteria for doctrinal eminence actually made it easier, as I indicated already, for the theological consultors to give a positive judgment in Thérèse's case. Recall that the very first requirement among the six proposed by the CDF is "the existence of a charism of *wisdom,* a fruit of the Holy Spirit." Several of the theological consultors latched on to this word "wisdom." They emphasized that one can distinguish two levels of theology: first, the original wisdom received from the Holy Spirit; and second, the elaboration of that wisdom in theological science. Thérèse may have fallen short in the latter department, since she was not a trained systematic theologian, but surely she was richly endowed with the former, that is, with a charism of wisdom rooted in the Scriptures and inspired by the Spirit. And so, many consultors argued, she more than satisfied the requirement.

These, then, were some of the general reasons given by the consultors in support of Thérèse's doctorate. In addition, many of them cited, as further evidence in her favor, certain particular contributions Thérèse had made to theology, spirituality, and pastoral practice. Let us now turn to these.

Theological and Pastoral Implications of Thérèse's Doctorate

What, then, has Thérèse's specific doctrinal and pastoral contribution already been, and what might it be in the future, especially now with the weight of the doctorate behind her? Clearly, beyond the question of what the pope might have intended in naming her a doctor, there is also the question of how that doctorate is received. We already know from the Church's past experience that simply naming someone a doctor does not automatically insure that he or she will exert a greater influence on the Church's theology and praxis. If Bernardine of Siena is named a doctor of the church tomorrow, for example, it won't necessarily mean that theologians will start measuring their teachings against his or that the ordinary faithful will start avidly reading his works. And even if we agree, as Pope John Paul II claims, that "doctors of the universal church" should be a "reference point" for theologians, they are only one "reference point" among many. No one is suggesting that the great theological works of the past and present, much less the Gospels, should be replaced by *Story of a Soul.* Many would argue nonetheless that she has something worthwhile to contribute, not only to specific fields of theological research such as Christology, ecclesiology, theology of grace, sacramental theology, and eschatology, but perhaps even to the way in which theologizing is done.

There are many points of entry into Thérèse's "doctrine," but let us start with the most obvious one, from which virtually all her other insights flow, namely, her rediscovery in the Scriptures of the God of merciful love, before whom the only proper human stance is utter filial love and confidence. It is important for Thérèse that the human and divine elements here always be taken together; otherwise the stress on merciful love can sound merely abstract, and the emphasis on humility and "littleness" can seem mere pious affectation. Thérèse came to her "rediscovery," as we know, through a long and painful process of lived experience and contemplative reflection on that experience. In a sense, we might say that hers is a "narrative" theology, a theology rooted in praxis and communicated in life-stories, parables, and images, like the message of the Gospel. In an era of devotion which put the emphasis on heroic saints and extraordinary deeds and experiences, Thérèse finally reached the point after several years in religious life of recognizing that not only was she still weak, but that in fact she would never by her own efforts reach the perfection to which she had aspired since childhood. And so, as she famously tells us, she searched the Scriptures and rejoiced to find, in Proverbs and Isaiah, the words "Whoever is a little one, let him come to me," and "As one whom a mother caresses, so will I comfort you; you shall be carried at the breasts, and upon the knees they shall caress you." (S, 208 [C 3r]) In a characteristic piece of Thérèsian logic, she reasoned that a loving God cannot inspire unrealizable desires, and so then if she could not grow up, God would have to come down to her level and raise her up. Indeed, as she came to understand, it is our very weakness and helplessness, coupled with utter dependence and trust, that places the greatest claim on God's compassion and gives us the greatest assurance of God's help. All we need do is remain like "little children," in the Gospel sense of that expression.

For Thérèse, this insight opened up fresh perspectives on virtually every article of faith. Not that she constructed any new theological "system"! Rather, as Cardinal Schönborn, one of the theological experts in the *Positio,* suggests, she in a sense helped to change the whole modern theological climate.[27]

Regarding the attributes of God, especially mercy and justice, for example, she reasons with one of her missionary brothers that God is all-merciful precisely because he is all-just and all-knowing; he understands our weakness.[28] She is blissfully unconcerned about purgatory, which she views in any case in terms of love rather than punishment.[29] At a time when so much Catholic piety focused on making reparation for offenses against God's justice, she offered herself instead as a "victim" to "Merciful Love."[30]

Regarding the theology of grace, within her own thoroughly Catholic context she nevertheless was able to move beyond the "mercenary spirituality" of her childhood, and its preoccupation with tallying up merits, to go to God "with empty hands," as she famously put it. Hans Urs von Balthasar has said that in her own way, without consciously intending to do so, Thérèse responds to Luther and Calvin point by point and even goes beyond them on the issue of faith and works.[31] Von Balthasar also credits her with finally overcoming the age-old dichotomizing of contemplation and action, by recognizing that a contemplative loving is itself the most fruitful action on behalf of the Church and the world.[32] Regarding ecclesiology, as William Thompson has argued, the well-known passage in *Story of a Soul* that ends with "In the heart of the Church, my mother, I shall be Love," is not merely about the personal discovery of her own vocation, but also sketches out a whole vision of the Church, an "ecclesiology of love," where structure and hierarchy are all preserved but all subordinated to the Gospel message of confidence in God's merciful love.[33] Thompson also credits her reflections on her own trial of faith as a rich source for Christology and soteriology.[34]

Again, in the area of sacramental theology, Thérèse advises her scrupulous cousin that sacraments are intended by God to be loving helps for sinners, not as rewards for sinlessness.[35] Pope Pius X, before Thérèse was ever canonized, praised her for advocating frequent (even daily) communion, something she unfortunately never lived to see in Carmel, and called her "the greatest saint of modern times." Or again, regarding Mariology, in an era which often stressed Mary's special privileges and often promoted Marian devotions based on private revelations and apocryphal stories, Thérèse returned to the Mary of the Gospel and of ordinary experience: "I must see her real life, not her imagined life," she said. "I'm sure that her real life was very simple. They show her to us as unapproachable, but they should present her to us as imitable. . . . We know very well that the Blessed Virgin is Queen of heaven and earth, but she is more Mother than Queen."[36] And as for eschatology, Thérèse boldly recasts even the traditional Christian understanding of eternal life. Instead of wanting endless rest in heaven, she hopes instead for unending activity on earth, helping to extend Jesus' salvific work. Once more, with familiar Thérèsian logic, she reasons that the God of merciful love could not have inspired her desire for a great posthumous mission without intending to satisfy it, and that if the angels can be ceaselessly active without ever losing the beatific vision, so can she. Indeed, she is firmly convinced that her evangelical mission will be far more fruitful *after* her death than before. And history seems to have proved her right! She offers us a dynamic vision of a resurrected life in Christ that does not separate us from ongoing care for the earth and the human family which gave us birth.

These, then, are but a few areas where Thérèse has made important contributions for others to explore and develop. If today we take some of them for granted, that only shows, I think, how much her ideas have already been absorbed by the Church of our time. They were by no means commonplace in her own day. For example, though she is never mentioned in *Lumen Gentium,* Thérèse is often credited as one of the major forces behind the Second Vatican Council's emphasis on the "universal call to holiness," which is hardly conceivable without the changes she helped bring about in the modern understanding of sanctity. Even today, major theologians are still "rediscovering," often without realizing it, points which Thérèse had made over a century ago.

Unfortunately, we cannot explore further here the deeper pastoral implications of Thérèse's doctorate, except to say that she not only shares a "doctrine" with us, but also models for us how it is to be lived. Anyone who reads the final chapters of *Story of a Soul* carefully cannot help being moved by her profound insights into Jesus' command at the Last Supper, to "love one another as I have loved you," and how we must learn to love our neighbor not by relying on our own feeble resources but by allowing Christ to love others *through* us. The pastoral fruitfulness of Thérèse's message is amply demonstrated by the extraordinary number of missions, pastoral groups, and active religious communities which have adopted her as their patron and teacher.

Conclusion

In closing, I would like to pay a brief tribute to Fr. Kieran Kavanaugh, a loyal disciple of St. Thérèse to whom this volume is dedicated. Alongside his numerous and widely publicized accomplishments, there are his many other kindnesses, less well known but equally important to their recipients. As my prior, it was Fr. Kieran who first strongly encouraged me to choose St. Thérèse's doctorate as the topic for my theology dissertation, which in turn gave rise to this essay (first delivered as a lecture at the Washington Theological Union) and to the book, *Saint Thérèse of Lisieux: Doctor of the Universal Church* (Staten Island, NY: Alba House, 2002). His excellent January 1998 presentation on this theme at the Washington archdiocese's "Convocation 2000" gave me important insights and direction in my own studies. For this and much more I am personally very grateful.

Obviously there is much more to be said about Thérèse's doctorate. My principal goal here has been not so much to defend Pope John Paul's decision to declare Thérèse a "doctor of the universal church"—a pope certainly doesn't need me to defend him!—but simply to explain how the declaration came about and what it might mean for us. Those who are already convinced that Thérèse should never have been made a doctor will probably not be persuaded by anything I have written above. But if their concern is that declaring Thérèse a doctor somehow separates her from the ranks of "little souls," I would suggest that the recent reaction to the relics has shown just the opposite; if anything, perhaps Thérèse is reminding the theological doctors of today that they, too, must stand among God's "poor and lowly." Or if you feel that this doctorate is simply an attempt on the Vatican's part to reinforce an old-fashioned brand of piety and passivity, I would advise you to look again at St. Thérèse of Lisieux. Thérèsian studies have come a long way in the last decades, and we are continuing to uncover beneath the sentimental images of the past a startlingly original, courageous, and wise woman. She still has much to teach us. May she continue to do so.

Notes

1 *Story of a Soul: The Autobiography of St. Thérèse of Lisieux,* trans. John Clarke, 3d ed. (Washington, DC: ICS Publications, 1997). All quotations from *Story of a Soul* are from this edition, hereafter cited as "S." The bracketed references are to the pagination in the original manuscripts, a referencing system now widely used in scholarly studies.

2 For a description of the ceremonies for her beatification and canonization, see Pierre Descouvemont and Raymond Zambelli, "Thérèse's Universal Influence," in *Saint Thérèse of Lisieux: Her Life, Times, and Teaching* (Washington, DC: ICS Publications, 1997), 263.

3 Cf. the audiotape series, *St. Thérèse of Lisieux: Her Mission Today*, published by ICS Publications, Washington, DC. Egan borrows this expression from Philippe de la Trinité; see the latter's *Thérèse de Lisieux, la sainte de l'enfance spirituelle, relecture des textes d'A. Combes* (Paris: P. Lethielleux, 1980), 124.

4 Congregatio de Causis Sanctorum (Prot. N. 2168), *Urbis et Orbis. Concessionis tituli Doctoris Ecclesiae universalis S. Teresiae Iesu Infante et a Sacro Vultu, moniali professae Ordinis Carmelitarum Discalceatorum* (1873-1897). 2 vols.
Vol. 1 (Pp. ix + 964): Includes *Positio* and votes of Cabellione (Ex Typis Rogeri Rimbaud, 1997).
Vol. 2 (Pp. 158): Includes votes of theological consultors (Roma: Tipografia Guerra, 1997).
A Spanish translation of major doctrinal portions of the *Positio* can be found in S.C.C.S., *La doctora más joven de la Iglesia,* ed. Gabriel Castro (Burgos: Editorial Monte Carmelo, 1998).

5 John Paul II, *Divini Amoris Scientia,* par. 8; quoted in *Carmel in the World* 37 (1998): 13.

6 John Paul II, *Homily During the Mass Proclaiming St. Thérèse a Doctor of*

the Church, par. 3; quoted in *Carmel in the World* 37 (1998): 25.

7 Ibid., 25-26.

8 For the biblical background I have drawn upon A. S. Kapelrud, "lamad," in *Theologial Dictionary of the Old Testament,* ed. G. Johannes Botterweck, Helmer Ringgren, and Heinz-Josef Fabry, trans. Douglas W. Scott, Vol. 8: lakad-mor (Grand Rapids, MI: Wm. B. Eerdmans Publishing Co., 1997); and Karl Heinrich Rengstorf, "διδασκω," in *Theological Dictionary of the New Testament,* ed. Gerhard Kittel and Gerhard Friedrich, trans. Geoffrey W. Bromiley, Vol. II: Δ-H (Grand Rapids, MI: Wm. B. Eerdmans Publishing Co., 1968). Scriptural quotation are taken from *The Oxford Annotated Bible with the Apocrypha,* Revised Standard Version, ed. Herbert G. May and Bruce M. Metzger (New York: Oxford University Press, 1965).

9 Bernard McGinn, *The Doctors of the Church: Thirty-Three Men and Women Who Shaped Christianity* (New York: Crossroad, 1999), 3. The entire first chapter of this book offers a useful overview of the history of the concept and title, "doctor of the church." For further background information, see especially Umberto Betti, "A Proposito del Conferimento del Titolo di Dottore della Chiesa," *Antonianum* 63 (1988): 278-91, and J. Madoz, "'Doctor Ecclesiae'," *Estudios Ecclesiasticos* 11 (January 1932): 26-43.

10 Betti, "A Proposito del Conferimento del Titolo di Dottore della Chiesa," 279-80.

11 Thus one year earlier than McGinn suggests in *The Doctors of the Church*, 13.

12 Betti, "A Proposito del Conferimento del Titolo di Dottore della Chiesa," 289.

13 Prospero Cardinal Lambertini, *De Servorum Dei Beatificatione et Beatorum Canonizatione*, new ed., Book IV, part 2, chap. 11, para. 13 (Prati: Typographia Aldina, 1841), 512.

14 Cited in Betti, "A Proposito del Conferimento del Titolo di Dottore della Chiesa," 284.

15 In his homily for the doctorate of St. Teresa, Paul VI insists that the doctorate does not entail "hierarchical teaching functions," and so does not violate the Pauline precept of 1 Corinthians 14:34. See Paul VI, "Teresa of Avila: The Message of Prayer," *The Pope Speaks* 15 (1970): 221.

16 See *L'Osservatore Romano*, English language edition (29 June 1981), 2-4.

17 Agostino Trape, "Community and Peculiarity," *L'Osservatore Romano,* English language edition (29 June 1981), 4.

18 Umberto Betti, "Preserve the true meaning of canonical requisites," *L'Osservatore Romano,* English language edition (29 June 1981), 3.

19 Pierre Descouvemont and Raymond Zambelli, "Thérèse's Universal

Influence," in *St. Thérèse of Lisieux: Her Life, Times, and Teaching,* 255.

20 For the history of this famous text, see especially *Manuscrits autobiographiques,* vol. 1: *Introduction,* ed. François de Sainte-Marie (Lisieux: Carmel de Lisieux, 1956); Sainte Thérèse de l'Enfant-Jésus et de la Sainte-Face, *La première "Histoire d'une âme" de 1898* (Paris: Éditions du Cerf, "Nouvelle édition du centenaire," 1992); Sainte Thérèse de l'Enfant-Jésus et de la Sainte-Face, *Manuscrits autobiographiques,* édition critique (Paris: Éditions du Cerf, "Nouvelle édition du centenaire," 1992); and *Histoire d'une âme de Sainte Thérèse de Lisieux, selon la disposition originale des autographes,* ed. Conrad De Meester (Moerzeke, Belgium: Carmel-Edit, 1999).

21 Descouvemont and Zambelli, "Thérèse's Universal Influence," in *St. Thérèse of Lisieux: Her Life, Times, and Teaching,* 257. The data given here are a bit confusing, since Descouvemont and Zambelli speak of a period of "seventeen years" between Thérèse's death and canonization, when in fact it was twenty-eight years.

22 See Sainte Thérèse, *La première "Histoire d'une âme"* de 1898, 16.

23 See Paul Droulers, "Le Doctorat de Sainte Thérèse de Lisieux Proposé en 1932," *Ephemerides Carmeliticae* 24 (1973): 86-129; Guy Gaucher, "le père Desbuquois et le doctorat de Thérèse," *Carmel* no. 87 (1988): 42-53.

24 See page 51 in the *Informatio* section of the *Positio.*

25 For a description of the final stages of the process, see Jesús Castellano Cervera, "El Doctorado de Santa Teresa del Niño Jesús: Memoria histórica y significado eclesial," *Revista de Espiritualidad* 57 (1998): 77-111; and the "Presentation du Rapporteur" in the opening pages of the *Positio*, iv-v.

26 *Informatio,* 588-603.

27 *Positio,* 829. This "vote" is not signed, but other consultors refer to its author by name.

28 See Letter 226 (9 May 1997) to P. Roulland, in Saint Thérèse of Lisieux, *General Correspondence, Vol. II: 1890-1897,* trans. John Clarke (Washington, DC: ICS Publications, 1988), 1093: ". . .it is this justice which frightens so many souls that is the object of my joy and confidence. To be just is not only to exercise severity in order to punish the guilty; it is also to recognize right intentions and to reward virtue. I expect as much from God's justice as from his mercy."

29 See, for example, S, 180-81 (A 84r-v), and LT 221 in L, 1072.

30 See S, 180-81 (A 84r-v), and the "Act of Oblation to Merciful Love" in *The Prayers of Saint Thérèse of Lisieux,* trans. Aletheia Kane (Washington, DC: ICS Publications, 1997), 53ff.

31 Hans Urs von Balthasar, *Two Sisters in the Spirit: Thérèse of Lisieux and Elizabeth of the Trinity,* trans. Donald Nichols, Anne Elizabeth Englund, and

Dennis Martin (San Francisco, CA: Ignatius Press, 1992), 283-84.

32 Ibid., 196-97.

33 William M. Thompson, *Fire and Light: The Saints and Theology* (New York: Paulist Press, 1987), 171ff.

34 Ibid., 89-93.

35 See LT 92 (30 May 1889) to Marie Guérin, in L, 567-69.

36 St. Thérèse of Lisieux, LC, 161.

Two Concentration Camp Carmelites: St. Edith Stein and Père Jacques Bunel

John Sullivan, O.C.D.
Institute of Carmelite Studies
Washington, DC

1. Introduction

At the origins of the Discalced Carmelite reform in Spain's *siglo de oro* a woman and man gave each other inspiration, as they attracted other Carmelites to join in their work of engrafting a new branch onto the then centuries-old trunk of the "vine of Carmel" or the Carmelite order.[1] Sts. Teresa of Avila and John of the Cross were exemplars of that productive gender mutuality so sought after today throughout the Church. The Discalced Carmelite order is blessed by the fascinating example of collaboration Teresa and John gave in their age. Though individually different in talents, both natural and graced, they go on attracting persons who thirst for guidance in the practice and art of contemplation, as does Fr. Kieran Kavanaugh, their reliable contemporary translator/ interpreter.

Fr. Kieran has coined expressions and crafted sentences to render their voices in contemporary idiom, and he has concluded the corpus of his St. Teresa translations as this festive volume in his honor makes its appearance. He has acted as an effective linguistic channel between cultures. In his life's work he has shown sustained interest in European proponents of the Teresian Carmelite vision of things: early on he personally experienced life in the desert house of the French Carmelites (1956-57), and more recently he served ably as vice-postulator of the cause for canonization of the German-Jew St. Teresa Benedicta of the Cross/Edith Stein.[2] Not limited to interest in just those two countries and their particular incarnations of the ideals of both Teresa and John, he stays in active contact with research emanating from scholarly sources "on the continent."

A comparison of the sufferings of a pair of twentieth-century Carmelite scions (Edith Stein and Père Jacques) with the two Spanish Discalced doctors of the church would likely offer, then, some small measure of tribute to him. Fr. Kieran lived through World War II on American soil; then, after study and a desert experience in Europe, he collaborated with Fr. Otilio Rodriguez who himself witnessed first-hand the agony of the Spanish Civil War.[3] Sheltered from the chaos unleashed by political confrontations, Fr. Kieran had for contemporaries in the "age of anxiety" both St. Edith Stein and Père Jacques Bunel, martyred by the machinery of the Nazi "insane ideology"(John Paul II).

"Martyred" though they were, they approached their fate in an eminently constructive way. True sources of hope because they drew hope out of their never-flagging contemplative stance toward reality, they showed others the human spirit could react, not just surrender, to the seemingly overwhelming destructive forces ruining their European continent. Both ultimately died from their stays in concentration camps, though differently–Edith in Auschwitz/Birkenau, Jacques soon after liberation from Mauthausen, Austria. This makes a comparison all the more interesting since several differences occurred that will afford better insights about the frequently beautiful ways the human spirit, aided by grace, can react to infernal situations like those provoked by the Nazis. They have left us useful indicators for a still uncertain future that can acquire new meaning, if we learn from what they went through. After situating them in their mid-century Carmelite milieu, we will go on to trace their paths through transforming suffering.

2. Convergence in the Lives of Two Religious

1. Commitment to Religious Life during the 1930s and Early 1940s

The ways of God's Providence sometimes create what look to us like coincidences, but they frequently offer symbolically interesting juxtapositions of destinies. This happened when both St. Edith and Père Jacques lived as professed Carmelites in practically the same time span. Père Jacques made profession of vows as a Discalced Carmelite religious earlier than Sr. Teresa Benedicta of the Cross: he entered the novitiate at Lille on the feast of the Exaltation of the Holy Cross, 14 September 1931.[4] He lived in the order for some thirteen years, eight months, and eighteen days. Death came for him in Linz, Austria on 2 June 1945.

Edith Stein embraced the life of a daughter of St. Teresa of Avila, foundress of the Discalced Carmelite family, entirely within the time-frame Père Jacques served as a friar son of the mystical Madre. She entered a little more than two years after Père Jacques, joining Cologne Carmel on 14 October 1933; then died on 9 August 1942, a little less than three years before Père Jacques' death.[5]

2. Educators in Carmel

Their respective curricula vitae prove both of them were devoted to imparting education before they entered the order, but also how they found ways to exercise their pedagogical talents, skills, and intuitions even within the context of their Carmelite contemplative lifestyles.

It is easy to see this in the case of Père Jacques, since he was asked by his superiors to cofound (in 1934) a boys' school from which vocations to the order were expected, as well as an establishment serving as a fine boarding school for children able to pay the tuition of similar private schools. At first it cost him a bit to meld duties of religious life with those of headmaster of a complex operation serving some 90 students—something he did not have when he was Monsieur l'Abbé Bunel and simply a diocesan priest.[6] Some pamphlets he wrote on such topics as character formation and the social virtues prove beyond a doubt, however, that he felt quite at home in the specialized ministry embraced by the Petit Collège de Ste. Thérèse at Avon in the far southeastern suburbs of Paris.[7]

For Edith Stein the forms and formats for passing on lessons as a pedagogue were much different in the two monastic cloisters she knew at Cologne in Germany and Echt in Holland; but she taught, just the same. She assisted others in ways that allowed her to apply her gifts as a bona fide educator. We see her at work in her correspondence, answering questions sent to her, but also offering true spiritual guidance for persons seeking advice. She made translations into German for the use of the nuns in the community. In exile from Germany at Echt, she gave classes in Latin to the novices. She composed communal exhortations to the community on the occasion of major feasts.[8] All throughout, she kept on writing essays of a popular nature that were published in significant periodicals likely to be seen by Catholic reading audiences.[9] Furthermore, she went on drafting book-length manuscripts—one reached the galley-proof stage but was not published due to the Third Reich's anti-Semitic laws—intended to be more didactic in style and aimed at more specialized readerships.[10]

3. Adverse Experiences as Preparation for Intense Periods of Assistance/Suffering

Flight into Exile for Edith Stein

In the fifth decade of St. Edith Stein's life anti-Semitic persecution emanating from the government of Germany drove her out of her homeland and into nearby Holland. Strangely, her years of exile among the Dutch prepared her for the ultimate persecution she endured on her *via crucis.* From the late hours of the last day of 1938, Edith was an exile, pursued by the injustices brought on her people by *Kristallanacht* between 9-10 November that year.

After transfer, she was in familiar surroundings and schedules since she spent her final three years and seven months in a monastery of her order, the Carmel of Echt in Limburg Province only fifty miles from Cologne as the crow flies. Nevertheless, she was not in her home monastery where she had conventual rights as a fully professed sister.[11] This is to say that Providence, once again the supplier of blessings in the midst of "dangerous times" (*"tiempos recios"* for St. Teresa of Avila), was getting her ready throughout her stay in that daughter monastery of Cologne Carmel for the peregrinations that filled the sad final week of her life: first around Holland and then along Germany's rail lines to Auschwitz in Poland. It is not enough to take note of the fact she was caught up in the maelstrom of World War II; no, while sharing in its uncertainties and terrors, she received a large measure of sadness from that period's upheavals (in excess of the share most Germans got), because Nazi hatred for Jews had succeeded in making her abandon her native land and seek shelter in another country.

Père Jacques, Prisoner Twice Over

In a parallel fashion, Père Jacques had undergone the moral sufferings of captivity several years before his arrest by the Gestapo for harboring Jewish teenagers. Like so many other clerics he was summoned by the secularist French Government to do military service when mobilization against the Nazis became inevitable. In the wake of the Czech crisis in the spring of 1938 he was stationed in the quartermaster's corps near Metz, but thereafter the army allowed him to return for the opening of school at Avon in the fall semester. Then, after the outbreak of hostilities between Germany and Poland on 1 September 1939, he was back in uniform again as a master sergeant (below see the letter he wrote from that vantage point). The outdated strategies of the French military establishment failed against Hitler's innovative *Blitzkrieg* tactics and Père Jacques served time as a prisoner of war in German custody. Fifteen long months of almost suspended animation far from Avon as a mess sergeant with the 21st Artillery Battery was his lot, including five months as a military prisoner in Stalag 152 at Lunéville, until he was allowed to return home.[12] This time the other soldiers he left were deported, as prisoners of war, to Germany and eventually made to work in war factories. Before long, in thirty-eight months' time, he would inescapably share a similar fate.

Caught up in what was so aptly called the "gathering storm," the stories of both Sr. Teresa Benedicta and Père Jacques followed a pathetic crescendo during the waning months of the 1930s that led to tragic destinies in the next decade: not so far apart in Central Europe, both acting as angels of consolation to their companions in suffering, and both showing compassion for Jewish children persecuted by the Nazis.

3. Edith Stein, Comforting Sister

St. Edith was arrested first, so we begin with her "Stations of the Cross," her "filling up what was wanting to the sufferings of Christ" (Col 1:24) caused by the Second World War. As the devotion of the *Via Crucis* describes Christ in one instance consoling those who worry for him, so too did Stein pray and act to console, calm, and encourage people known and unknown to her along the way they traveled during the seven last days of their lives.

First Station: Echt Monastery

Echt Carmel was her home of exile, as already indicated, for three years and seven months. Her sister Rosa, fifth of the surviving children in the Stein family (four died in infancy) and the only other member of Edith's generation to embrace Christianity, came to join Sr. Teresa Benedicta late in 1939. Rosa, her elder by eight years, became a lay assistant to the cloistered religious in the Echt monastery, who generally did not leave their enclosure. Neither of them returned home to Germany because the SS arrested them in retaliation against the pastoral letter by the Roman Catholic episcopate of the Netherlands read out at Sunday Masses on 26 July 1942 to defend a very persecuted Jewry. In the following terms (flowing from current usage in those times but not so ecumenical-sounding to modern ears) the Catholic bishops asked their people to resist the German occupation forces' inhumane and unjust treatment of their Jewish neighbors:

> Dear Brethren:
> When Jesus drew near to Jerusalem and saw the city before him, he wept over it and said, "O, if even today you understood the things that make for peace! But now they are concealed from your sight." . . . Dear brethren, let us begin by examining ourselves in a spirit of profound humility and sorrow. Are we not partly to blame for the calamities which we are suffering? Have we always sought first for God's kingdom and its righteousness? Have we always fulfilled the demands of justice and charity toward our fellowmen? . . . When we examine ourselves, we are forced to admit that all of us have failed . . . Let us beseech God . . . to swiftly bring about a just peace in the world and to strengthen the people of Israel so sorely tested in these days, leading them to true redemption in Jesus Christ. . . . [13]

With a ghastly outcome, the church leadership's *defense of the Jews* led to the arrest of several hundred Catholic Jews residing in a country that reacted bravely in opposition to the hatred-filled policies of the Nazi occupiers.[14] St. Edith showed contemplative concern through two acts of oblation made during her forty-three month stay: one early, then another later on in the spring of 1939 before World War II began.

The first gesture is captured in a note to her prioress requesting permission to offer herself. Significant to the spiritual impulse is the terminology she adopted. Thinking of a time-honored Carmelite usage that included such acts of oblation made by the sixteen nuns of Compiègne Carmel during the French Revolution and by St. Thérèse of Lisieux in that same country a century later, Edith requested her prioress's consent on 26 March 1939. Only one week earlier that month she set the stage for her oblation by writing lines of poetry imploring St. Joseph's benevolent assistance, since he was considered the "Protector of the Order" of Discalced Carmelites:

> Dark and heavy, the heavens loom o'er us.
> Is night to be eternal, and light ne'er ours again?
> Has our Father above turned 'way from us?
> As by a nightmare's throttling,
> Our hearts are choked from need,
> Is there no savior, near or far, who knows to help? . . . [15]

The text of the petition to her prioress deserves quoting in full:

> + Dear Mother: please, will Y[our] R[everence] allow me to offer myself to the heart of Jesus as a sacrifice of propitiation for true peace, that the dominion of the Antichrist may collapse, if

> possible, without a new world war, and that a new order may be established? I would like it [my request] granted this very day because it is the twelfth hour. I know that I am a nothing, but Jesus desires it, and surely he will call many others to do likewise in these days.[16]

At least three major spiritual realities are intended by the saint in her urgent text. First, a positive attitude predominates. She would see "true peace" take over and a "new order. . .be established"; and this is to come about through the always gracious prompting of God because "Jesus desires" it and he will call many others to the same generous act soon. Congruent with this "positive" outlook are the remarks about avoiding the harm of the "Antichrist" (unmistakably Hitler with the Nazis, on their way to unleashing war about a half year later on 1 September 1939), and the "new world war" that seemed so inevitable. The phrase "it is the twelfth hour" is inherently positive by its oblique reference to the New Testament idea of the "eleventh hour" workers who got their reward in spite of the lateness of their commitment.

Secondly, the Christological balance removes any fear she might be impelled by troubling messianic impulses: in the first sentence the sacred "heart of Jesus" is the one to whom she will offer herself so his reign, not the reign of his opponent the "Anti*christ*," may prevail; and in the second sentence she is careful to assign her inspiration to "Jesus [who] desires" this since she is aware her sufficiency comes from him, not from herself who "is a nothing."

Thirdly, she wants to offer herself not for her own well-being but "for true peace" in order to see "(that) a new order (may be) established." She stands to benefit from such a reversal of fortune in the face of the Nazi perversion of values and unjust societal structures, but essentially her desire tends toward the well-being of others. This offering is neither selfish nor morose; it is eminently constructive as it moves to stand in *for* others. Her attitude of vicarious offering would be restated with renewed urgency a mere three months later.[17]

The drafting of a last will and testament captured her desire to make a difference once again. In the will, as in the Passion Sunday offering, terminology reveals deep spiritual insight. This text is dated 9 June 1939 (on a day late in her annual retreat, therefore in the midst of intense reflection), and it allows us to see someone who has come to terms with an imminent end to life. It runs to 690 words in English, has practical instructions whose effects are now long past, but some of its passages definitely show how much St. Edith wanted to reach out spiritually and help others suffering in war-torn Europe and beyond.[18]

After explaining that this is the second will she has drawn up, she proceeds to leave instructions for disposal of her books–no longer in the amount of the legendary "six crates" she brought with her to Cologne Carmel when she entered on 14 October 1933. Then she leaves instructions for treatment of the manuscript of *Life in a Jewish Family,* an operation all the more sensitive because a number of her siblings had managed to escape Europe and set down roots elsewhere. Next she describes the status of *Finite and Eternal Being,* her as-yet-unpublished magnum opus which had reached the page-proof stage but was blocked by Nazi discriminatory laws against Jews. She thanks the nuns of Echt for the kindness of taking her in back in 1938 and for giving her a home away from home.

Then she expresses spiritual acceptance of the destiny God has in store for her. Some would call this a stock devotional formula recited by many a good Catholic, and thus not something deserving of any special personal significance for Sr. Teresa Benedicta at the time she included it. This could be the case, but the sentiments involved are of the same sort as the offering she made on Passion Sunday that same year. Key to them is the evocative small word "for" that shows her extending her caring and concerned intentionality to several groups in danger from the oncoming war (three months later):

> I accept even now, with joy, the death which God has in mind for me, in total submission to his most holy will. I beg the Lord, that he may accept my life and death *for* his honor and glory, *for* all the intentions of the Most Sacred Hearts of Jesus and Mary and of holy Church, especially *for* the preservation, sanctification and perfecting of our holy order, particularly of the Cologne and Echt Carmels, in reparation *for* the unbelief of the Jewish people and that the Lord may be accepted by his people and his Kingdom may come in glory; *for* the safety of Germany and the peace of the world; and finally, *for* relatives, living and deceased, and all whom God has given me: that none of them be lost.
>
> On Friday in the octave of Corpus Christi, 9 June 1939, the seventh day of my retreat.
>
> In the name of the Father and of the Son and of the Holy Spirit. Sr. Teresa Benedicta of the Cross, O.C.D. [italics mine]

Second Station: Amersfoort Camp

In all, Sr. Teresa Benedicta and her sister Rosa saw three concentration camps between 3-9 August 1942: they passed through two transit camps in Holland on their way to the death camp at Auschwitz. The first transit camp was in Amersfoort, a town 95 miles distant from Echt and 25 miles southwest of Amsterdam. Their stay there was brief, making a lengthy description of what they faced hardly possible, but two laymen recounted what Edith told them about the harsh treatment their group of prisoners received. These men had been sent by the nuns of Echt to deliver objects for personal use to Edith and Rosa at the stopover point after Amersfoort (at Westerbork transit camp), and their recollections were given soon after the completion of their mission. Both eyewitness accounts may be found in the volume *Never Forget,* seventh in the Carmelite Studies series. The Roermond Catholic Episcopal Newsletter editor Piet van Kempen gave in his own name the following statement (borne out also by his companion, Pierre Cuypers):

> From Echt the trip took them to the local headquarters in Roermond. That same evening two police vans left Roermond, destination unknown. Thirteen persons sat in one van, and fourteen in the other. Since the driver lost his way . . . the prisoners did not arrive in Amersfoort until 3 a.m. The guarding by the German soldiers had been friendly until now. In the camp of Amersfoort, treatment by the guards became brutal and hardhearted. The prisoners were hit in the back with rifle butts and driven to the dormitories. The non-Catholic Jews got something to eat, and after a "night rest" of several hours on bunk beds, the transport of Jews continued very early the next morning by freight train to Hooghalen. From the train station [they traveled] on foot to Camp Westerbork.[19]

Thanks to postwar efforts by the Carmelites of Cologne to obtain news about the Stein sisters we have an eyewitness account from within Amersfoort camp itself. In the first translation in English of the biography issued by the prioress of Cologne, Dr. Lenig (an active member of the Dutch resistance who was rescued from the Nazis and thus survived the war) gave similar harrowing details of what greeted the Catholic converts upon arrival at Amersfoort:

> . . . I met Sister Teresia Benedicta a Cruce, known in the camp as Edith Stein, on the 2nd [actually after midnight between the 2nd and the 3rd] of August 1942, when she came into the transit camp at Amersfoort, into Hut No. 9, if I am not mistaken. On this Sunday all Catholics of Jewish, or partly Jewish, ancestry were arrested by the German hangmen as a reprisal for the pastoral letter which had been read from the pulpits of all Dutch [Catholic] churches the previous Sunday. They were thrown into vans and assembled at Amersfoort before being carried off to the gas-chambers and crematoria. When your sister and the other three hundred men, women and children were once behind the barbed wire of the camp they had to stand waiting for a roll-call on the barrack-square, just as a pleasant welcome. As a punishment, so far as I remember—one of the internees had "stolen" some dry bread that had been thrown away—the whole camp was being made to stand there for several days. That is to say, part of them were still standing, the rest had collapsed and were being continually mishandled to get them on their feet again. Among those still standing I noticed an inflexible opponent of the Third Reich, Ministerial Director Dr. Lazarus, who, like the new arrivals, was an active and ardent Catholic. Nor can I forget how the day was one long series of kickings and beatings, although these were tolerable. The most distressing thing was the condition of the women. It was in this that Edith Stein showed her worth. . . . [20]

Dr. Lenig does not enlarge on which signs Edith Stein used to show "her worth" in those circumstances, but he helps us appreciate she must have been helping others in some practical way, if only by sustaining peaceful behavior like that shown back in Echt at her arrest.

She would continue her consoling influence at a site farther north the last three days of her stay in Holland (4-6 August).

Third Station: Westerbork Camp

The next transit camp was the Westerbork facility in northeastern Holland. What we know from eyewitness sources who testified after the war is confirmed by the contemporary collection of letters by Etty Hillesum that gained notoriety later on, *Letters from Westerbork.*[21] The arrival of Stein's group in the transit camp is even described by this woman working for the Jewish Council that was pressed into concentration camp service by the Nazis to induce a semblance of order and thus exclude any chance of rebellion from the prisoners. [22]

The camp had a railroad spur into it, and although this was not a death camp it had a "ramp" leading to and from the railroad cars that has become so symbolic of the death camps. Up the Westerbork ramp went the people sent away "to the East," to places like Sobibor and, of course, Auschwitz. Though the moment of truth would take place a long distance away, Westerbork imposed much misery on the detainees. Many of them were beside themselves with fear of what lay ahead. Especially affected were women with children. The mothers could well imagine they were on the brink of personal and family doom, so they were seized with a terror that left many of them depressed and unable to look after their own. Edith Stein quickly noticed what was going on and did not hesitate to pick up the slack. Her many years as an educator provided her with all the signals that indicate severe need for assistance; and the time spent in the monasteries of Cologne and Echt had not blunted her sharp powers of perception, quite the opposite. Perhaps harking back to her stint in World War I as a Red Cross volunteer nurse in a contagious disease hospital she pitched in to help the children.[23] She combed their hair, told them stories, did whatever else she could to keep their minds occupied. Someone who was allowed to visit the camp had this to say about her generous interventions. Julius Marcan, a survivor, testified that: "It was Edith Stein's complete calm and self–possession that marked her out from the rest of the prisoners. . . . Many of the mothers were on the brink of insanity and had sat moaning for days, without giving any thought to their children. Edith Stein immediately set about taking care of these little ones. She washed them, combed their hair and tried to make sure they were fed and cared for."[24]

From Westerbork Edith was able to send back a compelling message to the nuns at her monastery in Echt that included these words: ". . . we place our trust in your prayers. There are so many persons here in need of a little comfort, and they expect it from the sisters."[25] In this context, the term "sisters" refers to the religious nuns present among the Catholic Jews who had been rounded up on 2 August, and not the nursing personnel whose title "Sister" she shared during her volunteer service in World War I. Now Edith had no medications to dispense, nor could she deal with the other detainees from a nurse's position of authority. She had only herself to give: her attentiveness, the time she took away from her own worries, and her spirit of religious hope. She gave all that she had, because she was present with, present to the others; she was willing to do as much as she could to share their burden of suffering so as to lighten the load.

The freeing effects of her compassionate "comfort" did not go unnoticed. Mr. H. Wielek, a Dutch camp official who spoke with her in Westerbork left a description which confirms that letter she wrote as she contributed to this poor world's very limited reserves of compassion:

> I knew: here is someone truly great. For a couple of days she lived in that hellhole, walking, talking and praying . . . like a

> saint. And she really was one. That is the only fitting way to describe this middle–aged woman who struck everyone as so young, who was so whole and honest and genuine.
> She spoke so humbly . . . "I never knew people could actually be like this. . .and I honestly had no idea of how my brothers and sisters were being made to suffer. . . . I pray for them continually." . . . then I saw her go off to the train with her sister Rosa praying as she went, and smiling the smile of unbroken resolve that accompanied her to Auschwitz.[26]

These words of tribute deserve comment. Ten years after their encounter and therefore with sustained conviction, someone is using the word "saint" to describe Stein in the public forum of a Dutch newspaper. Mr. Wielek was and remained a Jew; and he certainly did not have an inkling people would be gathering up indications of acts of virtue suitable to promote an official cause for canonization at the time he wrote it (the diocesan process started officially in 1962). "She really was one." Second, he relates she was concerned for her "brothers and sisters." For Stein there is no intentional distance between her and these people, even though she is a Catholic who goes on praying for them within the religious mindset she had embraced twenty years previously (her baptism took place on the first day of the year 1922). She has no difficulty in calling all those who were being made to suffer her "brothers and sisters." Significant is that key word of imposed suffering: they "were being *made* to suffer." She shared in it, but I believe she bore it from a distinctly Christian point of view (as stated earlier); thus she felt all the more earnestly for the Jews around her, worried they might be giving in to distressing sentiments of abandonment.[27] Finally, Mr.Wielek says she went up the ramp to the train "praying as she went." You find no sign of despair in that picture: she even showed a smile of unbroken resolve as she moved into the train car. Her name as a nun was Teresa. Might she not have been reciting to herself, mantra like, the words attributed to the great St. Teresa of Avila: "Let nothing trouble you / let nothing frighten you / whoever has God lacks nothing?" Or did she remember lines from St. John of the Cross, still fresh in her mind from her recent work on his writings in *The Science of the Cross?*[28] Or was it a verse of Scripture like the one from Romans 8:28 that she attested she relied on at crisis points in her life, "All things work to the good of those who love God"?[29]

Surely she was deriving "resolve" from her progressive assimilation of the Carmelite vocation, whatever the tension she was undergoing at the moment.[30] All the years of self-denial and detachment were paying off, because she was able to forget herself especially as she was now communing with the sufferings of Christ; and she wanted to go on acting as a source of peace, a center of calm in the storm of fearfulness around her.[31]

Fourth Station: Schifferstadt Railroad Station

St. Teresa Benedicta's calm alerted her to her surroundings at the fourth and final station we know about, viz., a train stop on Friday, 7 August, at Schifferstadt near Speyer, the theater of so many years of her professional activities during the 1920s. Schifferstadt was a change-over point from long-distance trains for persons heading on to the less central station at Speyer, lying along a spur-line approximately seven miles to the southeast.

Much research, including work in the German national railways archives in Mainz, went into a recent study by Fr. Joachim Feldes titled *Edith Stein and Schifferstadt*.[32] The study sets out two major features of Edith's life: her relationship to Canon Schwind of Speyer Cathedral who was born in Schifferstadt and had family there; and the reported stop of her train from Westerbork to Auschwitz around noon on August 7th.

Aside from accurate data on train schedules or movements or their positions on train tracks that day—all uncovered by the painstaking research of Fr. Feldes, himself a native of Schifferstadt — the following two conclusions he draws shed light on the way Sr. Teresa Benedicta was dealing with her deportation, under armed guard, to the most infamous of all death camps constructed by the Nazis.

First, she was calm and concentrated enough to make contact with Valentin Fouquet, the station master. In spite of the danger, she furtively asked him to transmit greetings to relatives in Schifferstadt of Canon Schwind, her spiritual director immediately after baptism and until his death in 1927.[33] Next she recognized a priest on the platform, Fr. Ferdinand Meckes, whom she asked to greet a cathedral canon and her former colleagues, the sisters of St. Magdalena's in Speyer. She also had enough self-possession to throw a small piece of paper, ripped out of a pocket agenda, with her signature on it. Due to the vagaries of the war this paper no longer exists.[34]

These gestures betray no attempts to provoke intervention. Instead, she apparently wanted to inform old friends of her situation and perhaps supply them some comfort by being remembered by her. This was the last reported instance of what St. Edith said during her way of the cross. The gloomy end point of the journey of suffering was shrouded behind the curtain of secrecy maintained at the death camps by the Nazis, so to this date there is no more eyewitness evidence of what she faced on 9 August after arrival.[35]

"Endstation"

Earlier in the year of Edith and Rosa Stein's arrest in Holland, high German government officials decided at a conference held at Wannsee near Berlin to wipe out European Jewry by adopting what is known as the infamous "Final Solution."[36] Alongside an already infernal war effort the Nazis unleashed a firestorm of genocide within areas under the control of their occupation forces. The Stein sisters and their Catholic-convert companions were rounded up in the midst of an all-out mobilization mandated as a far-reaching effort to rid the Reich of its nemesis, the Jews.

Given the wide-ranging concentration camp system in place in several countries, we know "all roads did" not lead to Auschwitz, as the case of Père Jacques shows, but masses of Jews did meet their deaths there. They left the train under heavy guard, came down the "ramp," were not even admitted to the camp proper (so no identification numbers were tattooed on Edith or Rosa's forearms), and within hours were gassed expeditiously.

In that summer of 1942 their group was herded in even smaller-sized groups through the Birkenau section of the camp (called "Auschwitz II") to the building where zyklon-B gas was injected. Because the camp had not yet reached the industrialized proportions or smooth functioning of later on in the war, there were no crematoria at that spot. The bodies were stacked on top of each other, doused with fuel, and burned beyond recognition in the open air.[37] As for countless others, only post-wartime search services of the Red Cross issued a formal declaration of death to Sr. Teresa Benedicta/Edith Stein and Rosa Adelheid Stein.[38] A Carmelite professed nun and a Carmelite secular order member had met Christ and passed over into full possession of the Kingdom where his deep, deep peace swept aside the horrors they saw during the last week of their lives on earth.

4. Père Jacques Bunel, Martyr of Charity

Père Jacques Bunel, a friar of the Paris province of Discalced Carmelites, is known in the United States through a major feature film whose title captures his own words spoken at the moment he was placed under arrest and deported from France: "See you again, children" or *"Au revoir, les enfants."* The film director Louis Malle (famous for "Atlantic City," "Pretty Baby," "My Dinner with André," and, after a fashion, for his widow Candice Bergen) used Père Jacques's very words of farewell to title his film about his own school days in wartime France. The school in question was run by Père Jacques, in the village of Avon just a mile from the famous chateau of Fontainebleau. The dramatic interest of the film also flowed from the initiative of Père Jacques. It tells of the friendship one pupil creates with a newly arrived Jewish boy being protected by the headmaster, Père Jacques (called Père Jean in the film).[39]

In real life the three Jewish teenage boys—Jacques-France Halpern, Hans-Helmut Michel, and Maurice-David Schlosser—lived in Avon under Père Jacques's direct protection for twelve months (January 1943-January 1944).[40] Not a very long respite from persecution, some would say, but in a documentary about Père Jacques an older sister quoted Hans-Helmut Michel: "how lucky we are to be so well cared for; they even give us 'fresh eggs' on occasion." Given wartime rationing, his appreciation was sincere and an unsuspecting indicator of the exceptionally kind surroundings he came upon when received by the Carmelite friar at his school. Hans-Helmut Michel demonstrated his appreciation by gaining a prize during the spring term he studied with pupils like Louis Malle. In a year-end award booklet for academic achievement once placed on display at the U.S. Holocaust Museum as a wartime relic honoring Père Jacques, his name on the awards list was "Jean Bonnet," just as the other two

Jewish boys had been assigned the Christian names of Maurice Sabatier and Jacques Dupré as pseudonyms for protection. Unfortunately, Père Jacques's courageous gesture of protecting at great risk the three Jewish children became known, because a former lay associate of the school was tortured by the Gestapo to reveal the operation in the town of Avon and other underground secrets elsewhere.

Arrest was swift, deportation automatic, for Jacques-France Halpern, Hans-Helmut Michel, and Maurice-David Schlosser. On 15 January 1944 all three students were quickly sent to Auschwitz where their sufferings were terminated (in the manner we all have heard of); Père Jacques's sufferings were stretched out over some sixteen months at several stages of a true *via dolorosa.* In all, he stayed in two prisons and two concentration camps, and what he both tried and was able to do throughout that painful odyssey is the reason why they kept him moving from place to place. Like a squeaky wheel, or by adopting a "prophetic" stance as we'd put it nowadays, he called attention to himself as he did all he could to organize a resistance of the spirit against the demeaning and inhuman methods imposed on all prisoners by the German captors. This resistance sprang from the Christian sense of discipleship that he crystallized in a retort made to those who interrogated him after his arrest in Avon: "I know only one law: that of the Gospel and charity."[41]

First Station: The Prison at Fontainebleau

Avon is a small satellite village of the well-known royal chateau town of Fontainebleau outside Paris. Père Jacques spent seven weeks in Fontainebleau's prison.[42] Still close to his confreres in Avon he was helped along by them and by sympathetic people of the area. Although an attempt to free him fell through, his reaction to the attempt before seeing its failed outcome showed his self-sacrificing generosity. He remarked that far from wanting to be "sprung" from captivity he was convinced "there must be priests in the prisons" to assist the prisoners.

Bravado did not unleash that statement, nor did he have clear knowledge of what the ministry of prison chaplains required. He just came to realize others expected they could find much-needed and special support from a priest coprisoner. Père Jacques, not unlike Edith Stein, nurtured thoughts of active solidarity as he wished to be present *for* the victims of the Nazi injustice. In his case he did not only pray for, but he opted to be with them; and be for them a source of hope. He was applying, where needed, the ideas he expressed at greater length on 10 January 1940 in a small bulletin he created for his unit on the Maginot Line during what the French themselves call the "strange" or "funny" war, the lamented *"drôle de guerre":*

> Moreover, in the hearts of those whom it unites, camaraderie arouses and nourishes two very strong feelings: a sense of empathy, accompanied by an instinct of devotion.
>
> Without realizing it comrades who suffer from the same burden empathize with one another. Precisely because empathy is a form of charity, it generates spontaneous reflexes of devotion—sometimes even heroic devotion—that lead comrades to rescue one another. Moreover, since war is the harshest collective ordeal, it gives rise to the most ardent and enduring camaraderie. Comrades love one another strongly because they suffer intensely. Absorbed in distress, differences apparent in civilian life disappear. There remain only human beings, equally hurt in their innermost sensitivities and equally exposed to the same serious threats, as together they strive for the same goal. Their union grows deeper in this communion with the same ordeal.

> We are now living through such months of ordeal! Therefore, let us overflow with this strong spirit of true camaraderie, which teaches us to respect one another, to love one another, and to help one another for the rest of our lives.[43]

To say "there must be priests in the prisons" was brave of him, since the wardens could have been French collaborationists quite opposed to any relief for their noncompliant charges; but it was the Nazi occupiers who ultimately piped the tune. By 6 March of that year they moved him to another prison that served as a transit locale in the historic town of Compiègne, north of Paris.

Second Station: The Transit Camp at Compiègne Prison

Several centuries earlier, sixteen of his Carmelite sisters were expelled from the Carmel of Compiègne and killed in the French Revolution. One can imagine the heightened emotions swelling up in him when he realized he was being sent there. Nor would he likely have forgotten scenes of Nazi representatives accepting the surrender of their opposite numbers in the puppet Pétain French regime on 22 June 1940 in a railroad car brought to Compiègne, to symbolize their revenge for the defeat of Germany in World War I sealed by the signing of the armistice in the same car near Compiègne.

At this second place of detention he declared "now my place is with my comrades." A Communist described him as a Christian "as Christ wanted one to be."[44] He was growing quickly into a special missionary of mercy and service in spite of the unjust treatment he received. He did not give up, nor give in to the feelings of despair he saw around him. Helping him along, however, was the chance he had to offer Eucharist in the prison chapel; and he also swung into action by hearing confessions and giving catechism lessons. This priestly activity eased the pain of everyone's worries over chances of survival at the hands of the occupation forces in charge.

Though his activity had a distinctly religious tone to it, his captors noticed what he was up to and disliked the galvanizing results it had on the prisoners who were deriving so much spiritual support from him. As a result his stay was brief here, three weeks in all; worse still, his next destination was a bona fide concentration camp known as a reprisal camp for recalcitrant prisoners.

Third Station: Reprisal Camp at Neue Bremm (near Saarbrücken)

Not so very far from the French border stood this pitiful establishment. Père Jacques was swift to notice how the guards were overzealous in meting out punishment on the inmates, still, he soon earned from them the nickname of "agitator." No harm as far as he was concerned: he picked out and "cared for the neediest in whatever way he could," because he said they "were the men most in need of help."[45] Not only did he generate encouragement in this place, he shared in the punishments and displayed enormous reserves of solidarity in suffering. Never seeking or accepting special treatment offered him by other internees, he showed he could stand by and alongside them through it all. His willingness to keep nothing back was another form of "giving an account of the hope that was in him" (1Pt 3:15) as he gave others reasons to resist the dehumanizing treatment imposed upon them continually. Those reasons came from a mind and a heart that formulated thoughts like the following in his "*drôle de guerre*" bulletin called "*Centrale-Ecoute*" or the "Listening Post":

> To react against these trials means avoiding the useless muck in which some feel compelled to live. Instead, we have to find an alternative and discover the secret richness of patience.

> Patience! We know that it is useless to worry and to be sad. Sadness does not change a situation, except to increase its pain. Simply take each day as it comes, with its own share of sadness and joy. Do not try to guess what tomorrow will bring, and do not fall into fear. We have to do our work—all our work. We can be sure of only this: one day victory will come and then we will return to our homes and families. We must be intelligently patient! Not only must we live the war humanly, we must live it in such a way that each of us becomes more truly human. We must take advantage of the war and draw from it everything that can contribute to our personal moral growth. Admittedly, this personal growth is our only compensation. We will gather only crumbs, or pieces at best. But why should we ignore them?[46]

It is not clear what impelled the Nazis to intervene, but rather quickly, after just three weeks, they decided to ship him out "to the East" (just as Edith Stein went eastward deep into Hitler's thousand-year Reich) and send him to the horrendous city of death called Mauthausen concentration camp. This large camp lay in the river valleys near Linz, Austria. Actually, it was a series of subcamps named for the local emplacements they occupied. Père Jacques would thus be assigned to the Gusen I satellite camp.

Fourth Station: Mauthausen/Gusen Camp Complex

A full year and two weeks was the time he spent here, before the end of hostilities freed him from captivity. The history of Mauthausen, with its quarry, has been documented extensively.[47] Its infamous staircase of death was a particularly inhuman torture tool used grindingly by the SS guards: prisoners had to bring blocks of stone, some weighing as much as sixty-six pounds, in slings on their emaciated backs up

186 steps or face extermination, either by gunshot or by being pushed back headlong down the slope of the quarry.[48] Significantly, the main enlarged photo in the section of the U.S. Memorial Holocaust Museum's section explaining military liberation of World War II camps shows the front gate of Mauthausen. The camp was located east of the city of Linz, Austria, along the Danube River fabled in song for its blue waters. Smaller tributary rivers ran down from the hills into the Danube, and the Gusen River gave its name to the concentration camp subdivision where Père Jacques stayed most of the time he was held prisoner.

His experience of a real "hell-on-earth" was divided into three phases, with him thrown into a crucible of demeaning tortures that his indomitable generosity turned into bursts of light for those who interacted with him. An unexpected form his openhearted kindliness took were the efforts he made to learn enough Polish to minister the sacraments, on the sly entirely and at the risk of his own life, to Polish Catholic prisoners. Serving the other Frenchmen present was a constant concern, still, he interwove the brave encouragement he gave them with assistance to the Slavs interned with them but without a priest from their own country.

Second, he gave away frequently some of his daily rations so others could cheat death. He fretted a lot over the married men separated from their families. This emptying of himself to nourish others paralleled Christ's *kenosis*; and service of Christ was the ultimate motivational force of Père Jacques's generosity. This Christocentric compassion was preached by Père Jacques just a few months before his arrest when he gave a retreat to the Discalced Carmelite nuns of Le Havre from 6-12 September 1943: "Christ is a living being who is here, there, and everywhere. To see Christ, we must do as Zachaeus did. We must become poor. Formerly, the weight of wealth overpowered him and prevented him from rising. Riches drag down the soul. One has to become small in stature, that is, detached from the goods of this world, for such riches foster earthly desires."[49]

Third, the universal love he showed did not stop at the frontiers of faith: he even attracted Communists to informal discussions he conducted in the evening on inspiring topics. His credentials for interacting with the Communists were solid, and his actions of a few years previous during the *"drôle de guerre,"* show why. As pointed out above, the French futilely set up defenses unable to contain the ultramodern German Army. The French were outflanked and swiftly overcome by Nazi forces. Before this debacle Père Jacques was mobilized and he spent long, boring hours waiting at a French defensive position, not far from the border. He wrote a gem of a letter to his friend Fr. Maurice Lefèvre, O.C.D., that was also displayed in the Holocaust Museum in Washington D.C. It attests to how much Hitler was on Père Jacques' mind:

> 21 Sept. 1939
> Dearest Brother,
>
> Thank you for your most welcome letter. What a pleasure it was to relive so many memories as I read it! All that had been planned to mount the mobilization with such precision has amazed me. Everything went into place, hour by hour, according to plan, in perfect order.
>
> I am in a hurry to go into action and provide my small contribution to demolish Hitler. I am impatient from remaining "stagnant" on a border without German forces directly across from us. Getting back to Avon will be quite pleasant, but it is almost just as pleasant to die in order to see God. If I die, you should not say I "sacrificed my life," but that I joyfully left for heaven whence

- --

I will intently look after those I love.

Very affectionately.

fr. Jacques de Jésus o.c.d.
PS Every day I read my little ration of Pascal, and, when I can, a passage or two of Plato.[50]

In 1939 Père Jacques had been taken captive, interned, but then released enabling him to return to Avon and to do his charitable intervention work in favor of the Jewish children. Much can be derived about the character of Père Jacques from those words, but they at least prove he had an accurate "read" on the tremendous danger Hitler represented. He knew it was right to resist the neo-pagan worldview of the Nazis: why else would he use the strong word "*demolish* Hitler"? Unfortunately, Hitler's agents demolished his health in his second captivity.[51]

Just before liberation from Mauthausen by the Third U.S. Army's Eleventh Armored Division (shown in the photo at the U.S. Holocaust Memorial Museum), he was chosen by his countrymen to head all the French internees. Future research in American war archives might very well turn up traces of testimony he would have given to his liberators. He never lived to see France again, however, and remained in Austria due to the weakened condition he had fallen into. Only his body returned to Avon where it now rests in the monastery cemetery guarded faithfully by a plaque from the local Jewish community recognizing his goodness to them in the face of acute danger.

Aftermath

Père Jacques was indeed consumed by all he did and suffered by the end of the war, even though he lived to see the liberation of his camp by American Army troops. He was so emaciated that there was nothing their medical personnel could do to save him. Hence, he was transferred into the city of Linz to a private clinic run by the Sisters of St. Elizabeth. He died a mere twenty-eight days after he was freed from his captivity.

Thanks to a gift from his Austrian Discalced brothers living in that city his corpse was laid out in a Carmelite habit. Because his fellow citizens were so totally impressed by the man and all he had done to bring them through their hell-on-earth, they spoke to French authorities and word went to Paris. The government sent an air force plane to Linz and Père Jacques was brought back for a funeral, then interment at the Avon Carmelite monastery just next to the boys' school from which he was deported. He had finally come home, and there he rests to this day.

He "rests" after applying his great personal dynamism to alleviating suffering and in the meantime disregarding his own. The following prophetic words he wrote to his bother René two days before his arrest (15 January 1944) sum up his other-centered generosity: "It is very likely that in a short while some very serious things will overtake me. If I am shot, be glad over it because I will have attained my ideal of giving my life for those who suffer."[52] For his unstinting kindness the Israeli Government granted him their famous Medal of the Just, issued to rescuers of Jews during World War II like Oskar Schindler. A commemorative evergreen tree was planted for him by the Yad Vashem memorial museum on the outskirts of Jerusalem. It grows in section G (no. 1378), just north of the Children's Memorial that was built after it was planted. Strange dispensation of Providence this, that prompted the designers of the sad house of memories which is Yad Vashem, to erect a children's shrine so close to the verdant symbolic presence of the French friar who gave his life to lengthen the lives of three young Jewish boys.

5. Conclusion

By now many persons have seen images of the little girl who was cured through the intercession of Edith Stein. I think it extremely fitting that a *child* benefited from prayer to her: just as children were protected or nourished, even physically, by St. Edith and by Père Jacques, during their lives. It is always the defenseless little ones who suffer so in life.[53] We are fortunate as an Order to have such self-sacrificing members calling us to do our share of looking after "little ones" in our societies. May they pray for us, so that we can make a difference as they did.

Good educators/pedagogues that they were, they would welcome my concluding this reflection on their passing over from this life to life in the Kingdom with aphorisms that invite us to share their personal awareness of others in need. From Cologne Carmel St. Edith offered the following good advice to a friend who would ultimately accompany her on the train to Auschwitz: "Lay all your care for the future, confidently, in God's hands, and allow yourself to be led by him entirely, as a child would."[54] Père Jacques offers us a vision he undoubtedly let challenge himself: "True educators touch the hearts of all their students, and thus touch their entire lives. Such an approach requires a calm, firm, and balanced spirit. In one word, it requires gentleness."[55]

6. Epilogue: War and Remembrance in Carmel

1. The Case of Rosa Stein

Both Père Jacques and St. Edith Stein have had their share of posthumous honors: the State of Israel and the U.S. Holocaust Memorial Museum both have memorialized him; the Catholic Church declared her a martyr saint, while his cause for canonization is in the initial stages.

Alongside St. Edith at the moment of her martyrdom stood her blood sister Rosa Stein, a secular or "third" order member of Carmel, in the terminology of those days. Both of them had lived and served for a time with the Carmelite community of Echt, Holland.[56] Rosa desired to embrace the same kind of life her younger sister had been living from October 1933 on. However, since she had received baptism only late in 1936 the superior of that monastery suggested she delay entering the order as a nun when she asked admission sometime in 1939, soon after her departure from Nazi Germany. Time would tell, or would have told, how much longer she might wait before being admitted to formation to test her call to the cloistered life Sr. Teresa Benedicta was living there. Their shared cruel fate in Auschwitz/Birkenau destined them to die together, but it also swept away Rosa's longed-for goal of dedication to God in a religious vocation.

Nothing in her actions in Holland indicated she was not progressing in a generous lay vocation, however, and some eyewitnesses portray her as a very kind person representing the interests of the enclosed nuns to the outside world of the town of Echt.[57] I personally met one such eyewitness in rather unexpected surroundings, namely, Rome's Coliseum.

My pilgrimage group to the canonization of St. Edith in October 1998 met up with a similar group from the town of Echt inside the Coliseum. The touring pilgrims excitedly pointed out to me a Dutch gentleman they'd just learned had been an altar boy during World War II serving liturgies in the nuns' monastery. Of course he knew both the Stein sisters, but in different ways. This became apparent under the barrage of questions from the curious pilgrims eagerly asking if he had any recollections of the new saint, Sr. Teresa Benedicta of the Cross. "No," he replied, "not many memories of her because she lived within the enclosure and always wore a long, black veil. But, Miss Rosa, we all knew and liked Miss Rosa." In the course of performing her duties of running errands around the town, and accommodating requests from the people who came to the monastery door, Rosa had made many friends and won over a lot of hearts. Her goodness and kindness lived on in the elderly man who was speaking to us in the city of St. Edith's canonization.

It seems only fair to ask why couldn't the Order of Carmel, so keen nowadays on intently integrating the gifts, insights, and active collaboration of lay members into its life of service for the Church, also take up the cause of beatification of Rosa Stein? After all, her sister was beatified as a martyr who underwent the special kind of modern *collective* martyrdom that snuffed out the lives of so many Catholic convert Jews after the Dutch Bishops protested anti-Semitic persecution by the Nazis. She received no treatment different from St. Edith from the moment of their arrest, even though she was not a professed religious. Quite the contrary, she shared fully in what her nun sister underwent.

From the transit camp of Westerbork in northeast Holland Rosa even penned serene words as a postscript to a letter St. Edith sent back to Echt on the third day of their captivity. Her paragraph attests to a fully parallel experience as it sounds calming notes of its own:

> Sincere greetings to all. We are very sorry not to have seen Mother Otillia any more. In this brief time we have experienced a great deal; one lives together, with the others, and everywhere people help each other. We have slept very little, but have had a lot of good air and much traveling. Many greetings to Sophie [Meuwissen], Maria [Delsing] too, and to everyone; they were so upset; we not at all.
> *In Corde Jesu* we all find ourselves in gratitude.
>
> Rosa[58]

The final word "gratitude" is most evocative. It reveals a positive attitude in someone coping with downright threatening surroundings, hemmed in on all sides by forces unfriendly to her prisoner companions and intently bent on applying the infamous "final solution" to them (since January of that same year, though surely without their knowing it). Rosa also manages to accentuate the positive in her phrase "everywhere people help each other." Furthermore, in words of supreme kindliness, she lets us appreciate more accurately her frame of mind in the face of the violent events that accompanied her arrest at the Echt Carmel. She mentions Maria Delsing, one of the local women who had gathered near the Echt monastery door when the Stein sisters were being led away into the police van.[59]

Rosa tells us that Maria Delsing, Sophie Meuwissen and "everyone" were "so upset, we not at all." This makes her note all the more precious, since often-repeated accounts of that 2 August 1942 capture by the Nazis give another version of words and gestures exchanged by the Stein sisters. Rosa, as the tradition would have it, was so worried, that Sr. Teresa Benedicta was led to utter special words of comfort to her. We are told Sr. Teresa Benedicta had to intervene to reinstill calm in her elder sister. On the other hand, in her postscript to St. Edith's message, the very person concerned suggests she was doing fairly well: she noticed her friends in an agitated state of high concern for her well-being ("they were so upset"), but she was bearing up under the trying circumstances well enough to notice their fear and she apparently was as much in possession of herself as the circumstances could allow ("we not at all"). This makes it safe to assume that, at the distance of three days when she was writing the note, Rosa was not expressing just illusory or "stiff-upper-lip" type sentiments designed to cover up her real feelings. Besides, she wrote her words right after her sister's, thus making it unlikely she would have jotted down anything that Edith would have considered cloying or misleading.

Rosa's note is helpful in another way. It clarifies and underscores her own inherent significance in the story of the last days of her and her sister's life together. The now-accepted martyrdom of St. Edith Stein asserts she witnessed as a truly Christian vessel of grace to all around her in the concentration camps during her last week on earth. St. Edith spent herself in comforting others, as was explained above. Rosa's text indicates she acted similarly. "Everywhere people help each other," was one remark that described the mutual assistance she participated in as the group "experienced a great deal" (euphemistic phrase to describe their maltreatment, no doubt). The further remark that "one lives together" probably indicates a lack of privacy in the jumbled conditions of captivity on police vans and in camp barracks, but it also can be taken to mean she was sharing *actively* the lot of all the others. Her text describes a scene of people reaching out to each other, sustaining one another, giving of one's self to help the others along—things so much in character for her who years before had run the house for her busy mother, then was known for her friendly ways in Echt. Both she and her sainted sister were sources of Christian charity while moving through the concentration camps. Both were illumined by grace to shed perhaps small, but real, beams of light in the darkness around them. Both overcame the temptation to self-centeredness in the face of mortal danger, as they opened their hearts *("in corde Jesu")* to the other Jewish victims around them, sharing their burdens. Rosa's behavior was a mirror image of her sister's, however different they were as individuals. Ought they to remain distant in death for lack of equal recognition of how they witnessed to the presence of the suffering Christ in Nazi Germany's diabolical camp system? Can Rosa not qualify, in other words, for canonization?

The *sensus fidelium* or the *vox populi* counts for something in every age, and people of good will have the right to make their opinions known in the Church. Didn't St. Edith write a letter to Pius XI asking him to issue an encyclical against anti-Semitism?[60] I nourish the hope that everyone who reads this addendum to the thoughts above about St. Edith and Père Jacques might try to contact Fr. Ildefonso Moriones, the Discalced Carmelite in charge of causes for canonizations (his title is "Postulator General" and he is known for his writings about the Doria-Gratian controversies) to initiate a process to take up actively Rosa Stein's cause. Our order is the proper matrix or vehicle of such a cause, due to the fact that Rosa was a secular order member (as was, for instance, Bl. Josefa Naval Girbés before her). Carmel cannot answer for the other companions who accompanied them after the August 2nd roundup (some were Trappists and members of more modern congregations),[61] but we can, and ought, to feel a certain pride in Rosa's worth as a witness along with her sister. Not to do so is to lose an opportunity to show how widely the holiness of God in his servants shone forth at an hour of great darkness in the affairs of humankind.

2. Concentration Camp Carmels

This concluding segment concerns no longer individual Carmelites in concentration camps, but the postwar phenomenon of monasteries of Carmelites located near concentration camps. Since 1962 the Discalced branch of the Carmelites have founded and maintained three such houses. Two are in Germany, and a third in Poland. The controversial history of the latter, located near but not exactly at the perimeter of Auschwitz I concentration camp in the 1980's and 1990's, is so well known as not to require comment in itself.[62] It does deserve mention in this context with its sister Carmels on German soil—the first at Dachau, then the other in Berlin.

My purpose in describing this particular page of contemporary Carmelite history is twofold: 1) to provide accurate identification of each and, thus, 2) to turn aside accusations that they have been founded out of misguided or, worse, ignoble motivations. So often one has read or heard in the media that Auschwitz Carmel, for instance, was founded in memory of Edith Stein, perhaps now the most famous Catholic to die in the death camp's Birkenau section. Nothing could be further from the intentions of the sisters who opened their Carmel there.[63]

In gestures of solidarity with people who carry, still today, psychological wounds from either captivity in concentration camps or close association with people who suffered in them, the Carmelite Nuns of Dachau, Berlin/Plötzensee, and Auschwitz live precisely on those sites in order to be a balm in a world that smarts at the very mention of those names. They can do this because they believe in the spiritual and, it must be admitted even for a faith-vision of things, the mysterious nature of the contemplative life they lead as disciples of Christ. Theirs is not an interventionist or polemical vocation. Rather, they prefer to make prayer, primarily silent meditative prayer, the mainstay of their presence at places of great horror. They engage in praise of God and petitions to the Almighty to show that God's goodness deserves to be acknowledged today where so much evil prevailed in the 1930s and 1940s. Realism, not adulation for Edith Stein, marks the Carmels in an emblematic fashion through the actual titular patron or patroness selected for each monastery.

As already indicated, neither Auschwitz Carmel nor the other two have St. Edith Stein for their patron. In chronological order of foundation three distinct titles were chosen. Dachau was opened in 1964 under the patronage of "The Precious Blood" (of Christ) *[Heilige Blut].*[64] Nuns from Dachau thereafter founded a monastery in 1982 attached to Berlin's Resistance Church, not far from Plötzensee Prison with its execution unit that killed such opponents of the Nazi regime as Fr. Alfred Delp. Its title is "Queen of Martyrs" *[Regina Martyrum].*[65] And, from its inception in 1985 Auschwitz Carmel has been operating under the patronage of the "Communion of Saints" *[Communio Sanctorum],* a particularly positive choice as it indicates holiness in a place so shot through with the evil machinations of the SS and other Nazi agents.[66] So, none of the three are in any way a platform, either triumphalistic or proselytizing, for Edith Stein. None of them underscore directly, either, any other particular Carmelite who might have been interned in the camps they watch over today.

This ought to reassure persons who, haunted by the fallout of untold sufferings in their family, fear that the Catholic Church is somehow trying to "appropriate" the Holocaust, or otherwise soften the degree of loss among the groups that were hardest hit by Nazi hatred. The above-mentioned patrons, at least in the Catholic spiritual vision of things, represent broad-ranging mysteries of the faith. They do not target any one person who would serve as a kind of Trojan Horse in the midst of all who still mourn the disaster brought upon themselves or their loved ones. Dachau does not commemorate Edith

Stein's blood; nor is it Edith Stein the martyr who is remembered in Berlin but Mary, the Queen of Martyrs; nor is the name of *Saint* Edith brandished in Auschwitz (she wasn't even beatified when the Carmel opened, as the record shows), but the full "communion" of saints—that band of unnamed holy ones who faced death drawing on their faith in God and who relied upon God's merciful grace to persevere to the last.

While we might not feel there is a need for other foundations of Carmelite monasteries at still other concentration camps, we can at least rest easy with the overall images that these three evoke. Another frequently missed positive point about them is this: during the war the Nazis did all they could to keep the concentration camp prisoners captive in a double isolation, i.e., physical separation from the world at large behind electrified barbed wire, but also psychological separation from each other through fear of betrayal or punishment in order to curtail the possibility of concerted rebellion. In spite of their captors' demonic stratagems the internees formed large communities of shared suffering. To commemorate them in an ongoing fashion at the site of their agony one could not place a better symbol than a living *community* in which mutual loving service of the members prevails. The communal witness of Carmelite monasteries at concentration camps (though not within the precincts of the camps) is an eloquent reminder and a presence aiming at healing memories of the most diabolically organized mayhem produced by our race. May they be given God's blessing for the light they kindle there.

Notes

1 See chap. 5, "With Teresa in Avila: Ministry Among the Nuns," Federico Ruiz et al. *God Speaks in the Night: The Life, Times, and Teaching of St. John of the Cross,* trans. Kieran Kavanaugh (Washington, DC: ICS Publications,

1991, repr. 2000), 125-56, and Margaret Wilson, "St. John of the Cross and St. Teresa: Collaboration in Castile," *Leeds Papers on Saint John of the Cross, Contributions to a Quatercentenary Celebration,* ed. Margaret A. Rees (Leeds: Trinity and All Saints College, 1991), 27-47.

2 Kieran Kavanaugh, *"The Canonization Miracle and Its Investigation," Never Forget: Christian and Jewish Perspectives on Edith Stein,* U.S. ed. Steven Payne (Washington, DC: ICS Publications, 1998), 185-96. Hereafter cited as "Never Forget."

3 The ICS Publications edition of *The Complete Works of St. John of the Cross* comes from the teamwork of K. Kavanaugh and O. Rodriguez, as were the three volumes of *The Complete Works of St. Teresa of Avila.* More recently, ICS Publications issued volume one of Fr. Kieran's translation of *The Collected Letters of St. Teresa of Avila* in 2002, after Fr. Otilio Rodriguez left us, having died in Rome on 17 June 1994.

4 Francis J. Murphy, *Père Jacques: Resplendent in Victory* (Washington, DC: ICS Publications, 1998), xiv + 200 pp. Gives chronology, life-story and selected texts from the writings of Jacques Bunel, O.C.D. Cited hereafter as *"Victory."*

5 English-language biographies rely basically on the first life, now out of print, written by the novice director, then prioress of St. Edith/Teresa Benedicta of the Cross Stein, viz., Teresa Renata Posselt, *Edith Stein,* trans. Cecily Hastings and Donald Nicholl (New York/London: Sheed and Ward, 1952), 238 pp. This book has recently been updated and reprinted in the light of recent research as *Edith Stein: The Life of a Philosopher and Carmelite,* ed. Susanne M. Batzdorff, Josephine Koeppel, and John Sullivan (Washington, DC: ICS Publications, 2005). Cited hereafter as "Posselt."

6 See *Victory,* 71.

7 See *Victory,* 132-40 for the section titled "Père Jacques, Educator" with selected texts such as "The Education of Youth," "The Framework of Education," and "Gentleness."

8 We presume familiarity by the readers of this volume with the writings of St. Edith in the series *The Collected Works of Edith Stein.* For the texts of exhortations, given in the monasteries of Cologne and Echt, see vol. 4, *The Hidden Life: Essays, Meditations, Spiritual Texts,* trans. Waltraut Stein (Washington, DC: ICS Publications, 1992), 91-115. Hereafter cited as "Hidden."

9 One such essay appeared in a diocesan Sunday paper in Augsburg. See "On the History and Spirit of Carmel," *Hidden,* 1-6.

10 The posthumous tomes are titled *Finite and Eternal Being* and *The Science of the Cross,* respectively.

11 See John Sullivan, "Newly Refound Transfer Document of Edith Stein," *The Catholic Historical Review* 81 (1995): 398-402.

12 See chap. 9, "The Son of France," *Victory,* 71-81.

13 Partial translation found in a book that requires careful use by Waltraud Herbstrith, *Edith Stein: A Biography,* trans. Bernard Bonowitz (San Francisco, CA: Harper and Row, 1985), 102. Hereafter cited as "Herbstrith."

14 Whereas the prophetic gesture of the bishops is somewhat well known, the text that preceded the pastoral letter is generally not readily available. So here, in its entirety, is the telegram sent by the Catholic hierarchy and eight other Christian churches to the Nazi occupation authorities, translated by Susanne Batzdorff in Jakob Schlafke, *Edith Stein: Documents Concerning Her Life and Death* (New York: Edith Stein Guild, 1980), 29:

> The undersigned Dutch churches, already deeply shaken by the measures against the Jews in the Netherlands by which they are excluded from participation in normal national life, have become aware with horror of the new regulations by which men, women and children and entire families are to be deported to the territory of the German Reich and areas under Germany's jurisdiction. The suffering that this will cause tens of thousands of people, the knowledge *that these measures contradict the deepest moral conscience of the Dutch people,* but above all the infringement these measures constitute into everything that we are commanded by God as right and justice, compel the churches to implore you not to carry out these measures. In addition, as far as the Christians among the Jews are concerned, it behooves us to make this urgent request because of the fact that by these measures their participation in the life of the church is being cut off. [underlining in original]

15 Poem "Saint Joseph Care" in Josephine Koeppel, *Edith Stein: Philosopher and Mystic,* The Way of the Christian Mystics, vol. 12 (Collegeville, MN: Liturgical Press, 1990), 160-61. Hereafter *"Philosopher and Mystic."*

16 Edith Stein, Letter 296 to Mother Ottilia Thannisch, 26 March 1939, *Self-Portrait in Letters, 1916-1942,* trans. Josephine Koeppel, vol. 5, *The Collected Works of Edith Stein* (Washington, DC: ICS Publications, 1993), 305. Hereafter cited as *"Letters."*

17 See "Love for Love," *Hidden Life,* 29 where she uses the term "vicarious atonement."

18 Not always easy to find, the entire text deserves inclusion here:

> [Last Will and] Testament
>
> As prescribed in our Constitutions, I made a Last Will and Testament before my first profession [of vows] on 21 April 1935. It was preserved in the Cologne Carmel with the rest of them [the nuns' wills]. Before my transfer to Echt in December of 1938 I destroyed it, with the consent of dear Mother Teresa Renata of the Holy Spirit, prioress of the Cologne Carmel. It could possibly have caused difficulties at the border. Besides,

because circumstances had changed, it had become obsolete.

This document may now count in place of a testament. Actually, I have hardly anything left which needs to be disposed of. But in case of my death, it may please my dear superiors to know my mind.

The books [I] brought along, insofar as they are not scholarly and of no use to the Sisters, I would naturally like, most of all, to leave for the house. The scholarly books would surely be happily accepted as gifts by our Fathers, the Trappists or the Jesuits. I ask that the manuscripts be examined and, as it is considered good, they be either destroyed, included in the library, or given away as mementos. There are two manuscripts by foreign friends (their essays) among them. Should they not have been collected before I die, I would request that they be returned to their owners and a small handwritten memento sent with them. The addresses are: Dr. Winthrop Bell, Chester, Nova Scotia, Canada; Prof. Dr. Roman Ingarden, Lwow, (Lemberg), Poland, Jattonowski 4.

I request that the story of my family be not published as long as my siblings are alive, nor that it be given over to them. Only Rosa could be allowed to glance at it, and after the others die, their children [be allowed to see it]. Even then the order shall decide about its publication. The manuscripts are identified by this name on the paper they are wrapped in.

Should the book *Finite and Eternal Being* not yet be published at my death, I would ask the Most Rev. Fr. Provincial to most kindly take responsibility to wind it up [i.e., make all the necessary final arrangements about] the book and have it published. For this purpose I am attaching a copy of the contract made with the publisher. Since the contract was agreed to by the Cologne Carmel, if a new one were made the consent of the Cologne Carmel as well as the publisher, Otto Borgmeyer, would probably be required.

I thank my dear superiors and all my dear sister companions with all my heart for the love with which they have received me, and for all the good which has been my portion in this house.

I accept even now, with joy, the death which God has in mind for me, in total submission to his most holy will. I beg the Lord, that he may accept my life and death for his honor and glory, for all the intentions of the Most Sacred Hearts of Jesus and Mary and of holy Church, especially for the preservation, sanctification and perfecting of our holy order, particularly of the Cologne and Echt Carmels, in reparation for the unbelief of the Jewish People and that the Lord may be accepted by his people and his Kingdom may come in glory; for the safety of Germany and the peace of the world; and finally, for relatives, living and deceased, and all whom God has given me: that none of them be lost.

On Friday in the octave of Corpus Christi, 9 June 1939, the seventh day of my retreat.

In the name of the Father and of the Son and of the Holy Spirit. Sr. Teresa Benedicta of the Cross, O.C.D. [in Latin]

19 P[iet]O. van Kampen, "Eyewitness in Westerbork," *Never Forget,* 274; see Pierre Cuypers, "Eyewitness in Westerbork," *Never Forget,* 277-78.

20 Posselt, 228-29.

21 See Etty Hillesum, *Letters from Westerbork* trans. Arnold J. Pomerans (New York: Pantheon Books, 1986).

22 Hillesum, *Letters from Westerbork,* 28-30.

23 See E. Stein, chap. 8 "Nursing Soldiers at Märisch-Weisskirchen," trans. Josephine Koeppel, *Life in a Jewish Family,* vol. 1, *The Collected Works of Edith Stein* (Washington, DC: ICS Publications, 1986), 318-67. Hereafter "Life."

24 Herbstrith, 105.

25 E. Stein, Letter 341 to Mother Ambrosia Antonia Engleman, 5 August 1942, *Letters,* 352.

26 H. Wielek (orig. name W. Kweksilber, born in Cologne) "Doden die Leven," *Als een brandende toorts* (Echt: Vrienden van Dr. Edith Stein, 1967), 158-59; and 276, note 33 for personal background information. Appeared originally as an article in Amsterdam's *De Tijd* newspaper, 5 August 1952 edition.

27 Sentiments of this kind were housed in a letter she wrote the first Easter she spent away from Cologne in her monastery of exile at Echt: "But much prayer is necessary in order to remain faithful in all situations. Especially [must we pray] for those who have heavier burdens to carry than I have, and are not so rooted in the Eternal. Therefore, I am sincerely grateful to all who help." (Letter 300, to Mother Petra Brüning, 16 April 1939, *Letters,* 309.)

28 The nuns of Echt gave testimony to the effect she had written something in *The Science of the Cross* manuscript the very day she was arrested. This need not mean she had a lot more to write, as none of the eyewitness accounts specify which part of the manuscript she wrote in. This uncertainty raises a still-debated exegetical point: Sr. Josephine Koeppel who has done a fresh translation of *The Science of the Cross,* for instance, is convinced St. Edith had for all practical purposes completed her book since all the works of St. John of the Cross are mentioned in the German text. Sr. Josephine would wish to dissuade people from accepting the oft-repeated opinion that the work remains, like Schubert's famous symphony, incomplete. She is probably correct, though one might think a brief, formal con-

clusion was still to be drafted due to the somewhat abrupt-sounding ending that describes the death of St. John of the Cross in the arms of Bro. Diego—a fully haunting and ironic outcome to the literary effort of someone whose life was untimely terminated alongside her own sister soon after the last jottings were put into its manuscript.

29 See E. Stein, Letter 225, to Mother Petra Brüning, 13 September 1936, *Letters,* 235; and Letter 145 where she quotes St. Paul to Jacques and Raïssa Maritain, 21 June 1933, Letters, 147.

30 See John Sullivan, "Edith Stein, Carmelite," *Studies in Spirituality* 10 (2000), 275-93, and Josephine Koeppel, *Philosopher and Mystic,* 92-161, for a wide-ranging discussion of life as a Carmelite nun.

31 Pope John Paul II, no. 8, "Homily at Canonization Eucharist," in *Holiness Befits Your House: Canonization of Edith Stein, A Documentation* (Washington: ICS Publications, 2000), 11: "Gradually, throughout her life, as she grew in the knowledge of God, worshipping him in spirit and truth, she experienced ever more clearly her specific vocation to ascend the cross with Christ, to embrace it with serenity and trust, to love it by following in the footsteps of her beloved Spouse. . . ."

32 Joachim Feldes, *Edith Stein und Schifferstadt* (Schifferstadt: Sparkasse Schifferstadt, 1998). Hereafter cited as "Feldes."

33 Feldes, 62. English translation by Susanne Batzdorff in *Never Forget,* 264. This account was written relatively close to the event described, as indicated by the year given:

> Schifferstadt, 1953
>
> On 7 August 1942 around noon, I was waiting for the express train from Saarbrücken to Ludwigshafen. The train arrived, and a prison car, which had been attached to it, halted in front of me. From this car, a lady in dark clothes spoke to me, asking whether I was from Schifferstadt and whether I might know the family of Fr. Schwind. I answered in the affirmative, that the family of Dean Konrad Schwind, my classmate, was well known to me. She then asked me to give them regards from Sr. Teresia Benedicta, that she was Edith Stein, and was traveling east. The lady appeared calm, friendly. Only a short time later, I was able to pass this message to Miss Schwind, the sister of the Dean and niece of Edith Stein's spiritual mentor, Vicar General Joseph Schwind. . . .

34 Feldes, 73-74, bases his version of the fate of this written message on the testimony of a Benedictine nun of St. Lioba's priory in Günterstal (Freiburg), Sr. Placida Laubhardt.

35 See art. "Auschwitz" in vol. 1 *Encyclopedia of the Holocaust,* ed. Israel Gutman (New York: Macmillan, 1990), 42 especially.

36 See "Appendix III "Wannsee Conference Minutes" in Steven Paskuly, ed. and Andrew Pollinger, trans. *Death Dealer: The Memoirs of the SS Kommandant at Auschwitz* (Buffalo, NY: Prometheus Books, 1992), 371-81.

37 The chilling description by Auschwitz camp director Rudolph Höß provides a startling eyewitness account in chap. 1, "The Final Solution of the Jewish Question in Concentration Camp Auschwitz," *Death Dealer,* 32:

> As late as the summer of 1942 the bodies were still buried in mass graves. Not until the end of the summer of 1942 did we start burning them. At first we put two thousand bodies on a large pile of wood. Then we opened up the mass graves and burned the new bodies on top of the old ones from the earlier burials. At first we poured waste oil over the bodies. Later on we used methanol. The burning went on continuously all day and all night. By the end of November all the mass graves were cleared. The number of buried bodies in the mass graves was 107,000. This number contains not only the first Jewish transports which were gassed when we started the burnings, but also the bodies of the prisoners who died in the main Auschwitz camp during the winter of 1941-42 because the crematory was out of order. The prisoners who died at Birkenau [Auschwitz II] are included in that number.

38 Translation of official text available in Josephine Koeppel's additional "Chronology 1916-1942" to E. Stein, *Life,* 432.

39 To appreciate the historical merits and/or limitations of the film in relation to Père Jacques see Francis J. Murphy, "Louis Malle's Portrayal of Père Jacques in *Au revoir les enfants," Proceedings of the Annual Meeting of the Western Society for French History* 24 (1997): 389-97.

40 A reliable enough source sets the arrival time of the boys in the school at the "end of January 1943." See Jacques Chegaray, *Un carme heroïque: La vie du Père Jacques* (Paris: Nouvelle Cité, 1988), 194. In other regards one ought always to verify against parallel sources the assertions of Mr. Chegaray, an associate of Père Jacques at Avon, who sometimes allows feelings of antipathy against his old boss to cloud his judgments.

41 Quote taken from an important volume of eyewitness sources collected by a close associate of his during the Avon war days, Père Philippe (Rambaud), *Le Père Jacques, Martyr de la Charité, Témoignages* (Paris: Descleé de Brouwer, 1947), 346 note 1.

42 For greater clarity the dates that saw him shift from place to place may be borrowed from the helpful "Chronology of the Life of Père Jacques (Lucien-Louis Bunel)" devised by Murphy in *Victory,* xiii:

1944	January 15	Arrest at Avon
		Incarceration in Fontainebleau Prison

	March 6	Transfer from Fontainebleau to camp at Compiègne
	March 28	Transfer to camp at Neue Bremm
	April 23	Arrival at Mauthausen concentration camp in Austria
	May	Assignment to Gusen I work camp
1945	April	Return to Mauthausen
	May 5	Liberation of Mauthausen
	June 2	Death in Linz, Austria

43 *Victory,* 147.

44 Emile Valley quoted in *Victory,* 100.

45 Words of fellow-prisoner Captain Petrou, *Victory,* 104.

46 Père Jacques, "Let us Live Humanly," March 1940 in *Victory,* 149.

47 Gordon J. Horwitz, *In the Shadow of Death: Living Outside the Gates of Mauthausen* (New York: The Free Press/Macmillan, 1990); also art. "Mauthausen" vol. 3, *Encyclopedia of the Holocaust,* 944-52.

48 See Horwitz, *In the Shadow of Death,* 16.

49 Père Jacques, "To See Christ (Conference 3)," *Victory,* 154. The phrase "Christ is *here*" evokes a striking thought of St. Edith about our neighbor: "For the Christian there is no such thing as a stranger. At any time it is our neighbor who *stands before* us, the one who needs us the most; regardless of whether he is related or not, whether we like him or not, whether he is 'morally deserving' or not." See *Mystery of Christmas,* trans. Susanne Batzdorff, *Edith Stein Daybook: To Live at the Hand of the Lord* (Springfield, IL: Templegate Publishers, 1994), 116. [italics mine]

50 Père Jacques traces his idea of reading selections from philosophers to a famous French general. See his remarks in "Let us Live Humanly," *Victory,* 148-49: "To live the war humanly means also to react against anything that threatens our true human values. While in Tonkin, General Gallieni used to purge his mind of war by reading a chapter of philosophy each day. We should follow his example."

51 Other instances of Père Jacques' aversion for Hitler and all he stood for from that same period are reported in *Le Père Jacques, Martyr de la Charité, Témoignages,* 244, showing two letters, one of which mentions "Hitler's *pride.*" [italics mine]

52 Letter of Père Jacques to René Bunel, 13 January 1944, excerpt in section "Arrestation...Déportation...15 Janvier 1944 - 2 Juin 1945" booklet issued for the fiftieth anniversary of the death of Père Jacques, *Lucien Bunel/Fr. Jacques de Jésus, O.C.D., 1900-1945* (Avon: private publication, June 1995), 42.

53 John Sullivan, "Of Arms and the Child," *Spiritual Life* 47 (2001): 41-44.

54 Letter 181 to Dr. Ruth Kantorowicz, 4 October 1934, *Letters,* 185.

55 "Gentleness," *Victory,* 139-40.

56 Carla Jungels, O.C.D. has done a fresh study titled simply "Rosa Stein,"

for *Edith-Stein-Jahrbuch* 5 (1999): 397-403 relying on archival material in Cologne. See also Susanne Batzdorff, *Aunt Edith: The Jewish Heritage of a Catholic Saint* (Springfield, IL; Templegate Publishers, 1998), 158-63 and passim.

57 "Rosa Stein," in *Als een brandende toorts,* 168-76.

58 Edith Stein, Letter 340 to Mother Ambrosia Antonia Engelmann, 4 August 1943, *Letters,* 351. The text of St. Edith preceding Rosa's words were the following:

> During the past night we left the transit-station A. [=Amersfoort] and landed here early this morning. We were given a very friendly reception here. They intended to do everything to enable us to be freed or at least that we may remain here.
>
> All the Catholics are together and in our dormitory we have all the nuns (two Trappistines, one Dominican), Ruth [Kantorowicz], Alice [Reis], Dr. [Lisamaria] Meirowsky, and others are here. Two Trappist fathers from T.[ilburg] are also with us. In any case, it will be necessary for you to send us our personal credentials, our ID cards, and other ration cards. So far we have lived entirely on the generosity of the others. We hope you have found the address of the Consul and have been in touch with him. We have asked many people to relay news to you. The two dear children from Koningsbosch [Annemarie and Elfriede Goldschmidt] are with us. We are very calm and cheerful. Of course, so far there has been no Mass and Communion, maybe that will come later. Now we have a chance to experience a little how to live purely from within. Sincerest greetings to all. We will probably write again soon. *In Corde Jesu,* your / B.[enedicta]

59 See biographical note accompanying letter written to her by Edith Stein, Letter 332, 22 January 1942, *Letters,* 343. Sophie Meuwissen is identified as a volunteer helper of Rosa's at the monastery outquarters in the newest edition of Edith Stein's correspondence in German. See Maria Amata Neyer, ed., *Selbstbildins in Briefen II, 1933-1942,* vol. 3, *Edith Stein Gesamtausgabe, Biographische Schriften* (Freiburg: Herder, 2000), 583, note 5.

60 See her own account of this gesture in "How I came to the Cologne Carmel," *Edith Stein: Selected Writings, With Comments, Reminiscences and Translations of Her Prayers and Poems by Her Niece,* trans. Susanne Batzdorff (Springfield, IL: Templegate Publishers, 1990), 16-17.

61 See above cited eyewitness account of the group by P.O. van Kempen, "Eyewitness in Westerbork," *Never Forget,* 272-76.

62 In English there is a useful monograph by Wladyslaw T. Bartoszewski, *The Convent at Auschwitz* (New York, NY: George Braziller, 1990); and a collection of published essays and documents by Carol Rittner and John K. Roth,

eds., *Memory Offended: The Auschwitz Convent Controversy* (New York/London: Praeger, 1991). Both, however, were published before the crisis ended in 1995 (at least for the Carmelite community) with evacuation of the first building by the nuns.

63 Out of place, therefore, are the opening remarks in Arthur Giron's "Edith Stein, The Play," where the prioress of Auschwitz Carmel is chided precisely for this—erroneous—reason: "Your convent must be closed. The name of Edith Stein must not be glorified in Auschwitz. To name a community of nuns after a convert leads many to believe what you are doing is praying for the conversion of all Jews." See text as found in Donald Marinelli, ed., *Arthur Giron's Edith Stein: A Dramaturgical Sourcebook* (Pittsburgh, PA: Carnegie Mellon University Press, 1994), 42.

64 See official list in Conspectus *Ordinis Carmelitarum Discalceatorum (Roma: Casa Generalizia Carmelitani Scalzi,* 1997), 165.

65 *Conspectus*, 164.

66 *Conspectus,* 204.

Learning How to Meditate: Fifty Years in Carmel

Kevin Culligan, O.C.D.
Carmelite Monastery
Hinton, West Virginia

In Teresian Carmel two hours each day are devoted to mental prayer, a practice that goes back to St. Teresa of Avila who prescribed these two hours in her constitutions.[1] The current constitutions of both the Discalced Carmelite nuns and friars uphold this practice to encourage Teresa's sons and daughters today to deepen their friendship with Christ through an intimate sharing of themselves with him who they know loves them.[2] While Eucharist and the Liturgy of the Hours are the center of their daily life in community, Teresian Carmelites seek to deepen their knowledge and love of Jesus Christ through these silent hours of mental prayer each day. Since 1955, these two hours have been a part of my daily life as a Discalced Carmelite friar. This chapter describes what these two hours each day have been like for me and how, after fifty years, I'm still learning how to meditate.

Novitiate

When I arrived at our novitiate in Brookline, Massachusetts, on 1 August 1955, I knew I was joining a contemplative order, but I had little idea what that meant in practice. I still remember that first day. After the novice master showed me to my room, he told me "mental prayer is at 5:00 p.m. in the chapel." I arrived there a few minutes early and was shown my place at the end of a line of friars on one side of the chapel. At five o'clock sharp, the prior intoned an opening prayer to the Holy Spirit, someone read a brief passage from a meditation book, and then all was quiet. The other friars in the chapel were on their knees, eyes closed, and, I presumed, meditating. I said to myself, "now what?" Ten minutes later, I was wondering what I had gotten myself into.

A fellow novice had been a little better prepared for prayer in Carmel. A priest back home had told him that as a Carmelite he would have to meditate a lot and that the best way to do this is to reflect on the life of Jesus. This novice later told me about his first hour of mental prayer in the novitiate. Once the opening prayer had been said and all was quiet, he began reflecting on the life of the Lord. He recalled his birth in the stable at Bethlehem, his hidden life in Nazareth, his baptism by John in the Jordan, his public life in Galilee, his transfiguration on Tabor, his triumphal entry into Jerusalem, followed by his passion, death, resurrection, and ascension into heaven. After briefly visualizing Jesus seated once again with his Father in Glory, the novice then rested, waiting quietly for the hour to end. Then he heard: bong, bong, bong—the quarter hour chimes on the choir clock. He still had forty-five minutes to wait before the hour was over.

Our novice master, obviously, believed that the best way to learn to meditate was to dive right in, like learning to swim by jumping into deep water. As the novitiate year continued, he instructed us on how to pray and how to use the two hours of mental prayer profitably, although now, fifty years later, I cannot recall any particular instruction he gave us on how to meditate. I do, however, still remember a valuable booklet he gave us entitled *Little Catechism of Prayer,* by Fr. Gabriel of St. Mary Magdalen,[3] a Belgian Carmelite who was professor of spiritual theology at the Discalced Carmelite International College in Rome and one of the outstanding writers on Carmelite spirituality in the twentieth century.

In his catechism, Fr. Gabriel explained in the simplest possible terms what he called the Carmelite order's "method of mental prayer," which was "drawn directly from the works of St. Teresa of Jesus and St. John of the Cross" and formulated into a specific method by their later disciples.[4] The catechism clearly describes the many parts of mental prayer—preparation, reading, meditation proper with a loving colloquy, thanksgiving, oblation, and petition. The colloquy is the high point. Here we express directly to Jesus our desire to love and serve him in response to a heightened awareness of his love for us. Preparing ourselves by consciously living in God's presence throughout the day, reading from a meditation book at the beginning of the formal prayer period, and then imagining and reflecting upon Jesus' love for us are all designed to lead us to the loving colloquy; thanking God for all God's gifts, offering ourselves to God, and asking God's blessings for ourselves and others naturally flow from it and conclude the period of prayer. As I gradually learned these various parts of the method and applied them during the time for mental prayer, these two hours eventually became the center of my day in the novitiate. In them I discovered peace, insight, joy, fervor, commitment, and gratitude that God had brought me to the Carmelites.

After the novitiate, I began my formal studies for the priesthood. I continued following the meditation method Fr. Gabriel described in his catechism. Three years later, when my provincial was examining my readiness to make final vows in the order, he asked me to name the parts of the Carmelite method of prayer. I proudly answered: "Preparation, reading, meditation with colloquy, thanksgiving, oblation, and petition." However, by this time, now a Carmelite for four years, I was no longer practicing the method. I cannot recall exactly when I stopped, but I do remember that the delights and insights of the daily mental prayer periods had ceased and were replaced—just as St. John of the Cross said they would be—by dryness. I found it hard to concentrate on the various steps of the meditation method. Both my confessor and my reading in St. John of the Cross helped me to understand that I was going through a predictable stage in the prayer journey, a purifying period called the dark night of sense, and that if I just hung in there, things would get better. How or when they would get better I had to wait and see.

In the meantime, the periods of mental prayer had now become two boring, restless, distracted, and often painful hours in my day. When I described my difficulties to my student master, he picked up a book off his desk and handed it to me. "Here," he said, "try this. It might help." The book was *The Sanctifier*,[5] by Luis Martinez, the late Archbishop of Mexico City, a book of meditations on the Holy Spirit.

This book saved my prayer life. For the next six years, like St. Teresa of Avila, who did so for eighteen years, "I never dared to begin prayer without a book."[6] I devoted my two hours of mental prayer each day to "meditative reading." As with Teresa, sometimes just a few lines from the book were enough to help me begin a conversation with God. At other times, I might read a whole chapter before I was inspired to set the book down and reflect on its contents or simply sit quietly with the Holy Spirit. Meditative reading also kept me from wasting the two hours of mental prayer examining the theological theories I was learning in my seminary classes or ruminating on my personal problems in community life. I used other books for meditation during these years, but my mainstay was *The Sanctifier*. For me, it was the perfect book, providing short chapters on true devotion to the Holy Spirit, the gifts and fruits of the Holy Spirit, and the Eight Beatitudes. Although now I have not read *The Sanctifier* in over forty years, this book was the basis of my present understanding of and devotion to the Holy Spirit. My meditative reading for nearly six years, *The Sanctifier* was also an excellent preparation for ordination to the priesthood on 8 June 1963.

Priesthood

My life changed radically after ordination. I was assigned both to one of our parishes to assist in its pastoral activities and to graduate studies in psychology to prepare to teach in our seminary. Suddenly, the peaceful, regulated life of the novitiate and houses of studies with their scheduled times for meditation each day was gone. Now I was scrambling to use every available moment to compose sermons, write papers, and prepare presentations for supervised internships. I decided I no longer had time for meditative reading; at the same time I felt I could not give up mental prayer altogether. This dilemma I solved by using the two hours of mental prayer each day to prepare my Sunday sermons. And so I began the practice of *Lectio Divina.*

Lectio, of course, is an old monastic prayer practice. In the middle ages, Guigo the Carthusian articulated its four steps as 1) *lectio* or reading a passage from Sacred Scripture, 2) *meditatio* or reflecting prayerfully on that passage, 3) *oratio* or prayer that comes into the heart from the reflective reading, and 4) *contemplatio* or contemplation, sitting quietly in openness to whatever movements the Holy Spirit may inspire in you as a result of the reading.[7] Although *Lectio Divina* is mostly identified with the Benedictine tradition, its influence was also felt among the early Carmelites. John of the Cross, for example, advised: "Seek in *reading* and you will find in *meditation;* knock in *prayer,* and it will be open to you in *contemplation.*"[8] *Lectio* was ideal for preparing Sunday sermons. More importantly, I discovered it was a simple, natural, and rewarding way to pray centered in God's word.

As I pray the Gospels in *Lectio Divina,* for instance, I feel the immediate presence of Jesus. There are no centuries separating us. He is sitting beside me, speaking directly to me, calling me to follow him, sending me on mission, asking for my love, giving me his peace. My most fervent moments in prayer always come during *Lectio Divina,* seated quietly with the Bible on my lap, reading, reflecting, praying, waiting for the Holy Spirit to stir in my soul. Every day, I try to do some *Lectio Divina,* whether as a part of the formal two hours of mental prayer or as preparation for daily Eucharist. And in teaching others to pray, I now first introduce them to the simple steps of *Lectio Divina.*

But back to my early years as a priest. These were revolutionary times. Vatican II's aftermath was shaking the foundations of the American church. Much of our country was in protest over the war in Viet Nam. In that chaotic world, two hours of mental prayer each day seemed irrelevant. Better to be in the streets protesting the war than wasting your time kneeling in meditation before the Blessed Sacrament. Even in the Church, private prayer was being de-emphasized in favor of communal liturgical prayer. By the mid-seventies I had pretty much lost interest in our Carmelite practice of two hours of mental prayer a day. I had not given it up entirely, but now I was more often devoting that time to study, writing, counseling, preparing homilies—all good works, but not exactly meditation.

The Relaxation Response

Around this time, I read a story in the *Boston Globe* about a Harvard cardiologist named Herbert Benson whose research suggested that meditation is good for the heart. Comparing persons who practiced Transcendental Meditation with a control group of non-meditators, Benson found that meditation apparently relieves inner tensions and helps people deal more effectively with stress, thereby reducing high blood pressure, heart attacks, and strokes. After reading that article, I said to myself: "So that's why our Carmelites live so long and die so peacefully—they've been meditating for two hours every day."

I became interested in Benson's work. He maintained that meditation induces within us a "relaxation response" that physiologically undoes the effects of the "flight or fight response." In our society, when the stress of daily living causes this response within us, we ordinarily cannot act on it. We have to internalize it. When feeling stressed at work, for example, it's too risky to walk away from our job or punch out the boss—either way, "fight or flight" may cost us our job. So we internalize the stress, which causes ulcers, high blood pressure, strokes, and heart attacks. Meditation, on the other hand, induces in the presence of stress a physiological "relaxation response" bringing about body changes that lead to a decrease in heart rate, lower metabolism, decreased rate of breathing, and generally a healthier balance in the body. Based on this research, Benson began prescribing meditation rather than medication as the treatment of choice for many of his heart patients.[9]

This is what he prescribed: Once or twice a day, for at least ten to twenty minutes, sit quietly in a comfortable position. Close your eyes, relax your body, become aware of your breathing. As you breathe out, say the word "one." Breathe easily and naturally. Assume a passive attitude. If other thoughts come into your mind, say, "oh, well!" and gently disregard them and continue saying the word "one" as you breathe out. Benson explained that he discovered this effective meditation technique by surveying the meditation practices of the great world religions—Hinduism, Buddhism, Taoism, Judaism, Islam, and Christianity, including the teaching of St. Teresa of Avila. He found that in all these religions there were four common characteristics to the practice of meditation—a quiet place, a comfortable position, an object of focus, and a passive attitude. He included these four elements in the meditation practice he prescribed for his patients. He maintained, furthermore, that the most beneficial of these four elements in reducing the "fight or flight" response and inducing the "relaxation response" is the passive attitude. This attitude in meditation slows down the racing mind with its uncontrolled thoughts and the relentless stream of consciousness that most often cause internal stress and anxiety.

Eventually, when prescribing this meditation practice, Benson began encouraging people of faith to substitute words from their religious tradition in place of the word "one" with the outbreath, words such as "Our Father," "Come Holy Spirit," "Shalom," "Allah," " the Lord is my Shepherd," "Joy is inward," "I surrender." By saying a sacred word, Benson thought, his patients might not only be faithful to the prescribed regular meditation practice with the physiological benefits for the heart, but they might also integrate meditation into their faith life with all the possible spiritual benefits that could bring. He subsequently called this the "faith factor" in good health,[10] a theme he continues to explore in annual seminars on spirituality and medicine sponsored by, surprisingly, the continuing education department of the Harvard Medical School.

The Jesus Prayer

Benson's work revived my interest in mental prayer. He convinced me that for the sake of both my spiritual and physical health, I would be foolish to give up the practice of meditation. Moreover, by the end of the seventies, I was now student master in our order's house of studies, teaching in a pastoral counseling program, writing a doctoral dissertation on spiritual direction, assisting our secular order Carmelites, and devoting more of my time and energy to the pastoral ministry of spiritual guidance. As a spiritual guide in the Carmelite tradition, I had the responsibility to teach others how to pray, especially how to meditate as a way to prepare for the gift of contemplation. For both personal and pastoral reasons, I could see that meditation had to be an essential part of my day, although I was uncertain about how best to proceed. About this time, one of my fellow Carmelites suggested that I read *The Way of a Pilgrim.*[11] This proved to be a moment of grace.

This book, written originally in Russian by an anonymous author around the middle of the nineteenth century, is a spiritual classic of the Eastern Orthodox tradition. It tells the story of a crippled man who wants to learn how to pray always in order to conform his life to the teachings of Jesus and the New Testament. He travels throughout Eastern Europe and the Holy Land searching for someone to teach him how to pray always. Finally, he discovers a holy man who introduces him to "The Jesus Prayer," which goes like this: "Lord Jesus Christ, Son of God, have mercy on me, a sinner." These words have been prayed in the Eastern Church from as early as the fourth century. The nineteenth-century pilgrim found that, by saying this prayer day and night, simultaneously with his breathing in and out, his dream of praying always was fulfilled.

I was immediately drawn to the Jesus Prayer. St. Teresa of Avila encouraged prayer without ceasing. She claimed, "unceasing prayer is the most important aspect of the [Carmelite] Rule."[12] The Jesus Prayer provides that. It coordinates easily with your breathing. As you breathe in, you say, "Lord Jesus Christ, Son of God"; as you breathe out, you say, "Have mercy on me, a sinner." It contains the four basic elements of meditation that Benson noted, especially an object of focus and a passive attitude. It can be said continuously as one is seated comfortably during the quiet of the formal mental prayer periods in the monastery; but it can also be recited inconspicuously riding in a city bus or walking down the street.

With the help of Fr. George Maloney's writing and audiotapes,[13]I began to learn the Jesus Prayer. Beyond teaching the technical aspects of coordinating the prayer with your breathing, Maloney points out the more important theological implications of the Jesus Prayer. It is, first of all, centered in the powerful healing and saving name of Jesus. By invoking his name, we become aware of Jesus' presence. When we say the name of Jesus, we refer not only to the historical person who centuries ago lived in Nazareth and died on Calvary, but we here and now bring Jesus, Our Risen Lord, into our minds and hearts. Moreover, with the name of Jesus we awaken to the Holy Spirit. "No one," writes St. Paul to the Corinthians, "can say 'Jesus is Lord' except in the Holy Spirit." (1Cor 12:3) The Holy Spirit, present within us, enables us to say the name of Jesus and, in fact, actually "prays" his name in us.

The Holy Spirit guides us as we say the Jesus Prayer. In his Discourse at the Last Supper, Jesus said: "The Paraclete, the Holy Spirit, whom the Father will give in my name will instruct you in everything, reminding you of all that I have told you." (Jn 14:26) When we pray the Jesus Prayer, the Holy Spirit is within us, praying in us, instructing us, always reminding us of Jesus' teachings.

Finally, Maloney points out that the Jesus Prayer incorporates the attitude of humility that Jesus encourages in prayer. Jesus tells a story recorded in the Gospel of St. Luke (Lk 18:9-14) about two men who went up to the temple to pray. One was a pharisee, the other a tax collector. The pharisee, standing by himself, prayed, "God, I thank you than I am not like other people—grasping, crooked, adulterous—or even like this tax collector. I fast twice a week; I give a tenth of all my income." But the tax collector kept his distance. He didn't dare even to raise his eyes to heaven. He beat his breast saying, "God, be merciful to me, a sinner." Then Jesus comments: "I tell you, this man went down to his home justified rather than the other; for all who exalt themselves will be humbled, and all who humble themselves will be exalted." Thus, in addition to bringing Jesus with His Spirit into our consciousness, the Jesus Prayer includes the attitude of humble prayer that Jesus taught.

Thomas Merton, in his comments on the Jesus Prayer,[14] emphasizes that the power of the prayer is not in the formula, but in the name of Jesus. As persons continue to say this prayer, it frequently becomes shortened simply to "Jesus" with the inbreath, and "mercy" with the outbreath. Or simply "Jesus" with the inbreath, and no word with the outbreath. Ordinarily, though, one both invokes the name of Jesus breathing in, and asks his mercy breathing out, understanding all along that the power of the prayer is not the formula, but the saving and healing name of Jesus.

Throughout the eighties, I was saying the Jesus Prayer regularly. For me, it seemed the perfect way to pray. It is primarily a prayer of the heart in which the contents of the head are emptied so that the Lord Jesus can descend into the depths of the heart bringing the soul to life in the Holy Spirit.[15] It expresses all that had become most important in my life through earlier meditative reading and *Lectio Divina*—the following of Jesus and the presence of the Holy Spirit. It provided a solid anchor in dealing with my wandering mind during periods of formal meditation; it was an easy way to practice the presence of God throughout the rest of the day. I was also, as the Eastern Orthodox taught, bringing Jesus to my world. Saying the Jesus Prayer while driving a car, I bring his blessing to an urban traffic jam. When I say the Jesus Prayer shopping for groceries, Jesus is present in a modern super market. Reciting quietly the Jesus Prayer waiting in a doctor's office or sitting in a meeting, I bring Jesus' healing and saving presence to the other people there beside me. At last, I thought, I had found my way of praying, or rather this way of praying had found me. Some thirty years after my novice master introduced me to Fr. Gabriel's *Little Catechism of Prayer,* I felt as though I had been given a way of praying that met my every need as a Christian, a Carmelite, and a priest. However, in June1986, something new developed.

Christian Insight Meditation

During that year's Carmelite Forum seminar at St. Mary's, College, Notre Dame, Indiana, Dr. Mary Jo Meadow, a friend and colleague with whom I had collaborated for some years in the psychology of religion, told me about *vipassana* or insight meditation, a spiritual practice from Theravadan Buddhism. Earlier that year, she had made a three-month retreat under Joseph Goldstein, one of the leading teachers of insight meditation in the United States. She was struck by the similarities between this meditation practice and St. John of the Cross's teaching that the emptying of sense and spirit is necessary for transforming union with God. She invited me to explore with her the similarities between Buddhist insight meditation practice and St. John's spiritual teachings.

This invitation led eventually to my making two retreats under Joseph Goldstein's guidance. I began to see from my own experience the congruence between *vipassana* and St. John of the Cross. Moreover, this meditation practice seemed ideally suited to promoting the self-emptying exemplified by Jesus Christ and counseled by St. Paul in his letter to the Philippians (Phil 2:5-8) and fostering an interior openness to the movements of the Holy Spirit. However, I hesitated to explore these possibilities for fear of confusing Carmelite prayer with Buddhist meditation until I read an article by Daniel O'Hanlon, a California Jesuit, in the 1981 volume of the *Journal of Transpersonal Psychology.*[16] O'Hanlon pointed out that the Second Vatican Council not only directed Catholics generally to "acknowledge, preserve, and promote" the spiritual and moral goods and cultural values of Hinduism and Buddhism (*Nostra Aetate,* no. 2), but more specifically challenged missionary members of religious institutes to reflect attentively "on how the Christian religious life might be able to assimilate the ascetic and contemplative traditions whose seeds were sometimes already planted by God in ancient cultures prior to the preaching of the Gospel." (*Ad Gentes*, no. 18) To my surprise, the Vatican Council fathers challenged Catholic religious not only "to respect" but "to assimilate" the ascetic and contemplative traditions of ancient cultures.

O'Hanlon's article freed me to explore fully the possibilities of integrating the twenty-five-hundred year old Buddhist insight meditation practice into Carmel's eight-century tradition of contemplative prayer. Dr. Meadow and I began writing on the similarities between Theravadan Buddhism and Carmelite spirituality.[17] We presented these similarities at meetings of the American Psychological Association and the Society for Buddhist-Christian Studies. With the help of Daniel Chowning, Anthony Haglof, and other Carmelite friars, we developed an eight-day retreat in which we teach insight meditation within the context of a traditional Carmelite retreat that includes daily Eucharist, the sacrament of reconciliation, and conferences comparing *vipassana* with the teachings of St. John of the Cross.[18]

The meditation taught in this retreat includes Benson's four essentials of meditation—quiet place, comfortable position, object of focus, passive attitude. In insight mediation, however, the meditator does not choose the object of focus; it is, rather, provided for the meditator by his or her ongoing mind-body process. In contrast with other forms of contemplative practice in which meditators choose the object of focus—the breath, a sacred word, a mantra, an icon—the meditator in *vipassana* focuses on whatever the mind-body process presents to conscious awareness—body sensations, sensory experiences, thinking, emotions and mind states. As this ever-changing flow of mind-body activity comes into consciousness, the meditator makes a soft mental note naming each experience and observes what happens in the experience until it ends. Insight meditation is thus an awareness meditation practice rather than a concentrative practice: you simply remain *aware* of and note what is happening in your mind-body process rather than *concentrate* on an object of focus which you select for your meditation. Yet, within the context of Christian prayer, the goal of awareness meditation is the same as concentrative meditation—to dispose oneself for the gift of contemplation by emptying the sense and spirit of attachments to everything that is not God. Because we use this ancient awareness meditation practice to grow in the self-emptying exemplified by Jesus Christ and in openness to the movements of Christ's Spirit in our mind-body process, we call it Christian insight meditation.

As these events unfolded during the 1990s, I began devoting more of my afternoon meditation periods to Christian insight meditation rather than to the repetition of the Jesus Prayer, while still using the morning prayer period for *Lectio Divina.* Gradually I began to notice some fruits—deeper quiet during prayer, closer attention to the first movements of my disordered attachments to or aversion for experiences and greater freedom to choose not to act on these attachments and aversions. I also began to see clearly, as John of the Cross says is necessary for our soul's purification in order to be united with God, some of my "soul's infirmities"—long-buried roots of selfishness—as they came into awareness to be painfully felt and finally healed.[19]

Recently, though, I began to notice something different during the time of mental prayer. In August 2003, I was transferred from our house of studies in Chicago to our hermitage monastery in southern West Virginia. Life in this monastery—which we call a "Carmelite desert," a name the folks in the lush mountains of Appalachia have difficulty comprehending—is patterned on the eremitical lifestyle of the thirteenth-century hermits on Mt. Carmel. Its purpose is to provide today's Carmelites with a place apart where they can come to revitalize themselves in solitude in the spirit of the early Carmelite hermits. We call our desert "Christ-on-the-Mountain" and the daily schedule there fosters silence, solitude, and prayer. Not long after I settled in, I noticed that whenever I began a sitting of Christian insight meditation, I soon found myself spontaneously repeating the Jesus Prayer—"Lord Jesus Christ, Son of God, have mercy on me, a sinner"—over and over again.

At first, I noted this as a distraction and gently returned my attention to observing the dominant event occurring in my mind-body process. Nonetheless, the Jesus Prayer persisted. I soon realized that this prayer was being given to me, that it was praying itself within me. I concluded that it was best to let go of my attempts to practice insight meditation and to accept the Holy Spirit's movement within me. For St. Paul reminds us: "The Spirit too helps us in our weakness, for we do not know how to pray as we ought; but that very Spirit intercedes for us with sighs too deep for words. God, who searches the heart, knows what is the mind of the Spirit, because the Spirit intercedes for the saints according to the will of God." (Rom 8:26-27) We do not always know how to pray as we ought, but fortunately the Holy Spirit prays within us, the Spirit who knows what God deserves from us and what our deepest needs are. I suspect my need to implore God's mercy was deeper than I realized.

For some time, though, I wondered how best to respond to this movement. I wanted to honor the action of the Holy Spirit; at the same time, I valued all the graces that have come to me through Christian insight meditation, particularly the uncovering of my selfish motives in my relationships with others. I somehow wanted to do both—the concentrative practice of the Jesus Prayer and the awareness practice of Christian insight meditation. I knew I couldn't do them both at the same time; however, thanks to the freedom and flexibility of the daily schedule in our desert community, I decided to devote the morning period of mental prayer to Christian insight meditation, the afternoon period to the repetition of the Jesus Prayer, and move *Lectio Divina* to another time of day. Within a very short time, I realized this was the perfect solution, at least for now. Yes, for now, fifty years after I first walked through the doors of the Carmelite novitiate, this is how I spend the two periods of mental prayer each day, but this too may change in the years ahead with new personal experiences or different promptings of the Holy Spirit.

In Retrospect

Fifty years of learning how to meditate has taught me a lot about prayer, especially mental or contemplative prayer. In the novitiate I naively expected to be given a tested method of meditation practiced by all Carmelites that would soon bring me to a state of infused contemplation and transforming union with God; however, my experience over the years has been totally different. Learning to meditate has been an on-again, off-again process, dependent on the circumstances of my daily life, continually filled with new discoveries from unexpected sources that always seemed to answer my current needs. I have found meditation in Carmel to be, as St. Teresa said it would be, a long, arduous journey, but nonetheless a "divine journey which is the royal road to heaven."[20] Now beginning my second half-century of this journey, I am grateful for the many blessings that have helped me along the way.

I am blessed, first of all, to be in the Discalced Carmelites, who have remained faithful to St. Teresa's insistence that prayer and contemplation are the heart of her reform. As Teresa considered prayer to be the primary response of her renewed communities to the problems facing the Church in the sixteenth century, so Teresian Carmel today through its renewed legislation following Vatican II reaffirmed prayer as its essential charism and its primary apostolic service to the Church and the world. Accordingly, the order has maintained its traditional two hours of mental prayer in its daily schedule, even in the face of pressure to replace this time with seemingly more relevant pastoral activities. This scheduled time for prayer has always bolstered my weakness; without this structured support, I would have given up the journey long ago as being simply too difficult. Following those periods when I neglected mental prayer, the daily schedule was always there to help me begin again.

I am grateful to my Carmelite brothers for their daily fidelity to the practice of mental prayer. Their example has always inspired me to keep trying. None has inspired me more than Fr. Kieran Kavanaugh whom we honor in these pages. Over the years, Kieran has influenced me in many ways: as a teacher who introduced me to the basic principles of Christian spirituality, as a scholar whose translations of and commentaries on the writings of St. Teresa and St. John of the Cross opened for me the spiritual richness of these Spanish mystics, as a colleague whose advice has always been invaluable, as a collaborator in promoting Carmelite spirituality who always brings both historical clarity and fresh new insight and learning to our work. However, what I value most about his presence in my life over the years is his quiet witness to the place of daily mental prayer in Carmelite life. Whenever I walk into our chapel at prayer time and see him seated there in meditation, my own resolve to continue the prayer journey is strengthened.

I have also been blessed by the Order's encouragement to find my own way of prayer. From Fr. Gabriel's *Little Catechism of Prayer* and Fr. Peter-Thomas Rohrbach's *Conversation with Christ,* I learned early in my religious life *a* method for mental prayer drawn from the writings of St. Teresa of Avila and St. John of the Cross, but I was never told that this was *the* method I had to follow. I have always enjoyed the freedom to discover the way of praying that best suits me. St. Teresa of Avila struggled with discursive meditation for eighteen years before she finally found her own prayer of active recollection in which "the soul collects its faculties together and enters within itself to be with its God."[21] Similarly, Carmelites today gradually discover their own way of praying. If six friars are together in chapel for the evening mental prayer hour, one may be repeating the Jesus Prayer, another practicing Christian meditation using the *maranatha* mantra, another saying the rosary, another gazing at the Blessed Sacrament in the tabernacle, another sleeping, another following Teresa's method of active recollection. They are not all expected to follow one method. The order insists, however, that every community provide two hours each day in its schedule for mental prayer and that each friar make his personal prayer during that time, either with others in the chapel or alone in some other place of his choice.[22]

I have also enjoyed the freedom to find teachers who could teach me about prayer and meditation, whether they are Christian, Buddhist, Jewish, or of no declared religious tradition. I am particularly grateful to my novice master, Fr. Christopher Latimer, and to Fr. Kieran, my teacher in spiritual theology and student master in our house of studies when I was a seminarian. I am also indebted to Archbishop Martinez for his book on the Holy Spirit, to Herbert Benson for introducing me to the relaxation response, to Mary Jo Meadow and Joseph Goldstein for their instructions on the meditation practices of Theravadan Buddhism, and to George Maloney for teaching me the theology and practice of the Jesus Prayer. These teachers and many others, especially other Carmelites, have shown me the multifaceted ways of meditation and sustained me on my journey.

Above all, I am grateful to the Church, east and west. Over the centuries she has built a treasury of prayer that today provides amply for our need "to pray always and never lose heart" as Jesus instructed. (Lk 18:1) This treasury reveals prayer as an organic, dynamic reality that continually grows and adapts to the demands of different personalities and changing times. When I entered the Carmelites in 1955, our exclusivist attitude toward other religions made it unthinkable that the Church would one day officially tell religious institutes to "assimilate" the ascetic and contemplative practices of Hindus and Buddhists. Yet, in 1965 the *Ad Gentes* document on missions from Vatican II encouraged us to do precisely that.

Furthermore, in 2003, our own order's most recent general chapter directed our friars in Asia to enter "an open-ended dialogue with the major non-Christian religions, especially in the area of spirituality."[23] We now see clearly how the Word of God and the Holy Spirit teach us about the interior life through these traditions. The *vipassana* meditation practice of the Theravadan Buddhist tradition, for example, provides Carmelites with a reliable method for implementing the self-emptying counseled by John of the Cross for growth in faith, hope, and love that are the means for union with God. Quite possibly the next ecumenical council will instruct us to assimilate into Christian prayer what we have learned about the human person and our universe from contemporary studies in human sexuality, the life and social sciences, astronomy and quantum physics, economics and international relations. I probably will not live to see this development, but I have no doubt that it will happen, for Christian prayer always assimilates and accommodates to truth from whatever source.

But other than gratitude, do I have anything else to show for fifty years of daily mental prayer? Two hours a day for fifty years adds up to over thirty-five thousand hours of formal meditation. Am I in any way different today than I would have been had I invested these hours in study, or writing, or spiritual guidance, or pastoral counseling? This question is more difficult to answer. Daily meditation has surely helped me remain a Carmelite. Throughout these years, no matter what was going on within me or around me, in the order or in the Church, daily mental prayer reassured me that I am where I belong. I have never seriously questioned that God called me to Carmel.

Daily meditation may also explain the pride I feel in being a Carmelite. I live in a contemplative tradition that dates back eight centuries to the early hermits on Mt. Carmel in the Holy Land and includes three church doctors of spirituality—Teresa of Avila, John of the Cross, and Thérèse of Lisieux. I feel privileged to share this heritage with contemporary Americans. I also know that I am one with the entire Carmelite family throughout the world in prayer for the problems of the world. I am convinced that simply praying for the human family in all its needs is the best thing I can do with my life. And there are those times when in the deep stillness and quiet of mental prayer I have felt in complete harmony with God and all of creation, breathing in and out in union with God and the entire universe.

Awareness of God may be the main fruit of daily mental prayer. In prayer I come before the mystery of God. I see God's transcendence, the total otherness of God. No image, no thought, no feeling of mine captures God. "For my thoughts are not your thoughts, nor are your ways my ways, says the Lord. As high as the heavens are above the earth, so high are my ways above your ways, and my thoughts above your thoughts." (Is 55:8-9) Because God is Totally Other than I think or imagine, I am very cautious in interpreting God's action in my life, in the lives of others, or in our world today. Nonetheless, God does speak to me. "The Father spoke one Word," writes John of the Cross, "which was his Son, and this Word he speaks always in eternal silence, and in silence must it be heard by the soul."[24] Meditation enables me to know God's Word.

Over the years, Jesus, God's Word made flesh, has become the center of my life. I attribute this largely to meditation, for there in silence the mystery of the Risen Christ becomes real to me. I understand why Teresa of Avila insisted that our prayer always be centered in the humanity of Jesus. God is fully present in Jesus. My surest way to union with God is through Jesus' human nature, which of course involves accepting fully my own human condition as well. As a priest, I try always to live *in persona Christi*—to be Christ's presence for others wherever I go—and the more fully I can embrace my humanity, the more closely I believe I approach that ideal. This also involves imitating Jesus' life on earth and attempting to "behave in all events as he would."[25] John of the Cross insists, though, that we must imitate especially Jesus' emptying of self in sense and spirit on the cross, because on Calvary Jesus, under the guidance of the Holy Spirit, reconciled the human family with God.[26] For this reason, I value Buddhist *vipassana* meditation because, more than any other meditation method I have found, it helps me imitate more consciously in time of prayer the self-emptying of Jesus Christ.

Meditation also reveals me to myself. Gradually I have come to see myself more as I really am rather than as I had hoped myself to be. Meditation gives me a deeper insight into my true motivation for the things I choose to do. I ordinarily tell myself that I always do what I do for the best of reasons, whereas meditation often reveals the hidden self-seeking in my most seemingly altruistic decisions. I want to think I am collaborating with others in projects that are for the good of the order and of the Church; in actuality I am often using others to advance my own reputation. This perhaps has been the greatest benefit of Christian insight or awareness mediation, to see more clearly the true motives of my behavior and my continual need to be purified of my inveterate self-seeking.

I have come to appreciate how difficult the process of human transformation really is. I can clearly teach others that the goal of the contemplative life, at least as Carmelites see it, is the transformation of the total personality in God through love, to become even in this life, as St. John of the Cross puts it, "God through participation in God,"[27] to see reality with God's eyes, to respond to daily events with the heart of Christ Jesus; yet, when I observe my own first interior movements in response to persons and events, I can readily see how far removed I am from this transformation, how hard my heart is, how unconverted to the Gospel most of my life still remains. I now understand why St. Teresa insists that humility is a necessary foundation for the life of prayer. The unending self-discovery that comes through prayer and meditation forces me to admit how far I am from the perfection Christ calls us to in the Gospel and how much I depend on God's grace for the little good I actually do in this life.

If the fruits are so slow in coming, is mental prayer really worth all the effort? After fifty years in Carmel, as I see my time in this world coming quickly to an end, I know of no better way to prepare for Jesus when he comes for me. It no longer embarrasses me that my understanding of God is so limited and my life so untransformed, for I believe that will all be remedied in an instant at the moment of death when I see the Lord. I am, however, embarrassed by the irrational fears that still grip my soul—fear of disapproval, fear of failure, fear of intimacy, fear of final damnation. "There is no fear in love," writes St. John the Evangelist, " but perfect love casts out fear; for fear has to do with punishment, and whoever fears has not reached perfection in love." (1Jn 4:18) Sadly, fifty years of mediation in Carmel have not yet brought me to perfect love. Nonetheless, meditation prepares me to enter fully into God, the Abyss of Love, because each day it provides me another opportunity to abandon myself with total confidence to God's infinite mercy, as my sister Thérèse of Lisieux counsels.[28] In this surrender, I shall eventually see God, and that, after all, is why, as Christians, as Carmelites, we learn how to meditate—to see God.

Notes

1 Constitutions, 2 & 7, in "The Constitutions," in *The Collected Works of St. Teresa of Avila,* trans. Kieran Kavanaugh and Otilio Rodriguez, vol. 3 (Washington DC: ICS Publications, 1985), 319-20.

2 *Rule and Constitutions of the Discalced Nuns of the Order of the Blessed Virgin Mary of Mount Carmel adapted according to the Directives of the Second Vatican Council and the Canonical Norms in force and approved by the Apostolic See in the Year of our Lord 1991,* Const. no. 79, (Rome: Casa Generalizia OCD, 1991), 78-79; OCD Friars, *Constitutions and Norms,* Const. no. 64. (Dublin: Conference of OCD English-Speaking Provincials, 1988), 65-66. See also St. Teresa of Avila, *The Book of Her Life,* 8.5, in *Collected Works* vol. 1 (Washington, DC: ICS Publications, 1976), 67.

3 Fr. Gabriel of St. Mary Magdalen, O.C.D., *Little Catechism of Prayer,* trans. Discalced Carmelite Nuns of Concord, New Hampshire (Concord, NH: Monastery of Discalced Carmelites, 1949). A similar, but much larger book that was being written by one of the friars stationed in our novitiate at this time is Peter-Thomas Rohrbach, *Conversation with Christ: An Introduction to Mental Prayer* (Chicago: Fides Publishers, 1956).

4 Ibid., 10.

5 Luis M. Martinez, *The Sanctifier*, trans. Sr. M. Aquinas, O.S.U. (Paterson, NJ: St. Anthony Guild Press, 1957).

6 *The Book of Her Life,* in *Collected Works* 1, 44.

7 Guigo the Carthusian, *Scala Paradisi,* chap. 2, in Migne PL 40, 998. Recommended readings on *Lectio Divina* are: Michael Casey, *Sacred Reading: The Ancient Art of* Lectio Divina (Liguori, MO: Liguori/Triumph, 1995); Mariano Magrassi, *Praying the Bible: An Introduction to* Lectio Divina, trans. Edward Hagman (Collegeville, MN: The Liturgical Press, 1998.)

8 St. John of the Cross, *The Sayings of Light and Love,* no. 158, in *The Collected Works of St. John of the Cross,* rev. ed., trans. Kieran Kavanaugh and Otilio Rodriguez (Washington DC: ICS Publications, 1991), 97. [italics mine]

9 Herbert Benson, *The Relaxation Response* (New York: William Morrow and Company, Inc., 1975).

10 Herbert Benson, *Beyond the Relaxation Response* (New York: Berkley Books, 1985).

11 *The Way of a Pilgrim,* trans. R.M. French (New York: Seabury Press, 1965).

12 St. Teresa of Avila, *The Way of Perfection,* in *Collected Works* 2, 53.

13 George Maloney, *Prayer of the Heart* (Notre Dame, IN: Ave Maria Press, 1981); *The Jesus Prayer: Practicing Both a Method of Prayer and a Way of Life* (Bronx, NY: John XXIII Center for Eastern Christian Studies/Fordham University, 1972), audiocassette, JF-2.

14 Thomas Merton, *The Jesus Prayer* (Kansas City, MO: Credence Communications, 2000), audiocassette, A4363.

15 Maloney, *The Jesus Prayer.*

16 Daniel J. O'Hanlon, "Integration of Spiritual Practices: A Western Christian Looks East," *Journal of Transpersonal Psychology* 13 (1981): 91-112.

17 Mary Jo Meadow and Kevin Culligan, "Congruent Spiritual Paths: Christian Carmelite and Theravadan Buddhist *Vipassana,*" *Journal of Transpersonal Psychology* 19 (1987): 181-96.

18 Kevin Culligan, Mary Jo Meadow, and Daniel Chowning, *Purifying the Heart: Buddhist Insight Meditation for Christians* (New York: Crossroad, 1994).

19 St. John of the Cross, *The Living Flame of Love* 1.21, in *Collected Works,* 649.

20 St. Teresa of Avila, *The Way of Perfection*, in *Collected Works* 2, 117.

21 Ibid., 141.

22 Discalced Carmelites, *Constitutions*, no. 64, p. 65; and *Norms* no. 29, p. 150.

23 General Chapter of the Discalced Carmelites, *Journeying with St Teresa of Avila and St John of the Cross: Setting out from Essentials,* Avila, Spain, May 2003, no. 67.

24 St. John of the Cross. *The Sayings of Light and Love*, no. 100, in *Collected Works,* 92.

25 St. John of the Cross, *The Ascent of Mount Carmel* A.1.13.3, in *Collected Works,* 148.

26 Ibid., A.2.7.11, 172.

27 St. John of the Cross, *The Living Flame of Love* F.2.34, in *Collected Works,* 671.

28 St. Thérèse of Lisieux, *Story of a Soul,* trans. John Clarke, 3rd rev. ed. (Washington, DC: ICS Publications, 1996), 200.

The Influence of the Carmelite Mystical School

Denis Read, O.C.D.
Spiritual Center of Our Lady of Mount Carmel
Miami, Florida

Fr. Kieran Kavanaugh, O.C.D., practitioner of the spirituality of Sts. Teresa of Avila and John of the Cross and translator of their writings, deserves a special niche in the history of the Carmelite school of mystical theology. Through his prodigious labors in translating the writings of these two Carmelite saints and church doctors of spirituality from their original Spanish into standard American English, he, perhaps more that any other English-speaking Carmelite, has brought the enormously influential Carmelite school of mystical theology to bear on the English-speaking world.

We can perhaps best appreciate the importance of Fr. Kieran's quiet, behind-the-scenes Carmelite work when we compare it to the labors of Fr. Silverio of St. Teresa, O.C.D., a twentieth-century European Carmelite who was involved in the same apostolate of diffusing the writings of the Carmelite mystical tradition. Fr. Silverio was the editor of the immense fourteen volume *Biblioteca Mistica Carmelitana,* published in Burgos, Spain, by the Editorial El Monte Carmelo. As a researcher into the texts of Teresa and John and a master of the fine points of textual criticism, Fr. Silverio established the best manuscripts of the two Spanish doctors that served as a basis for Fr. Kieran's translations.

During his long and varied career, Fr. Silverio inspired a new generation of younger Discalced Carmelites such as Fr. Crisógono of the Blessed Sacrament, Fr. Efrén of the Mother of God, Fr. Eulogio

Pacho, Fr. Teófanes Egido, Fr. Federico Ruiz, and their successors in the European Carmelite world. Since 1950, but especially after the "return to the mystics" following Vatican II, these men have collaborated in preparing for the ecumenical success of the Carmelite mystical school wherever the Gospel is preached today.

This success rests primarily upon the authority of Sts. Teresa of Avila and John of the Cross. Both are proclaimed doctors of the Catholic Church. Both are mentors in the spiritual life. They are often the final authorities in numerous disputed questions on the mystical knowledge of God that is of fundamental importance for the theoretical and practical understanding of the Christian life. Through their textual criticism and commentaries on the writings of Teresa and John, Fr. Silverio and his students have influenced all of Catholic theology today. By that important contribution, they have also affected the inner life and even the public face of the Roman Catholic Church.

The Influence of the Carmelite Mystical School in the Last Fifty Years

We can approach the subject of theological influence from several angles. First, there is the historical angle, which would show how various authors during the last four hundred years have profited by the mystical theology of the Carmelite school. The *Dictionnaire de Spiritualité,* for example, pursued this avenue in its treatment of Teresa and John. A more devotional approach, which we follow in this essay, would illustrate how the mysticism of Teresa and John influences popular religiosity. Their writings, for instance, greatly influenced the young nineteenth-century Carmelite genius, St. Thérèse of Lisieux, who, in turn, through her own writings popularized the doctrines of her holy parents and introduced mystical theology into everyday life. St. Thérèse, very aptly called "St. John of the Cross with a smile," expressed popularly what Karl Rahner, S.J., some years later would articulate more intellectually.

Bookshelves are now full of books on "spirituality" which record the dimensions of living religion all the way from Thomas Merton's monastic journey to the charismatic movement's latest intuitions. Spirituality, today, has indeed become a buzzword—a substitute perhaps for rigorous theological analysis and careful attention to the doctrine of the mystics recommended by the Catholic Church. But sound Christian spirituality presupposes spiritual theology. Spiritual theology is *theology*—a rigorous, definable, and communicable knowledge of God and the things of God. Spirituality's current popularity must not blind us to the movements of the Holy Spirit in our day impelling men and women everywhere to seek the Spirit of God and to discover the Spirit's ways to find God.

This is what mysticism is all about: finding and experiencing God in spirit and truth. Here the Carmelite school finds its indispensable mission to bring the good news of experienced faith, hope, and love to the world, and thus to evangelize "all of creation" with the mystical Gospel of Jesus Christ, of St. Paul the Apostle, of St. John the Evangelist, and of their successors in the Catholic mystical tradition. This is not popularizing a "school of thought" among other such schools as Thomism or phenomenology or "the new theology." This is a return to the biblical and experiential sources of theology. It is what Yves Congar calls a *"ressourcement,"* a return to the sources of the eternal Gospel of Jesus himself, and its continuing relevance for every facet of life today. "I came that they may have life and have it more abundantly . . . . Everyone who lives and believes in me will never die." (Jn 10:10 and 11:26)

The Carmelite mystical school's greatest achievement before 1950 was to bring this message to light. Both before and after the

Protestant Reformation, this message was often kept under a bushel basket. In this age of rationalism, devotions, visions, and private revelations were staples of Catholic piety. Even after the epoch-making works of Teresa of Jesus and John of the Cross, mysticism was held in low esteem. Beginning in the nineteenth century, translators such as Benedict Zimmerman, O.C.D., David Lewis, and E. Allison Peers labored to acquaint the English-speaking world with the two great Carmelite mystics. However, with the Church's theological schools in disarray due largely to the Vatican's fear of modernism, it was not until St. Thérèse of Lisieux's canonization in 1925 that the theological world became aware of St. John of the Cross. Because John was Thérèse's mentor and she followed his principles and developed them into her own "little way," her "storm of glory" paved the way for his being declared Doctor of the Church the following year in 1926.

After the terrible devastation and human angst wrought by two world wars and the Holocaust, St. Thérèse's amazing popularity, helped by the interest in the contemplative life created by Thomas Merton, prompted the English-speaking world to look to Sts. Teresa and John for inspiration. This interest in mystical—now called "spiritual"—theology became a source for a mystical awakening, not only in the Roman Catholic, but also in the Orthodox and Protestant churches.

John Paul II's Influence in the Turn toward Mysticism

No one has been more central to this interreligious rediscovery of mysticism than our late pope, John Paul II. He was primarily a mystic and a man of prayer, secondarily a philosopher, and finally a mystical theologian in the tradition of John of the Cross. Quoting John, John Paul II maintained that "when God is not known, nothing is known."[1] Conversely, when God is known by experiential faith, there is much about the human person that is known. This mystical knowledge decisively influenced his own thinking and his pontificate. It put his personal stamp on his actions as bishop of Krakow at Vatican II, later as the cardinal of Krakow in the Polish Solidarity movement, and finally as a pope with a new style for over twenty-five years. This made him a man of surprises. He was unique and original.

We can document John Paul II's originality in his dealing with philosophical and ethical issues. In treating the Church's social philosophy of work, for example, he starts with the basic findings of Scriptural revelation. He first analyzes Genesis for the anthropological data on the nature of work. Then he probes the *meaning* and discovers the *values* revealed in Adam's dominion of creation by means of his work. Finally, he proceeds to recognize the difference between the worker's objective product and the subjective *virtue and effects of the work on the worker.* The pope thus sees work as a process of growing in self-determination or liberty and of pursuing truth, goodness, beauty, and communion. This process is the reason for a work ethic and becomes the Church's social philosophy in the new millennium. The transcendentals of truth, beauty, and communion—manifest in the Catholic community—thus characterize the pope's doctrinal, moral, and catechetical teaching.

This unifying synthesis, with a new philosophical integrity, articulates a holistic social doctrine that surpasses the rationality of a former moral theology founded on the "principles of morality" taken from Aristotle and St. Thomas Aquinas. An example of this difference may be seen in comparing the article on "Papal Social Teaching" in the *New Catholic Encyclopedia* by Msgr. Pietro Pavan, Pope John XXIII's moralist and ghost writer, with Samuel Gregg's more recent *Challenging the Modern World: Karol Wojtyla/John Paul II and the Development of Catholic Social Teaching.*[2] What has happened to papal social teaching? Still based on the dignity of every human person, it is now recognized as a *datum of faith* following the meaning of Genesis and becomes a full-blown *social philosophy* with roots in a mystical vision of Genesis. The same procedure is followed in John Paul's *Theology of the Body,* a study of human sexuality. John Paul II gave the Church the beginning of a *mystical philosophy of life.* It is a beginning of mystical reasoning, and a mystical ethic: he has shown us the way to think mystically, without leaving us a "summa philosophiae mysticae."

In his rethinking of Catholic philosophy, John Paul II employed a phenomenological method by which he could perceive and critique the values of human and religious experience. This experience is the same mystical phenomena that John of the Cross brought to the mystical enterprise. As a young layman, Karol Wojtyla had discovered St. John of the Cross through his acquaintance with a Krakow tailor. He even wanted to join the Discalced Carmelites there, but Cardinal Sapieha advised him to enter the underground seminary that was then active in Krakow.

After ordination, Karol followed up his interest by writing "Faith in St. John of the Cross," his doctoral dissertation at the Dominican Angelicum University in Rome. Returning to Krakow for pastoral ministry, he continued to study and teach in various Polish universities. He did a second doctorate on the phenomenology of Max Scheler and its usefulness in understanding the philosophies of Thomas Aquinas, Emmanuel Kant, and Edmund Husserl. This included a critique of traditional Thomistic ethics from the perspective of mystical and moral experience.

This study brought him into a new world he called "the world of values," which was instrumental in his formation as a mystical theologian. This new world consists, above all, in *the values of the good.* It involves perceiving these values and experiencing these goods, together with perceiving and experiencing the gifts and charisms of the Holy Spirit. With this background, he analyzed the problems faced in Vatican II, such as the value of religious freedom, the fundamental importance of the body in our creation as incarnate spirits, and work as the starting point for the dialogue with the modern world on economics and politics. These everyday realities and their newly understood meanings became the categories of Vatican II's *Gaudium et Spes, The Pastoral Constitution on the Church in the Modern World.* We still await a developed history of this mystical philosopher and theologian's influence on the deliberations of the Second Vatican Council. Yet, Karol Wojtyla's phenomenology of mysticism, which he had used in his own pastoral ministry both before and after Vatican II to formulate solutions to the problems raised at Vatican II, was decisive.

Vatican II did not solve many of the Catholic Church's problems in confronting modernity, but it did frame them. Coming from the tyranny of the Polish communist state, Karol Wojtyla had long confronted the issues associated with liberty, ethical renewal, family, and global poverty. He was passionately involved in formulating the *Declaration on Religious Freedom* at Vatican II. In Poland, he deliberated often on the violations of human rights. This experience made him the protagonist for human rights and an opponent of human wrongs. His phenomenology helped him to recognize and ponder rights and wrongs as spiritual realities within moral philosophy and theology. Because mysticism is a branch of Thomistic moral theology, Karol Wojtyla integrated his "world of values" into the Thomistic synthesis, which he recognized as superior to Scheler's system, although in doing so he gave Thomism a new turn to subjectivity.

During his formative intellectual years, Karol also confronted some of the historical facts of the Catholic Counter-Reformation and the effect of its rationalism upon the Church's mystical tradition that led to the decline of theology. He saw clearly the need for a *renaissance* of Catholic theological life and culture. As any human institution would be, the Roman Catholic Church had been frightened to its very core by Martin Luther and the *devotio moderna* that followed the charismatic and mystical flowering in the Rhine and German provinces of the Hapsburg dominions in the fifteenth and sixteenth centuries. (John Paul II would later beg pardon of Protestants for the now historically evident Catholic sins and mistakes during and after the Reformation.)

Most of the Counter-Reformation theologians suffocated the ideas of a direct experience of God, of contemplative prayer beyond the liturgical and devotional practices of the day, and especially of Luther's "freedom of the Christian man" to accept the lights, movements, graces, and inspirations of the Holy Spirit. However, sixteenth-century mystical saints like Ignatius of Loyola, Teresa of Avila, and John of the Cross recognized such spiritual gifts as substantial words, or the influence of good and evil spirits upon our souls, substantial touches, and the seven Gifts of the Spirit—all within the most profound orthodoxy that these same theologians had ever encountered. These Catholic mystics experienced, perceived, and practiced the Church's doctrines in a way that instructed the Church herself, confirmed her faith, and anchored the realities of that hitherto abstract science of mystical theology in the sober reality of a discerning, experienced faith. This was a profound realization for the ancient Western Catholic Church, so much in need of reform and renewal.

The young priest, Karol Wojtyla, later bishop and archbishop of Krakow, thus entered with zest into the Church's updating after John XXIII called the Second Vatican Council. (As John Paul II, he later beatified John XXIII in September 2000.) He had already discovered what Vatican II confirmed: the proper stance of a truly Catholic theology is the experiential life of faith, hope, and love. He translated this as *communion.* It is a spirituality of communion for bishops (the depth reality behind collegiality), for his beloved and frequently worrisome priests (the ministers of sacramental, ecclesial communion), and especially for young religious and laity who are called to be the new evangelists of mystical communion with the Father, Son, and Holy Spirit (cf. *Lumen Gentium,* 1). This, in a nutshell, is John Paul II's mystical vision, his theological stance from which he did his theology and philosophy. His mysticism undergirds all his philosophy and theology. It is his point of view, his horizon whence he looks for engagement to a critical reception or dialogue with both his critics and his colleagues. (I speak here only of John Paul II's thought and prescind from his, or the Church's, opinions of its *moral normativity*. Indeed, this is a further question which requires, if his thought is to come to maturity, an additional theological critique, grounded in a similar philosophy of the experience of work, of economic entrepreneurship, and of the evangelization of the Third World.)

The Carmelite Mystical School's Influence on John Paul II's Teaching

St. John of the Cross's influence on the thought and, more deeply, the life of Fr. Karol Wojtyla was pervasive. The young workingman, and then priest, became a mystic, experiencing the living flame of love in his spirit and expressing it in his poetry. He recognized the overall primacy of love in all human desiring, seeking, longing, and finding. In his pastoral ministry to young couples, he found the broken nature of sexual love which would one day give rise to his great "theology of the body," a spiritual phenomenology of human sexuality. As Pope John Paul II, he continued to root his spiritual life in the mystery of the Trinity, indwelling and activating him.

Intellectually, he developed a spirituality that will characterize his influence in future Catholic life and thought by taking Mary, all mother, as his *Totus Tuus* motto, so characteristic of a Carmelite mystic. He even joined the Carmelite secular order to assure his continuance in the Carmelite school. He once had dreamed of being a Carmelite before Cardinal Sapieha of Krakow saw that he was made for another vocation. As he became older, the pope saw that his spiritual family home was the mystical school of Sts. Teresa of Avila and John of the Cross.

This family horizon in Pope John Paul's prophetic vision explains much of his doctrine of the Holy Spirit who spoke through the prophets and its expression in the phrase "Lord and Giver of Life" as he calls the Spirit in the encyclical *Dominum et Vivificantem.* The pope's recognition of the Holy Spirit as "the communion of the Father and the Son" (St. Augustine's phrase) reveals in depth his spirituality of communion that is the source of the following: 1) our prayer life of communion with the Trinity; 2) ecclesial communion—"I believe in . . . the communion of saints"; 3) the ecclesial mission of evangelization—John Paul II's constant plea to everyone to work for communion with lapsed Catholics and separated Christians; 4) the communion of faith and reason in our human makeup; 5) dialogue with those who are different from Catholics—with separated Christians in fellowship; and with men and women of good will in interreligious dialogue and human support, understanding, and forgiveness; 6) and, perhaps most importantly, recognizing the importance of the saints, their personal example, and their teachings on mysticism.

These six expressions of the Holy Spirit as "the communion of the Father and the Son" are all implicit in the writings of St. John of the Cross. John's poetry and prose give a dynamism and a fresh originality to his theology, breaking open the classical molds of scholastic theology to find fresh means of theological expression. His poetry and prose, and sometimes prose-poetry, return to a biblical language of symbol, image, and lyric poetry. "This is what the thought and the language (of St. John of the Cross) have brought to the beginnings of a new theology" and Pope John Paul II has been more influential than any other person in bringing out these hidden riches of the Carmelite mystical school.[3]

In his analysis of modern life, the pope recognized the importance of St. John of the Cross and the entire Carmelite school for renewing the Church, theology, and human culture. With the rise of atheism and secular humanist agnosticism in the modern world, an even more profound movement has grown up out of all the wars, the holocausts, the sufferings, and the birth pangs of a new world order during this last and most violent of all centuries. John Paul II called these terrible signs of the times "a collective experience . . . of the dark night which is an experience which is simply human and Christian. . . . The doctrine of the saint is newly relevant today to make sense of this incomprehensible mystery of human suffering."[4]

John Paul II had the contemplative insight to recognize that a tremendous turn has taken place in the teaching of the Church catholic: the dark night has become democratized and is now part and parcel of the ordinary life of every man and woman, believer and unbeliever. Pope John Paul promoted as an integral element in official church teaching what I call "the recognition factor" of the presence or absence of God, so evident in the Scriptures. His study of the Carmelite mystical school and its turn toward the subject's experiential faith—a doctrine of the spirituality of faith, hope, and love—has made his theology different from what it was before. John Paul himself notes this in his 1990 apostolic letter when he writes, alluding to St. John of the Cross: "I desire, with the light of the 'Holy Spirit, the

Teacher' (A.2.29.1) and writing in the same spirit and sapiential style which Fray John of the Cross used, to comment on some aspects of his doctrine of faith, sharing his message with men and women of today, who are living in this particular historical time, full of challenges and hope."[5]

"The Church and the world of culture know John of the Cross in many fields: a literary giant and a Castilian poet; an artist and a humanist; and a man of profound mystical experiences; a theologian and spiritual exegete; a master of souls and a director of consciences. As a master on the road of faith, his person and his writings have given us a great synthesis of spirituality and Christian mystical experience. His central message is living faith, the guide of Christians, their only light in the dark nights of trial, and the burning flame nourished by the Spirit. 'Faith is the only possible and proportional way to union with God.'"[6]

Pope John Paul cites Vatican II. He says that John of the Cross "has been our companion during this period of history, twenty-five years after the closing of Vatican II, which gave the impulse and fomented the renewal of the Church: 'It is the function of the Church to make God the Father and His Incarnate Son present and, as it were, almost visible, through continuous renovation and purification, under the guidance of the Holy Spirit. This renovation is brought about chiefly by the witness of a living, mature faith, one namely that is so well formed that it can see difficulties clearly and overcome them.'"[7] According to John Paul, St. John of the Cross was one of those persons who made God present and visible to his contemporaries. The pope goes so far as to say that ever since "he entered into an intimate dialogue with this 'master of the faith,' dialoguing with his language and his thought, . . . I have found in him a friend and a master who pointed out to me the light that shines in the darkness, so that I could always walk toward God,

with no other light or guide
than the one that burned in my heart.
This guided me
more surely than the light of noon."[8]

John Paul II thus acknowledges his personal debt to St. John of the Cross. However, the Carmelite school's influence extends far beyond John of the Cross's impact on the Polish pontiff's worldview.

The Influence of the Carmelite School in the Churches of Europe

This history is vast. Since 1961, for example, the *Bibliographia Internationalis Spiritualitatis (BIS),* located in the Teresianum, the Discalced Carmelite college in Rome, has tracked the explosion of written records and other evidences of the worldwide growth of spirituality. Even though the precise standing of spirituality and its scientific normativity is still in dispute, *BIS* has recorded the Carmelite school's influence that has permeated the studies of spirituality and its allied sciences since the end of the World War II.

The doctorates of St. Teresa of Avila and St. Thérèse of Lisieux have also added prestige to the mystical theology of the Carmelite school and increased its influence in the cultural life of the churches of Europe and the world. The writings of Edith Stein have added to this luster, especially since the opening of the synod of European bishops in Rome on 1 October 1999, when John Paul II proclaimed her co-patroness of Europe along with St. Bridget of Sweden and St. Catherine of Siena. The *Catechism of the Catholic Church* also attests to the range of influence of the Carmelite mystics, citing St. Thérèse of Lisieux six times, Sts. Teresa of Jesus and John of the Cross five times each, and Blessed Elizabeth of the Trinity once. Part Four of the

Catechism on Christian prayer, in particular, draws upon the Carmelite doctors to explain the nature of prayer and the qualities of a good spiritual director. However, more than anywhere else, Carmel's mystical influence in Europe emerged in Vatican II's rediscovery of the Holy Spirit.

Pope John XXIII prepared the way for the Vatican II Church's mystical rediscovery of the Holy Spirit. Before Vatican II, Père Marie Michel Philipon, O.P., a leading Catholic spiritual theologian, had written *The Great Unknown: The Holy Spirit and His Gifts,* an outstanding work in the Thomistic tradition. Influenced by his reading of this book, John XXIII simply accepted the Spirit's inspiration, which he sensed as "a simple word: an ecumenical council, coming up from our heart and onto our lips. An unexpected touch, a gift of light from on high, a great savor in the eyes and in the heart . . ." (Discourse opening the Council, 11 Oct. 1962, 7). He challenged the council fathers to make the council "a new Pentecost, which would make the interior riches of the Church break into flower" (Discourse closing the first session, 8 December1962). A "flowering" did indeed occur, for which Europeans found an American word, "a revival." Henceforth, spirituality became a course in all seminaries and most Catholic universities. A hunger for spirituality broke out all over the world. In the United States, the Catholic charismatic renewal began at Duquesne University in Pittsburgh. As Cardinal Suenens had foretold at the council—and repeated in lectures in this country after the council—the Roman Catholic Church was rediscovering the charisms of the Holy Spirit.

At the Council, there had been two schools of thought on the nature of the charisms of the Holy Spirit. One, preferred by Cardinal Ruffini of Palermo, Italy, considered the charisms extraordinary gifts; the other, sponsored by Cardinal Suenens of Malines, Belgium, thought them ordinary. The council fathers accepted Suenens's theology. From that day on, the charisms of the Holy Spirit, both of service and of prayer, became a new movement. This movement is now ecumenical, with the Protestant churches joining in, and has spread to the other nations of Europe, as can be seen in groups like the *Cursillo de la Cristianidad, Communione e Liberazione,* the growth of renewed secular orders in all the mendicant orders, Taizé in France, and many other centers of prayer and spiritual life throughout Europe. These and other signs of the times brought with them a return to the writings of the mystics as the classics of spirituality, leading Karl Rahner to coin the phrase: "We can say the Christian of the future will be a mystic or he will not be a Christian."[9] An Association of Friends of Christian Mysticism began in Europe using Rahner's phrase as a slogan.

In the crisis of conscience following Vatican II, the mystics became guides and directors of the spiritual life, bringing about a remarriage of theologians and spiritual men and women after three centuries of divorce. As Rahner put it in his fundamental book, *Spirit in the World,* the spiritual life was restored to be known as "life in the spirit," pneumatology. His books on everyday spirituality, a la St. Thérèse of Lisieux, became best sellers. The Carmelites Thérèse of Lisieux and Elizabeth of the Trinity, even more than Rahner, became new evangelists of the spirit. They gave the world "a little way," a popular spirituality of abandonment to the Trinity dwelling within us. A new integration was seen in European spirituality. Passive receptivity, under the influence of the gifts of the Holy Spirit, again became part of the Christian life. Hyperactivism was seen for what it is: a flight from prayer and spirituality. Contemplation and action were now complementary, not conflictual. American authors such as Thomas Merton and Dorothy Day received a more welcome reception. European churches were becoming international and ecumenical under the influence of Vatican II's Holy Spirit.[10] With spirituality alive again in Europe, the Church looked to the Carmelite mystical tradition for spiritual nourishment and guidance.

The Carmelite Mystical School's Influence in English-Speaking Churches in the Modern World

Pope John Paul II's avowed purpose in his entire pontificate was to put Vatican II's teachings and initiatives into pastoral practice. His mystical dynamism was a major influence on the pastoral life of the entire Catholic Church during the past fifty years. His "spirituality"—the word he prefers to describe his mystical teaching—is evident in his catechesis and in his summaries of the synods that have dealt with every aspect of the Church: priestly life, religious life, and the mission of the laity. He was not alone, however, in infusing spirituality into the Church's pastoral life. My final exhibit of the Carmelite mystical school's influence is its pastoral importance for the English-speaking world.

Here Fr. Kieran Kavanaugh's work has had its greatest impact. Together with Fr. Otilio Rodriguez, O.C.D., he has translated into standard American English the collected writings of both St. John of the Cross and St. Teresa of Avila. Following Fr. Otilio's departure for Rome in the late 1960s to become the rector of the Teresianum and founder of *BIS,* Fr. Kieran continued the major share of their translation project under the auspices of the Institute of Carmelite Studies, of which he was a founding father in 1966 and to which he has given decisive leadership over the years.

This translation ministry has provided pastoral tools for the English-speaking churches of the United States, Ireland, the United Kingdom, the Philippines, Oceania, India, and Africa. In addition to translating the texts of Sts. John and Teresa, Fr. Kieran has also helped the reader to understand their spirit and teaching. His striking introductions to the various books of John and Teresa are themselves jewels of mystical and spiritual direction. His footnotes, glossaries, and indices have further clarified the translated texts. His translations and accompanying interpretative tools have thus introduced many teachers, priests, religious, formation masters, and lay persons into the riches of the Carmelite tradition of spirituality.

Throughout the years of translation, Fr. Kieran has worked within the Institute of Carmelite Studies. He has labored alongside the Institute's other translators and editors such as the late John Clarke, O.C.D., principal translator of the writings of St. Thérèse of Lisieux, Salvatore Sciurba, O.C.D., translator of *The Practice of the Presence of God* of Br. Lawrence of the Resurrection, and both John Sullivan, O.C.D., then Steven Payne, O.C.D., series editor of I.C.S.'s multivolume translation of *The Collected Works of Edith Stein*. Together, these and other members of the Institute have committed themselves to share the Carmelite mystical heritage with the English-speaking world, a collective effort that has produced over one million volumes of translation and commentary.

Even with the support and assistance of fellow members of the Institute, translating is a solitary, demanding, and underestimated ministry, especially when, as in Fr. Kieran's case, done over an entire lifetime. On the one hand, everyone would undoubtedly prefer to read a lyric poet like John of the Cross in the original Spanish; on the other hand, faithful, literate, and comprehensible translations of St. John's writings are necessary to make him known, loved, and followed by English-speaking people who cannot read him in the original language. While the Latin phrase *Omnis traductor, traditor* (every translator is a traitor) contains a grain of truth, it is equally true that without the help of skilled translators, non-Greek-speaking gentiles could not read the Bible.

Fr. Kieran, for example, has worked steadily over the years to improve their translation of John of the Cross through research, revision, and reordering of the saint's writings. When Doubleday first published the Kavanaugh and Rodriguez translation of *The Collected Works of St. John of the Cross* in 1964, the 740 page volume was without index and two subsequently discovered letters. In 1979, ICS Publications produced a second edition of the translation that included the two newly found autographs of John's letters to Maria de Soto (1582) and to a Carmelite nun in Segovia (1591). Also added were a topical index, an index of Sacred Scripture, and a list of the saint's own references. Finally, in 1991, to commemorate the fourth centenary of John's death, ICS Publications published a new revised edition of the translation.

Fr. Kieran tells the story of this revision:

> During the years that our [Kavanaugh and Rodriguez] English translation [of *The Collected Works of St. John of the Cross*] has been in print, major advances in sanjuanist scholarship have occurred, and new popular critical editions of John's works have come out. Now, at the fourth centenary celebration of the death of St. John of the Cross in 1591, seems the appropriate time to provide further enlightenment for his readers by incorporating the recent research into a revised English translation.
>
> To begin with, I have followed the practice in the new Spanish editions of changing the order in which John's works appear. Editors are now reminding readers of the benefit of *reading the poems first* and letting the symbolism speak, before going on to treatises and commentaries. John never intended his

> readers to restrict themselves to his commentaries, although certainly his explanations are of inestimable value; they greatly expand our horizons. Also, in the new Spanish editions, the *Sayings of Light and Love* precede the larger works. Before undertaking the latter, John gave spiritual guidance in writing through brief, compact counsels that were like dense summaries of his oral teaching. These maxims overflow with spiritual wisdom and whet the appetite for more; they prepare the way for his major works.
>
> With the passing of years, I began thinking that it would be more beneficial to the reader if some of the information in the introductions were in footnotes at the appropriate place. Doing so in this edition gave me an opportunity to include new information about doctrine and sources and some helpful cross-references. Also, in the back of the book is a glossary of terms that gives the reader further explanations and references to some of John of the Cross's terminology. . . .
>
> . . . . My hope is that this revised volume will continue to inspire and enlighten students and devotees of the teachings of St. John of the Cross, the Church's Mystical Doctor.[11]

"To inspire and enlighten"—certainly the goals of mystical theology! Through his translations of St. John and St. Teresa and his other writings, Fr. Kieran has inspired and enlightened many in the English-speaking world. Together with his ICS colleagues, he has provided the inspiration and enlightenment of the Carmelite mystical school for countless English readers. By his work and example, Fr. Kieran has increased the influence of the Carmelite school of mystical theology in the churches of both the United States and the entire English-speaking world, churches with growing numbers and increasing responsibilities throughout today's world. Into these churches, once "nourished by an austere creed,"[12] Fr. Kieran has placed the warmth of the mystical heart of Jesus, casting the living flame of the Holy Spirit's love upon the face of the earth. That Spirit, the influence of the Father and the Son in the renewal of the Church, gives the Gospel of Jesus to the whole world.

Such is Fr. Kieran Kavanaugh's service to God, the Church, and the worldwide Carmelite family. He has cooperated in handing on our sacred Carmelite mystical tradition to our present English-speaking generation and to all generations to come. A remarkable achievement! With the help of the Holy Spirit, may his achievements continue. May he continue "to inspire and enlighten" us for many more years.

Notes

1 Apostolic Letter, *Maestro de la fe,* 14 December 1990, quoting St. John of the Cross's *The SpiritualCanticle,* 26.13 [redaction B]. See *The Collected Works of St. John of the Cross,* trans. Kieran Kavanaugh and Otilio Rodriguez, rev.ed. (Washington, DC: ICS Publications, 1991), 578.

2 Petro Pavan, "Social Thought, Papal," *New Catholic Encyclopedia,* XIII, 352-61; Samuel Gregg, *Challenging the Modern World: John Paul II/ Karol Wojtyla and the Development of Catholic Social Teaching* (Lanham, MD: Lexington Books, 1999).

3 Ciro García, "San Juan de la Cruz entre la 'escolastica' y la nueva teología," in *Dottore Mistico-San Giovanni della Croce: Simposio nel IV Centenario della sua Morte,* ed. Eulogio Pacho (Rome: Teresianum, 1992), 129.

4 *Maestro de la fe,* no. 14.

5 Ibid., no. 4.

6 Ibid., nos. 4 & 2, quoting *The Ascent of Mt Carmel* 2.9.1 (see *Collected Works,* 177). [emphasis added]

7 Ibid., no. 3, quoting *Gaudium et Spes*, no. 21. See Austin Flannery, ed., *The Basic Sixteen Documents of Vatican Council II* (Northport. NY: Costello, 1996), 183-85. [emphasis added]

8 John Paul II, Sermon on St. John of the Cross in Segovia, Spain, 3 November 1982.

9 Karl Rahner, *Geist und Leben* 39 (1966): 335.

10 Daniel de Pablo Maroto, *Historia de la espiritualidad cristiana* (Madrid: Editorial de Espiritualidad, 1990), 352-58.

11 *Collected Works,* 7-8. [emphasis added]

12 Cornelia Otis Skinner, Hymn to Mary.

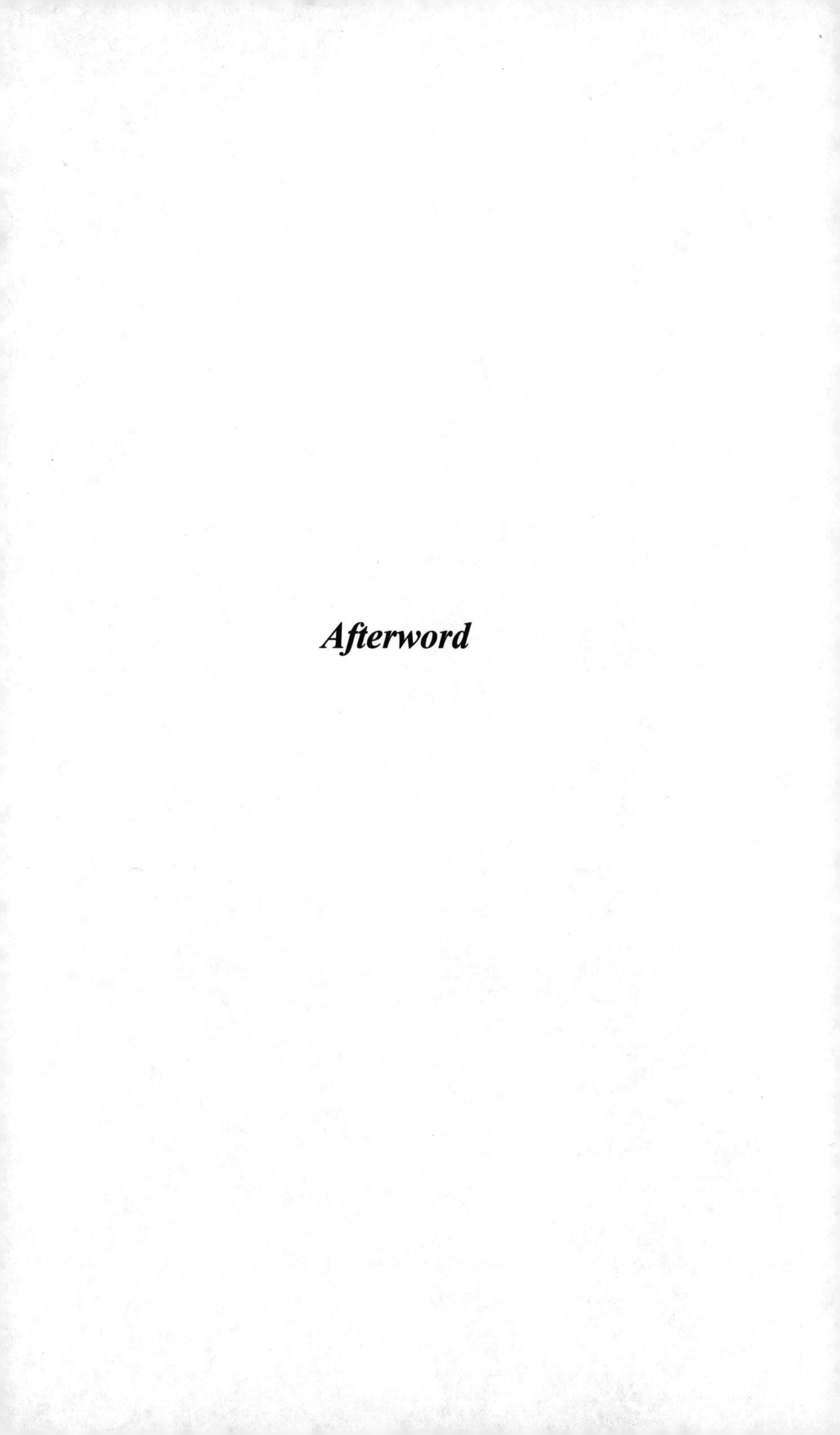

Afterword

St. John of the Cross and Interreligious Dialogue in Asia

William Johnston, S.J.
Jesuit House
Tokyo, Japan

As we enter the third millennium, it becomes increasingly clear that the great theological challenge of the future will be interreligious dialogue. At the end of the twentieth century we insisted that dialogue between the religions was necessary for world peace. Now we can say that dialogue between the religions is necessary for world survival. Without friendship and cooperation between the religions our planet will fall into chaos.

The starting point must be mysticism. In their deepest religious experience, Muslim, Jew, Christian, Buddhist, and Hindu are silent before the mystery. They enter into the unknown world of emptiness and darkness where they can meet one another in silent communion and love. It is here that the Carmelite mystics, whom Fr. Kieran has brought so beautifully to the English-speaking world, will play a key role.

That St. John of the Cross can speak to Islamic and Jewish mystics is clear. Scholars tell us of Spain's enormous debt to Arab culture during eight centuries of Islamic presence; the poetry of St. John of the Cross, they tell us, has distinct Islamic features. As for Judaism, John's love for the Song of Songs, which he knew by heart, and his appeal to the prophet Ezekiel bring him close to the Qabbalists. Here, then, a fruitful dialogue can take place. In this essay, however, I would like to speak of the dialogue with Asia and Asian religions.

St. John of the Cross

Having lived for many decades in Japan, I have come to the conclusion that the Christian mystic who speaks most powerfully to Asia is St. John of the Cross. At present, it is true, the most popular Christian mystic is Meister Eckhart whose paradoxes are remarkably similar to the Zen koan. The great Dr. D.T. Suzuki loved Eckhart; and Japanese scholars of the Kyoto school have written very fine studies of the German mystic, emphasizing his capacity to transcend dualism, reconcile opposites, and find the unity of all things. But what about St. John of the Cross?

In the middle of the nineteenth century, in the Meiji era when Western culture poured into Japan, Spain was neglected. Britain, Germany, and France, deeply prejudiced against Spain, brought their prejudice to Japan. The American Protestant missionaries, who established the powerful universities that dominated Japanese education, glorified Luther and Queen Elizabeth, paying little attention to Catholic Spain and its Catholic mystics. Only Pedro Arrupe, who later became superior general of the Jesuits, seeing that Japanese Christian contemplatives needed guidance, translated St. John of the Cross into Japanese. Arrupe's translations were not known outside a narrow Catholic circle, but his work was carried on by a brilliant Japanese Carmelite. Ichiro Okumura, a convert from Zen, never lost his great love and respect for Buddhism; he has brought St. John of the Cross into the Zen-Christian dialogue. Surely there is here a great future.

For St. John of the Cross reconciles opposites and glories in paradox, while centering his mysticism on love. He can be called both *Doctor of Nothing* and *Doctor of Love.* "To arrive at being all desire to be nothing" is complimented by "Seeking my Love I will head for the mountains. . . ." Love and nothingness go hand in hand. Now dialogue is a two-way street. We learn and we give. Christians can learn humbly from Zen while offering to Buddhism "the living flame of love." What a wonderful exchange that could be!

The Sketch of Mount Carmel

At the beginning of *The Ascent of Mount Carmel* St. John of the Cross draws a sketch of the ascent which, I believe, will appeal to the Zen master, the Hindu sannyasin, the Muslim Sufi, and the Jewish Qabbalist. At the center of the picture is the famous *nada:*

Nothing, nothing, nothing,
nothing, nothing, nothing.
And even on the mountain, nothing.

Here is the radical detachment that characterizes all mysticism. One must be detached from all things in order to live in utter poverty of spirit. One must be detached not only from material things but also from all thoughts and images and feelings. One must be detached from spiritual experiences and even from God's gifts. One must be detached from Church and sacrament. St. John of the Cross quotes St. Paul: "Let those who have wives be as though they had none, and those who mourn as though they were not mourning, and those who rejoice as though they were not rejoicing, and those who buy as though they had no possessions, and those who deal with the world as though they had no dealings with it. . . . I want you to be free from anxieties." (1 Cor 7:29-32)

One who would embark on this journey must be detached from all feelings and thoughts about God. For God transcends everything we can see or hear or feel or touch. At the center of the sketch are the words, "Neither this, nor this, nor this, nor this, nor this, nor this." These words remind us immediately of the "neti, neti, neti . . ." of the

English translation of terms used in St. John's original drawing.

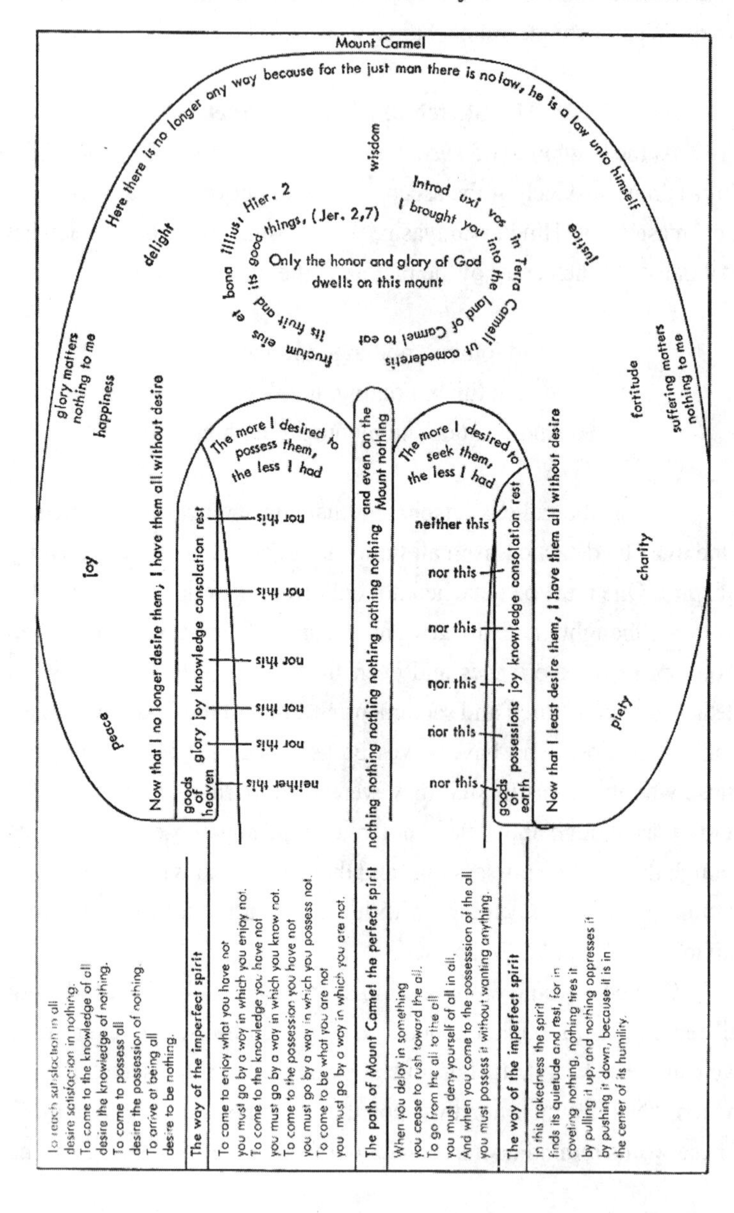

Hindu sannyasin and the "mu, mu, mu" of the Zen master. God, the mystery of mysteries, is neither this nor that.

This radical renunciation may sound inhuman and repellant; but it is the source of true peace: "In this nakedness the spirit finds its quietude and rest. For in coveting nothing, nothing tires it by pulling it up, and nothing oppresses it by pushing it down, because it is in the center of its humility." (A.1.13.13)

Let me, then, quote two characteristics of this mystical journey that make it eminently attractive. First there are the words:

Now that I least desire them
I have them all without desire.

This important sentence brings to our attention the distinction between *detachment* and *rejection.* The mystic is detached from all things, but he or she rejects nothing. Indeed, the mystic is the one who really enjoys life and revels in its beauty. "My Beloved, the mountains, and lonely wooded valleys, strange islands, and resounding rivers, the whistling of love-stirring breezes." (C, stanza 14; C.14 & 15,1). This is the immortal *todo y nada.* This is the Pauline, "Having nothing but possessing all things." (2 Cor 6:10) Does it not remind us of that other mystic who sang joyfully of Brother Sun and Sister Moon and conversed with the little birds? And does it not remind us of the Zen poet Basho who was delighted by the sight of the frog jumping into the pond? In becoming nothing the mystic becomes everything.

The second sentence I wish to emphasize is inscribed at the top of the mountain:

Here there is no longer any way
Because for the just man there is no law
He is a law unto himself

To some this may sound shocking. Is St. John of the Cross doing away with law and rules and regulations?

Yet this is traditional doctrine. St. Ignatius of Loyola tells us that he is reluctant to write rules because what really matters is "the interior law of charity and love which the Holy Spirit writes and imprints on the human heart." Likewise, the Second Vatican Council stresses that we will be judged not by exterior laws but by the interior law of conscience. Speaking of freedom of religion, the Council insists that we must always recognize and respect the faith of another person, even when it is different from our own. Such is the central importance of the law of the heart. From exterior laws we can be *detached*; but the interior law is the voice of God.

Needless to say, this sentence of St. John of the Cross will win the approval of Buddhists, for whom the only norm of morality is obedience to the true self. Rules and regulations are useful and should be obeyed; but they are no more than "skillful means," controlling the little ego. We come to truth when we are enlightened and discover the true self.

From all that has been said, it will be clear that mystics of all religions will accept the sanjuanist sketch of Mount Carmel. Buddhists and Hindus may follow it more conscientiously than many Christians. Now, however, let me add an important principle: each mystic has his or her distinctive faith. *The nada of St. John of the Cross can never be separated from his faith in and love for the crucified Jesus.* Indeed, the *nada* of St. John of the Cross is unintelligible without the cross of Jesus.

The Sketch of Christ Crucified

Giving concrete advice to one who would climb the mountain, St. John of the Cross writes: "First, have a habitual desire to imitate

Christ in all your deeds by bringing your life into conformity with his. You must then study his life in order to know how to imitate him and behave in all events as he would." (A.1.13. 3) The saint goes on to tell the would-be mystic to renounce sensory satisfaction out of love for Jesus Christ and "for Christ, desire to enter into complete nakedness, emptiness, and poverty in everything in the world." (A.1.13.6)

Nor is this imitation of Christ something external, pertaining to the early stages of the mystical ascent. In one of his most profound experiences the saint had a vision of Christ crucified, which he immediately sketched on a small piece of paper. This extraordinary sketch baffles the critics, who claim that the artist knew nothing of the rules of his day. He was writing from the very core of his being. One is reminded of St. Francis of Assisi and Padre Pio on whose hands and feet the wounds of Christ appeared. Like St. John of the Cross they were not just imitating a Christ outside; they were living the words of St. Paul: "I live, now not I, but Christ lives in me." (Gal 2:20) This quotation from Galatians St. John of the Cross loved. He quotes it several times.

What I say here is of the greatest importance for our dialogue. Buddhists often speak enthusiastically about Jesus. Zen masters see the death and resurrection of Jesus as a great koan. However, the Buddhist faith and the Christian faith are quite different. For the Buddhist, the death and resurrection of Jesus is a symbolic story, a "skillful means" that leads to enlightenment. For St. John of the Cross, on the other hand, the death and resurrection of Jesus is an event. The risen Jesus is alive in the world today.

The Living Flame of Love and Passive Purification

The Ascent of Mount Carmel treats of the "active purification" that emphasizes human effort. We are told to let go of all attachments. "Let go! Let go! Let go! Nothing. Nothing. Nothing." However necessary this human effort may be, it alone will not bring us to the summit of the mountain. It needs to be complemented by *The Dark Night of the Soul,* which treats of "passive purification," about which I shall now speak briefly.

One who enters the path of Christian contemplation abandons reasoning and thinking to enter into an interior silence in which one experiences an obscure sense of God's presence. There then arises in the mind and heart a movement of love so gentle, so delicate that one may scarcely notice it. Indeed, St. John of the Cross warns contemplatives and their directors that they could easily crush this precious stirring in the depth of their being. He tells the contemplatives to remain quietly "doing nothing" in order that this tiny flame may grow and develop.

As it grows, it purifies and causes pain. John of the Cross uses the very traditional metaphor of the fire applied to the damp and sodden log of wood. The fire is divine love: the damp log of wood is the unpurified soul. As the flame is applied, the log burns and crackles, and belches off smoke. This is the agonizing dark night. The pain is caused not by the fire of love but by the impurity of the log. Finally, the log catches fire. It bursts into flame; and the poet can sing:

O living flame of love
that tenderly wounds my soul
in its deepest center!

St. John of the Cross writes that the living flame of love is the Holy Spirit. Through this living flame of love, the human person is divinized, becoming God by participation.

Passive purification is vitally necessary because many of our attachments are in the unconscious mind. Sometimes they are real addictions that no amount of human effort will eradicate. Only the fire of love will burn them out and bring us peace of soul. The question now arises: Is there anything resembling the living flame of love in Asian mysticism? I have found nothing like this in Zen.

However, there may be scope for dialogue in the *kundalini* of tantric yoga and Tibetan mysticism. Here we read of the feminine energy or *shakti* or "serpent power" which lies dormant at the base of the spine. Once awakened, this powerful energy passes through the energy centers or *chakras*, reaching a climax at the crown of the head, where one experiences extraordinary bliss in the marriage of Shiva and Shakti.

At some future time there will surely be dialogue between those who have experienced the living flame and those who have experienced *kundalini* arousal. At present, however, to attempt this dialogue would be premature and beyond the scope of this essay. Only let me say that Fr. Kieran Kavanaugh's work on the Carmelite mystics opens the door to a dialogue with Asia that may dominate the theology of the third millennium. We sincerely thank him for his work of love, and we pray that it will continue in the years that lie ahead.

Finally, let me add a personal note. I have benefited immensely from the work of Fr. Kieran. I have never felt any contradiction between my life as a Jesuit and the spirituality of the Carmelites. I recall how, as a young scholastic in Ireland, I told my spiritual father that I was reading St. John of the Cross. The holy man commented: "St. John of the Cross needs to be adapted for Jesuits. But to adapt a principle is not to water it down."

In a world that is moving toward mysticism, the little Spanish friar will speak not only to Christians but also to Muslims and Jews, Buddhists and Hindus. As we thank Fr. Kieran, we pray that his work will help bring unity to our troubled world.

Bibliography of Kieran Kavanaugh, O.C.D.

Compiled by
Regis Jordan, O.C.D.
Institute of Carmelite Studies
Washington, DC

1959

"St. John of the Cross: On Faith." *Spiritual Life* 5 (1959): 277-87.

1962

"St. John of the Cross: On Aridity and Contemplation." *Spiritual Life* 8 (1962): 182-93.

1963

Director, The Carmel Series on Christian Life. Vol. 1, *The Simple Steps to God,* by François of St. Mary. Translated by Harold Evans. Introduction by Thomas Merton. 1963. Vol. 2, *Anguish and Joy in the Christian Life,* by François Mauriac. Translated by Harold Evans. 1964. Vol. 3, *The Secret Ways of Prayer,* by R. L. Bruckberger. Wilkes-Barre, PA: Dimension Books.

1964

The Collected Works of St. John of the Cross. Translated by Kieran Kavanaugh and Otilio Rodriguez. Introduction by Kieran Kavanaugh. Garden City, NY: Doubleday, 1964.

1966

"Death of God and John of the Cross." *Spiritual Life* 12 (1966): 260-69.

1967

"LSD and Religious Experience-II: A Theologian's Viewpoint." *Spiritual Life* 13 (1967): 54-63.

Review of *Functional Asceticism,* by Donald L. Gelpi (Sheed and Ward). *Spiritual Life* 13 (1967): 67-68.

Review of *The Nature of Mysticism,* by David Knowles (Hawthorn Books). *Spiritual Life* 13 (1967): 262-63.

"Is de God-is-dood-Theologie wel zo nieuw?" *Carmel* (Merkelbeek) 19 (1967): 361-71.

New Catholic Encyclopedia. S.v. "Abandonment, Spiritual"; "Aridity, Spiritual"; "Dark Night of the Soul"; "John of the Cross, St."; "Purification, Spiritual"; "Self-Abandonment, Spiritual"; "Spirituality (History of)."

1968

Review of *Histoire spirituelle de la France: Spiritualité du Catholicisme en France et dans les pays de langue française des origines à 1914,* [Bibliothèque de Spiritualité, vol. 1] (Paris: Beauchesne). *The Catholic Historical Review* 53 (1968): 685-86.

Review of *A New Catechism: Catholic Faith for Adults* (Herder and Herder). *Spiritual Life* 14 (1968): 125-27.

"Hope and Change." *Spiritual Life* 14 (1968): 158-65.

1971

Review of American *Mysticism from William James to Zen,* by Hal Bridges (Harper and Row). *Spiritual Life* 17 (1971): 19.

Review of *Tiempo y vida de Santa Teresa,* by Efrén de la Madre de Dios and Otger Steggink (Madrid: Biblioteca de Autores Cristianos). *The Catholic Historical Review* 57 (1971): 532-33.

1973

The Collected Works of St. John of the Cross. Translated by Kieran Kavanaugh and Otilio Rodriquez. First paperback edition. Washington, DC: ICS Publications, 1973.

Review of *Eastern Christian Prayer and Spirituality: A Series of Ten One-Hour Cassettes* (Fordham University). *Spiritual Life* 19 (1973): 71-72.

"St. Thérèse and the Mystery of Jesus." *Spiritual Life* 19 (1973): 151-62.

1976

The Collected Works of St. Teresa of Avila. Vol. 1, *The Book of Her Life, Spiritual Testimonies, Soliloquies.* Translated by Kieran Kavanaugh and Otilio Rodriguez. Introductions by Kieran Kavanaugh. Washington, DC: ICS Publications, 1976.

1977

Review of *Monumenta Historica Carmeli Teresiani: Documenta Primigenia, vol. 1: 1560-1577, vol. 2: 1578-1581.* Edited by Institutum Historicum Teresianum (Rome: Edizioni del Teresianum). *The Catholic Historical Review* 63 (1977): 310-11.

Review of *St. John of the Cross: His Life and Poetry,* by Gerald Brenan and poetry translated by Linda Nicholson (Cambridge University Press). *The Catholic Historical Review* 63 (1977): 311-12.

1979

The Collected Works of St. John of the Cross. Translated by Kieran Kavanaugh and Otilio Rodriguez. Introductions by Kieran Kavanaugh. 2nd ed. Washington, DC: ICS Publications, 1979.

Teresa of Avila: The Interior Castle. Translated by Kieran Kavanaugh and Otilio Rodriguez. Preface by Raimundo Panikkar. The

Classics of Western Spirituality. New York: Paulist Press, 1979.

1980

The Collected Works of St. Teresa of Avila. Vol. 2, *The Way of Perfection, Meditations on the Song of Songs, The Interior Castle.* Translated by Kieran Kavanaugh and Otilio Rodriguez. Introductions by Kieran Kavanaugh. Washington, DC: ICS Publications, 1980.

1981

The Collected Works of St. John of the Cross. Translated by Kieran Kavanaugh and Otilio Rodriguez. Introductions by Kieran Kavanaugh. Bangalore, India: AVP Publications, 1981.

Review of *Espejo de bien vivir y para ayudar a bien morir,* by Jaime Montanés (Madrid: Universidad Pontificia de Salamanca). *The Catholic Historical Review* 67 (1981): 152-53.

Preface to Francisco de Osuna, *The Third Spiritual Alphabet.* Translation and introduction by Mary E. Giles. The Classics of Western Spirituality. New York and Ramsey, NJ: Paulist Press, 1981.

1982

The Collected Works of St. Teresa of Avila. Vols. 1 & 2. Translated by Kieran Kavanaugh and Otilio Rodriguez. Introductions by Kieran Kavanaugh. First Indian Edition. Bangalore, India: AVP Publications, 1982.

1984

"St Teresa and the Spirituality of Sixteenth-Century Spain." *In The Roots of the Modern Christian Tradition.* Edited by E. Rozanne Elder. Introduction by Jean Leclercq. *The Spirituality of Western Christendom, II* (Cistercian Studies Series; 55). Kalamazoo, MI: Cistercian Publications, 1984.

1985

The Collected Works of St. Teresa of Avila. Vol. 3, The Book of Her Foundations, Minor Works. Translated by Kieran Kavanaugh and Otilio Rodriguez. Introductions by Kieran Kavanaugh. Washington, DC: ICS Publications, 1985.

1986

The Collected Works of St. Teresa of Avila. Vol. 3, The Book of Her Foundations, Minor Works. Translated by Kieran Kavanaugh and Otilio Rodriguez. Introductions by Kieran Kavanaugh. First Indian Edition. Bangalore, India: AVP Publications, 1986.

1987

John of the Cross: Selected Writings. Edited with an introduction by Kieran Kavanaugh. Preface by Ernest Larkin. The Classics of Western Spirituality. Mahwah, NJ: Paulist Press, 1987.

1988

Review of *Le origini dei Carmelitani Scalzi (1567-1593): storia e storiografia,* by Ludovico Saggi (Rome: Institutum Carmelitanum). *The Catholic Historical Review* 74 (1988): 506-07.

1989

"Spanish Sixteenth Century: Carmel and Surrounding Movements." In *Christian Spirituality: Post-Reformation and Modern.* Edited by Louis Dupré and Don E. Saliers in collaboration with John Meyendorff. Vol. 18 of *World Spirituality: An Encyclopedic History of the Religious Quest.* New York: Crossroad, 1989, 69-92.

1990

"Jessica Powers in the Tradition of St. John of the Cross: Carmelite and Poet." *Spiritual Life* 36 (1990): 161-76.

1991

Review of *Edith Stein: Philosopher and Mystic*, by Josephine Koeppel (Liturgical Press). *Spiritual Life* 37 (1991): 239-41.

The Collected Works of St. John of the Cross. Rev. ed. Translated by Kieran Kavanaugh and Otilio Rodriguez. Introductions by Kieran Kavanaugh. Washington, DC: ICS Publications, 1991.

"The Garden." *Living Prayer* 24 (1991): 8-12.

Ruiz, Federico, and others. *God Speaks in the Night: The Life, Times, and Teaching of St. John of the Cross.* Translated by Kieran Kavanaugh. Washington, DC: ICS Publications, 1991.

1992

"Faith and the Experience of God in the University Town of Baeza." In *John of the Cross: Conferences and Essays by Members of the Institute of Carmelite Studies, and Others. Carmelite Studies,* vol. 6. Edited by Steven Payne. Washington, DC: ICS Publications, 1992, 48-64.

1995

The Autobiography of St. Teresa of Avila. Translated by Kieran Kavanaugh and Otilio Rodriguez. By arrangement with ICS Publications. New York: Book of the Month Club, 1995.

1996

Preface to Susan Muto, *Words of Wisdom for our World: The Precautions and Counsels of St. John of the Cross.* Translation of the Saint's Texts by Kieran Kavanaugh. Washington, DC: ICS Publications, 1996.

1997

The Wisdom of Teresa of Avila: Selections from the Interior Castle. Edited by Stephen J. Connor. Translated by Kieran Kavanaugh and Otilio Rodriguez. Introduction by Kieran Kavanaugh. Mahwah, NJ: Paulist Press, 1997.

1998

"The Canonization Miracle and Its Investigations." In *Never Forget: Christian and Jewish Perspectives on Edith Stein. Carmelite Studies,* vol. 7. Edited by Waltraud Herbstrith. Translated by Susanne Batzdorff. Washington, DC: ICS Publications, 1998, 185-96.

"Deserto." In *Dizionario di Mistica.* Edited by Luigi Borriello, Edmundo Caruana, Maria Rosario Del Genio, and Nicolo Suffi. Vatican City: Libreria Editrice Vaticana, 1998.

1999

John of the Cross: Doctor of Light and Love. Spiritual Legacy Series. New York: Crossroad, 1999.

Foreword to Angel de les Gavarres, *Thérèse, The Little Child of God's Mercy: Her Spiritual Itinerary in the Light of Her Autobiographical Manuscripts.* Translated by Michael Gaughran. Washington, DC: ICS Publications, 1999.

2000

"How to Pray: From the Life and Teachings of St. Teresa." In *Carmel and Contemplation: Transforming Human Consciousness. Carmelite Studies*, vol. 8. Edited by Kevin Culligan and Regis Jordan. Washington, DC: ICS Publications, 2000, 115-35.

St. Teresa of Avila. The *Way of Perfection.* Study Edition. Prepared by Kieran Kavanaugh. Washington, DC: ICS Publications, 2000.

Preface to ICS Publications' 2000 reprint of Peter–Thomas Rohrbach, *Journey to Carith: The Sources and Story of the Discalced Carmelites.* New York: Doubleday, 1966.

2001

The Collected Letters of St. Teresa of Avila. Vol. 1. Translated by Kieran Kavanaugh. Washington, DC: ICS Publications, 2001.

2002

Introduction to Edith Stein, *The Science of the Cross.* Translated by Josephine Koeppel. *The Collected Works of Edith Stein,* vol. 6. Edited by L. Gelber and Romaeus Leuven. Washington, DC: ICS Publications, 2002, xi-xxxvii.

Foreword to *Drink of the Stream: Prayers of Carmelites.* Edited by Penny Hickey. San Francisco: Ignatius Press, 2002, 9-10.

2003

Teresa of Avila. *The Way of Prayer: Selected Spiritual Writings.* Edited and introduced by Kieran Kavanaugh. Hyde Park, NY: New City Press, 2003.

"Contemplation and the Stream of Consciousness." In *Carmelite Prayer: A Tradition for the 21st Century.* Edited by Keith J. Egan. New York/Mahwah, NJ: Paulist Press, 2003, 101-18.

"Jessica Powers." *Carmel Clarion* 19 (April-May, 2003): 6-12.

"Understanding Carmelite Spirituality." *Magnificat* 5 (October, 2003): 58.

Translation of *St. Teresa's Manner of Prayer,* by Salvador Ros García. Salamanca [Spain]: Kadmos, 2003.

2004

Review of *St. John of the Cross: Songs in the Night,* by Colin Thompson, (The Catholic University Press). *Spiritual Life* 50 (2004): 183-85.

2005

Introduction to Vilma Seelaus, *Distractions in Prayer: Blessing or Curse?* Staten Island, NY: Alba House, 2005.

Review of *John of the Cross: Man and Mystic*, by Richard Hardy (Pauline Books), and *Silent Music: The Life, Work, and Thought of St. John of the Cross,* by R.A. Herrera, (Eerdmans Publishing Co.). *Spiritual Life* 51 (2005): 185-86.

2006

St. Teresa of Avila for Eveyday. Edited by Kieran Kavanaugh. Mahwah, NJ: Paulist Press, in press.

The Collected Letters of St. Teresa of Avila. Vol. 2. Translated by Kieran Kavanaugh. Washington, DC: ICS Publications, in press.

"Blessed Anne of St. Bartholomew." In *The Heirs of St. Teresa of Avila: Defenders and Disseminators of the Founding Mother's Legacy. Carmelite Studies,* vol. 9. Edited by Christopher C. Wilson. In press.

ELECTRONIC MEDIA

Audiocassettes

Teresa and Her Censors. Canfield, OH: Alba House. 1987. TAH192.

Teresa and Her Spiritual Directors. Canfield, OH. Alba House. 1988. TAH212.

John and the Inquisition. Canfield, OH. Alba House. 1992. TAH284.

St. John of the Cross: The Person, His Life and Times. Tape #91447 0070 of OCDS Congress, Philadelphia, PA, 1991. Elkridge, MD: Chesapeake Audio/Visual Communications, Inc.

Listening and Loving: A Carmelite Response. Tape #2 of OCDS Congress, Louisville, KY, 1994.West Covina, CA: St Joseph's Communications.

"St Teresa of Jesus." In *Establishing God's Kingdom Within and Without: OCDS Regional Cngress 2004.* Tehachapi, CA: St. Joseph Communication, Inc.. Tampa, FL0104-2.

St. Thérèse of Lisieux: Her Life and Spirituality. Washington, DC: ICS Publications. T131.

"The Revolution of Thérèse" and "The Little Way." In *St. Thérèse: Her Mission Today 1897-1997.* Washington, DC: ICS Publications. TND.

"Eros and the Experience of God." In *The Experience of God Today.* Washington, DC: ICS Publications. T99 3.

"The Holy Spirit: The Bond of Divine Friendship in John of the Cross." In *Carmel Faces the New Millennium.* Washington, DC: ICS Publications. T140.

"The Steam of Consciousness and Carmelite Prayer." In *Carmelite Prayer.* Washington, DC: ICS Publications. T148 3.

"The Meaning of Meditation and Contemplation in the Carmelite Tradition." In *Prayer and Meditation in Carmelite Tradtion.* Washington, DC: ICS Pubications. T157-2.

"'The Little Arab': Blessed Myriam's Prayer." In T*he Faces of Prayer in Carmel.* Washington, DC: ICS Publications. T158-7.

Videocassettes

Prehistory of Carmel in the United States. Presentation given 14 August 1990, at "Carmel 200: Contemplation and the Recovery of the American Soul." Available through the Carmelite Monastery, Baltimore MD.

The Revolution of St. Thérèse (54 minutes) and *The Little Way* (55 minutes) . Presentations given in 1996 at the Carmelite Forum seminar, St. Mary's College, Notre Dame, IN. Available through The Carmelite Institute, Washington, DC.

Eros and the Experience of God (56 minutes). Presentation given in 1997 at the Carmelite Forum seminar, St. Mary's College, Notre Dame, IN. Available through the Carmelite Institute, Washington, DC.

Compact Disks

St. John of the Cross: A Digital Library. Spanish text and translations of the writings of St. John of the Cross, including the translation by Kieran Kavanaugh and Otilio Rodriguez. Washington, DC: ICS Publications. CD.

Contributors

Daniel Chowning, O.C.D., is novice master for the Washington province of the Immaculate Heart of Mary and prior of the St. Florian community in Milwaukee, Wisconsin. He studied at the International Center for Teresian/Sanjuanist Studies in Avila, Spain, and obtained a licentiate in theology at the University of Salamanca, Spain. He preaches retreats, lectures, and publishes on themes of Carmelite spirituality. His popular talk "Freedom to Love: The Role of Negation in St. John of the Cross" is available on CD. He coauthored *Purifying the Heart: Buddhist Insight Meditation for Christians* with Kevin Culligan and Mary Jo Meadow (Crossroad, 1994).

Kevin Culligan, O.C.D., lives in the Carmelite community in Hinton, West Virginia. He is a charter member and former chairman of the Institute of Carmelite Studies, as well as a member of the Carmelite Forum. He is an instructor in the Carmelite Institute's Distance Education Certificate Program and in the Spiritual Director Training Program at Mount Carmel Spiritual Centre, Niagara Falls, Ont., Canada. His articles have appeared in *Spiritual Life, America, National Catholic Reporter, Review for Religious,* and *The Way.* He is coeditor with Regis Jordan of *Carmel and Contemplation: Transforming Human Consciousness* (ICS Publications, 2000)

Michael Dodd studied Spanish in Mexico City, theology at the University of Dallas (Irving, TX), and spiritual theology at The Catholic University of America. He has published articles on St. John of the Cross and Carmelite spirituality in the United States and in Spain. He contributed to *The New Dictionary of Catholic Spirituality* (Michael Glazier Press, 1993). An experienced spiritual director and pubic speaker, he is an instructor in the Distance Education Program of the Carmelite Institute at the Washington Theological Union in Washington, DC. He has recently completed a mystery novel based on the life of St. John of the Cross.

Marc Foley, O.C.D., is a Discalced Carmelite priest living in Washington, D.C. He teaches courses on St. John of the Cross and St. Thérèse of Lisieux at the Washington Theological Union in Washington, D.C., does spiritual direction, and leads retreats. He is an active member of the Institute of Carmelite Studies, currently serving as its secretary. Fr. Marc is the author of three books: *Study Guide of "The Story of a Soul" by St. Thérèse of Lisieux* (ICS Publications, 2005), *John of the Cross: The Ascent to Joy* (New City Press, 2002), and *The Love That Keeps Us Sane: Living the Little Way of St. Thérèse of Lisieux* (Paulist Press, 2000).

William Johnston, S.J., was born in Belfast, Northern Ireland in 1925. He joined the Jesuit noviceship in Ireland in 1943. After studies in Greek and Latin at University College, Dublin, he went to the Jesuit mission in Japan in 1951 and was ordained to the priesthood in Tokyo in 1957. He received his doctorate in theology at Sophia University, Tokyo, writing a thesis later published as a book entitled *The Mysticism of "The Cloud of Unknowing."* While teaching religious studies at Sophia University, Fr. Johnston wrote extensively about mysticism. His autobiography, *Mystical Journey,* was published in the United States in 2006 by Orbis Books.

Regis Jordan, O.C.D., was born in Boston in 1936 and entered the Carmelite novitiate at Brookline, Massachusetts in 1956. Following ordination to the priesthood in 1964, Fr. Regis has served the order in a variety of positions: seminary vice–rector, vocation director, local community treasurer, and superior of the communities in Washington, DC, and Hinton, WV. In the 1990s, he was chairman of the Institute of Carmelite Studies and publisher of ICS Publications and directed the development of the audio cassettes/compact disks division of ICS Publications. He is now stationed in Washington, DC, and serves as the mid-Atlantic Provincial Delegate to the Discalced Carmelite Secular Order.

Steven Payne, O.C.D., a priest of the Washington Province of the Discalced Carmelite friars, holds doctorates in philosophy and theology. He has taught theology and spirituality at several academic institutions in the United States. He is currently stationed in the Carmelite community in Nairobi, Kenya, East Africa, where he also serves as Director of the Institute of Spirituality and Religious Formation in Tangaza College. Past president of the Carmelite Institute, Steven is also a former editor of both *Spiritual Life* and ICS Publications. His numerous writings on Carmelite themes include *Saint Thérèse of Lisieux: Doctor of the Universal Church* (Alba House, 2002).

Denis Read, O.C.D. was born in Seattle, Washington in 1927. He entered the Discalced Carmelites in Brookline, MA, in 1944 and was ordained a priest in 1952. After terms as minor seminary rector and director of philosophy students, Denis received his doctorate in theology from the Alphonsianum in Rome, writing his dissertation on the moral theology of John Henry Cardinal Newman. His talk "St John of the Cross for Carpenters: The Ordinary Way of the Dark Night of Faith" remains a best selling audiotape for ICS Publications. In recent years, Fr. Denis served the Hispanic Carmelite Secular Order communities in Florida and the Caribbean. Fr. Denis died on 18 October 2004.

Salvatore Sciurba, O.C.D., a native of New Jersey, made his first profession of religious vows as a member of the Washington Province of Discalced Carmelite friars in 1974. He is now prior of the order's community in Brighton, MA. He is the translator of the ICS edition of *Brother Lawrence of the Resurrection: The Practice of the Presence of God* and the album *Thérèse and Lisieux*. In addition to his translations, Fr. Salvatore has served as teacher, director of formation, retreat master, and spiritual director. In recent years he has worked largely with the Secular Carmelites and Carmelite nuns.

Emmanuel Sullivan, O.C.D. is a member of the Discalced Carmelite community in Brighton, MA. He received his Ph.D. from The Catholic University of America and is a professor emeritus of philosophy and religious studies. He has taught in the Carmelite houses of study in Washington, DC, Massachusetts, and Wisconsin, as well as at The Catholic University of America, Boston College, and St. Joseph's College in Maine. He is past president of the Mariological Society of America. His Carmelite Marian lectures —"Mary and the Holy Spirit in the Writings of John of the Cross" (1991), "Teresa, Mary, and the Reform of Carmel" (1993), "Blessed Elizabeth of the Trinity: Mary in Her Interior Life" (1994), "Three Heroic Women: Mary, Teresa, and Thérèse" (1997)—are all available on CD.

John Sullivan, O.C.D., is currently chairman the Institute of Carmelite Studies and publisher of ICS Publications, as well as the prior of the Discalced Carmelite community in Washington, DC. He has served his Order in many capacities, including six years on the general council in Rome from 1991 to1997. Presently he is the Order's NGO representative at the United Nations. He was the first series editor for ICS's *Collected Works of Edith Stein* in English and contributed *Edith Stein: Essential Writings* to the Modern Spiritual Masters Series (Orbis Books, 2002). In 1995, the Edith Stein Guild honored him with the Edith Stein Award.

The Institute of Carmelite Studies promotes research and publication in the field of Carmelite spirituality. Its members are Discalced Carmelites, part of a Roman Catholic community—friars, nuns, and laity—who are heirs to the teaching and way of life of Teresa of Jesus and John of the Cross, men and women dedicated to contemplation and to ministry in the Church and the world. Information concerning their way of life is available through local diocesan Vocation Offices or from the Vocation Directors' Offices:

1233 So. 45th Street, W. Milwaukee, WI 53214

P.O. Box 3420, San Jose, CA 95156-3420

5151 Marylake Drive, Little Rock, AR 72206